BRAND WHITLOCK'S THE BUCKEYES

Edited with an Introduction by Paul W. Miller

Brand Whitlock's

THE BUCKEYES

Politics and Abolitionism
in an Ohio Town, 1836-1845

Edited with an Introduction by
Paul W. Miller

OHIO UNIVERSITY PRESS ATHENS

To my cousin Marjorie, who first taught me the joy of learning; to my son Gary, who first instructed me in the art of being a parent; and to Joyce and Walt, who proved beyond cavil that the gracious hospitality of Queen Arete and King Alcinoüs still flourishes in Greece.

CONTENTS

ILLUSTRATIONS
(Facing page 54 and following)

ACKNOWLEDGEMENTS

In the summer of 1973, Mrs. Charlotte Hupp of the Champaign County Historical Society showed me the Society's Brand Whitlock collection in Urbana, Ohio. Among the items in this collection was a supposedly lost manuscript of *The Buckeyes,* Whitlock's last, incomplete, unpublished novel. From that summer of 1973 to the present I have received many kindnesses from the Society's members, who include Attorney Charles B. English, Attorney and Mrs. Edwin L. English, Sr., Mr. and Mrs. Edwin English, Jr., Mr. Lawrence Little, Mr. Robert Park and Mr. John J. Steinberger. To the Society as a whole I want to express my thanks for permission to publish *The Buckeyes.* I especially wish to thank Charles English for the use of his taped lecture on Whitlock delivered to the Society on December 4, 1969, and for the initiative he took in securing my permission to publish. I also want to give special thanks to Mr. and Mrs. Edwin English, Sr. for granting me permission to record their recollections of the Brand and Whitlock families and for generously offering me the fruit of their study of the Brand family history in response to my numerous queries.

I am grateful to the Meredith Corporation for permission to quote from *The Letters and Journal of Brand Whitlock,* ed. Allan Nevins (New York: D. Appleton-Century, 1936). My thanks also go to the following institutions providing assistance in my research: the Ohio Historical Society, the Library of Congress (Manuscript Division), Thomas Library at Wittenberg University, and the Warren County Historical Society Museum. In addition I have a great debt to Professor Jack Matthews of Ohio University for his interest in and support of my project. Other individuals assisting me in my research and the preparation of my manuscript include Mr. Richard Rademacher and the late Mrs. Rademacher, who graciously invited me into their home, the Ward house; Mrs. Suzanne White and Miss Kristin Fippin of the Wittenberg University English Department staff; and Mary Jo, my most valued critic.

Paul W. Miller
Department of English
Wittenberg University
Springfield, Ohio 45501
December 15, 1975

The Buckeyes:

A Story of Politics and Abolitionism
in an Ohio Town, 1836-1845

By Brand Whitlock

Introduction by Paul W. Miller

The Buckeyes is the last novel of Brand
Whitlock (1869-1934), set in Ohio two decades
before the Civil War. Written over a period of several years and
left unfinished at his death, the nearly 100,000 word manuscript
of *The Buckeyes* is now printed for the first time.

Though Robert M. Crunden, Whitlock's most recent biographer,
indicated that the manuscript of *The Buckeyes* had disappeared,[1]
its carefully revised typescript was recently found in the collection of the Champaign County Historical Society, Urbana, Ohio,
to which it was presented in 1942 along with other Whitlock man-
uscripts, photographs and memorabilia relating to Ohio.[2]

Like two of his previous novels and seven short stories, *The
Buckeyes* is set in the town of Macochee,[3] Ohio, a thinly dis-
guised representation of Urbana, Whitlock's birthplace and early
childhood home. Whitlock was born at 510 South Main Street,
Urbana, in a modest, two-story frame house still standing. His
father, Elias Whitlock, A.B. and A.M. from Ohio Wesleyan University, had married Mallie Lavinia Brand, daughter of Joseph
Carter Brand, in 1868. Her home, at the corner of 132 W. Reynolds and Walnut Streets, was just a short walk round the corner
from the Whitlock house. The Brand home of white painted brick
with green shutters is also still standing, though no longer owned
by the Brands or their descendants (see fig. 2).[4]

In Urbana Elias Whitlock was principal of the local high school
but soon became a Methodist minister moving from town to town

1

in Ohio. Ordained in 1874, he had probably moved his family away from Urbana by 1875, when his second child, Mary Bell, was born in Degraff, some 20 miles north west of Urbana. Brand, however, the first of the four children born to the Whitlocks,[5] came back to Urbana from his father's ministerial homes in such Ohio towns as Delaware, Findlay and Kenton to spend summers with his beloved grandfather Brand, on whom the protagonist of *The Buckeyes* is modeled.

Whitlock never attended college. After finishing high school in Toledo, he worked for the Toledo *Blade* as a reporter 1887-90, and for the Chicago *Herald* 1891-93, during which latter period he also tried writing fiction. In 1892 he married Susan Brainerd of Springfield, Illinois, who died four months later of what was diagnosed as "vomiting of pregnancy." In 1894 he was admitted to the bar in Illinois and began a brief political career there, serving Governor John Altgeld's administration in a minor capacity. In 1895 he married Ella Brainerd, Susan's nineteen year old sister, to whom he was happily married till his death in 1934.[6]

In 1897 he passed the Ohio bar exams and set up practice in Toledo. His first novel, *The Thirteenth District*, was published in 1902. Beginning in 1906, he served four terms as reform mayor of Toledo, continuing to write fiction in whatever spare time he could find. He was U.S. Minister (later Ambassador) to Belgium from 1914 to 1921; thereafter he devoted himself to full-time writing in Cannes on the French Riviera. *J. Hardin & Son* (1923) is generally regarded as his best novel; *Lafayette* (1929) is his outstanding biography. He lived in France till his death on May 24, 1934.

Whitlock's Urbana is now a city of 11,000, located in west central Ohio 14 miles north of Springfield and Interstate 70, between Dayton and Columbus. The county seat of Champaign County, Urbana still boasts an old-fashioned square, at the center of which stands the contemplative, bronze statue of a dismounted Union cavalryman facing "homeward," i.e. northward. Erected in 1871 by a Monument Committee of which Whitlock's grandfather was president, this statue is among the most distinctive features of the town, as Whitlock's repeated references to it in his fiction suggest. This monument symbolizes Champaign County's deep involvement in the Civil War; according to a list compiled in 1876, 151 of nearly 3,000 volunteers (from a total population of 22,700) were killed in battle; 427 others died of war-related causes such as wounds, imprisonment or disease, for a total of 578, approximately 20% of those enlisted.[7]

Situated in rich, rolling farm land, Urbana is now known for light manufacturing of such items as aircraft lights as well as for farm products. Its stately, green-shuttered, white-columned homes set well back from spacious main streets provide an attractive if static reminder of the city's late nineteenth century heyday as a railroad, industrial, and even theatrical center with travelling stage plays.

In 1868, the year before Whitlock was born, Urbana became a city as defined by the Legislature of Ohio, with a population of 5,124 according to a feverish one-man census that counted even "the tombstones and everything that had any relation to the human race."[8] But despite its gradual growth in population, its "atmosphere of culture" influenced by the Swedenborgian Urbana University, and its mild celebrity as the boyhood home of the famous American sculptor John Quincy Adams Ward (1830-1910), Urbana always remained in Whitlock's memory a somewhat complacent, essentially conservative town: "It was a rather self-sufficient town, I fancy, and it cared so little for change that it has scarcely changed at all, save as one misses the faces and the forms one used to see there in other days."[9] In spite of such gentle expressions of animadversion against the town, Whitlock must have been strongly attracted to Urbana, as his frequent return to it in his imagination indicates. As scholars have generally agreed, the town of Macochee bears a striking resemblance to the town of Urbana as Whitlock knew it and as he read about its past in the sources at his disposal.

Providing the setting for some of Whitlock's best fiction, the town of Macochee commands attention because of its particular hold on Whitlock's imagination over a period of 30 years (1904-1934). But the chief interest of this fiction today, and the increasingly insistent impulse behind successive Macochee stories including *The Buckeyes*, lies in the attempt to portray the town before and after its apparent opportunities for heroic vision and action had narrowed, before and after it had lost its Garden of Eden purity and freshness. Whitlock seems ever to have been in pursuit of "the dearest freshness deep down things" that Gerard Manley Hopkins celebrated; unlike Hopkins', however, Whitlock's vision of the beauty he so desired was flickering, partial, and largely confined to the vanished Midwestern American frontier, as when he writes in *The Buckeyes:*

> Everything was going on well; everything was growing, developing, like the elms he [Carter Blair, the protagonist] had planted along the street before his house; they were high enough now to

cast a bit of shade, and the rose-vine that Lucretia [his wife] had brought from Virginia was climbing one of the pillars of the verandah. Along the side of the house her beds of pinks were blooming, their spicy odour scenting the air. Behind the house there was a great vegetable garden, and when they went into supper presently its produce would be hot upon the table—the new potatoes and golden ears of sweet corn, and spoon bread or beaten biscuits (p. 243).

Perusal of *The Buckeyes* initially gratifies one's curiosity as to the nature of Whitlock's last portrait of the town of his imagination. But further examination of this substantial, though incomplete, novel is rewarding in other respects as well. Besides having considerable intrinsic interest as a story of the vanishing frontier which Whitlock knew intimately through the tales of his grandfather, *The Buckeyes* sheds light on the abolition movement. It also examines such important political figures as President William Henry Harrison (1773-1841) and Ohio Governor Thomas Corwin (1794-1865) from Whitlock's varied perspectives as a reformer, diplomat and professional biographer. Whitlock's own description of *The Buckeyes* as a "novelized history of Ohio in the middle of last century" is apt.[10]

Almost as interesting as the novel itself, however, is Whitlock's inability to complete it, or even to give it a wholly satisfactory direction, despite his efforts to write it in two different versions over a period of three years. Thus, in a letter to an old friend in 1932 he writes: "I have had another novel [*The Buckeyes*] on the stocks for a long while; I began it two years ago—in fact, began it twice in different ways. When I wrote it one way I thought it ought to be written the other, and vice-versa."[11] "The one way" and "the other" evidently refer to the two drafts which are now in Urbana—the 100,000 word version of the novel printed here, and a 12,500 word fragment also in the Historical Society's collection. Among other differences between the two, the longer version presents a much less idealistic picture of the protagonist than the shorter one.

Though the novel was left untitled in the version printed here, the 12,500 word fragment is introduced with the following pencilled notation in Mrs. Whitlock's hand: "one beginning of the Buckeyes (novel never finished)." I have accepted the title assigned this fragment as the title of the longer version printed here, not only because it is sufficiently representative of the intention and spirit of the novel, but because it is probably the title that Whitlock himself used for the novel, as Mrs. Whitlock's notation suggests. In the longer MS Whitlock portrays the novel's protagonist Carter Blair as a proud Kentuckian from Bourbon County becoming a proud Ohioan of Macochee: "He [Blair] was beginning to take a pride in Ohio too, now that he had a stake in the country. He was beginning to think of himself not so much as a Kentuckian as an Ohioan: not a Corn Cracker but a Buckeye, as Ohioans had begun to call themselves..." (p. 175). The process of Blair's becoming an Ohioan culminates in his successful candidacy for the State Assembly in 1840, the year when Presidential candidate William Henry Harrison reviewed a Macochee parade that included a buckeye log cabin of the kind in which "Old Tip" himself was supposedly born (p. 184). The Tippecanoe Glee Club, also in the parade, reinforces the patriotic fervor of The Buckeye State with a popular campaign song of the day, sung to the tune of "Highland Laddie" (p. 185):

> Oh where, tell me where, was your Buckeye Cabin made?
> [Repeat]
> 'Twas built among the merry boys who wield the plow and spade;
> Where the Log-Cabins stand in the bonnie Buckeye shade.

In his protagonist Carter Blair of *The Buckeyes* Whitlock planted the seeds of an idealism which, though observed in his grandfather's abolitionism, was also an important part of his own life as a member of the Progressive movement and as a reformer. Whitlock also portrayed in Blair the political realism bordering on cynicism which was a vital part of his own make-up—especially in the Post World War I era[12]—as well as a probable facet of his grandfather's nature, which served as a model for Blair's character. Of Blair's disillusionment with politics following his idol Henry Clay's defeat in 1844, Whitlock wrote: "He was disgusted with politics and all the nasty mess of their [politicians'] deceits and betrayals; he would have nothing more to do with them; he was out of politics" (p. 253). Despite his best efforts, however, Whitlock was unable finally to resolve the central conflict in his protagonist and in his novel by allowing either the idealistic or the realistic strain to dominate.

Had Whitlock presented the character of his protagonist as a more idealistic figure, as he seems to have been tempted to do in the short, first version of the novel, he would have done violence to his political sensibility as well as his artistic insight. Had he followed the politically realistic, sometimes almost deterministic vein further into the longer version, the idealistic image of his grandfather, so carefully preserved over a lifetime, would have collapsed. The result of this conflict between his idealistic and realistic perceptions was a dilemma, the only escape from which, if he were to preserve his few remaining ideals about public life (and incidentally, about his grandfather) was to lay aside the novel, which he ultimately did. The catalyst of this traumatic decision to give up the novel, as revealed by Whitlock in his letters, was a memorable luncheon engagement with the American novelist Edith Wharton in 1931.[13] This encounter, described later in the introduction, shook Whitlock's confidence in his novel as well as in his ability to complete it.

But *The Buckeyes* was the last, not the first of the Macochee fictions created by Whitlock. To get some perspective on the beginnings, the development and the eventual abandonment of *The Buckeyes*, we need to go back to the first years of the twentieth century, when Whitlock was just beginning his career as a fiction writer.

Following the first Macochee novel, *The Happy Average* (1904), the first Macochee short story, entitled "Macochee's First Campaign Fund," was included in a collection called *The Gold Brick* (1910); six more Macochee stories were included in *The Fall Guy* (1912). Eleven years later, in 1923, the second Macochee novel, *J. Hardin & Son*, appeared.[14] Last came *The Buckeyes*, begun in 1930 and worked on intermittently till the project was finally abandoned late in 1933, a few months before Whitlock's death.

In *The Happy Average*, set in the 1890's, the protagonist rejects the town as devoid of opportunity. In the Macochee short stories, collected in *The Gold Brick* and *The Fall Guy*, Whitlock's pursuit of the Golden Age of Macochee leads him farther into the past, to the period of the Civil War; emphatically rejected is the era of railroad monopoly following the Civil War. But even Whitlock's vision of the Golden Age of dedication, self-sacrifice and heroism during the War is clouded at times by doubt or cynicism. In the second Macochee novel, *J. Hardin & Son*, Whitlock returns to the town's more recent past but with a new severity of outlook. Whereas the Macochee of *The Happy Average* possessed several redeeming features, including its easy familiarity and scenic beauty, the Macochee of *J. Hardin & Son* can perhaps best be described as a spiritual wasteland like T. S. Eliot's, but without the faint hope provided by a Fisher King. Finally, in *The Buckeyes*, Whitlock plunges still further into the past to the decades preceding the Civil War. But even here, alas, he finds that his vision of the Golden Age cannot be sustained.

Reviewing the history of the Macochee fiction in more detail, one notes that as Whitlock pursues his vision of a Golden Age of Macochee further into the past, his attitude toward the town's

6

more recent past gradually hardens from nostalgia into contempt. Thus, though Macochee in *The Happy Average* is portrayed as a *cul de sac* for youth, it is also presented as a pleasant town to live in, nestled in a beautiful river valley. Its hero, Glenn Marley, has the impossible dream of some day establishing himself as a successful Macochee lawyer devoted to the cause of justice. By so doing, he hopes to satisfy his social conscience, aroused by his impecunious but compassionate legal mentor Wade Powell; simultaneously he hopes to provide for the material needs of his fiancee Lavinia, daughter of the prosperous, worldly-wise Judge Blair, Powell's legal antithesis in the town.

What Marley fails to recognize is, first, that the town is glutted with lawyers, and, second, that even if one were to work up a successful law practice over the years, it would have to be done by cultivating the rich, not ministering to the poor. The end product of this realization is Marley's and Lavinia's departure for Chicago, portrayed as a city of great opportunity. It is left to the cynical Wade Powell to sum up the disadvantages of life in Macochee of the 1890's: "No one with ambition can stay here now. The town, like all these old county-seats, is good for nothing but impecunious old age and cemeteries. It was nothing but a country cross-roads before the railroad came, and since then it's been nothing but a water tank; if it keeps on it'll be nothing but a whistling post, and the trains won't be bothered to stop at all."[15] In the view of Powell, even the remote past of Macochee is depressing; the present, with declining opportunities for youth, is more depressing still. Though some of what Powell says here can be faulted as over-statement, sour grapes and temperamental cynicism, his words add up to a compelling indictment of life in Macochee of the 1890's.

The Macochee short stories and sketches published a few years after *The Happy Average* develop a series of contrasts, explicit or implicit, between the past and the present of Macochee, mostly to the detriment of the present or recent past. One can discern everywhere in these stories Whitlock's search into the remote past for a Golden Age.

"Macochee's First Campaign Fund" is set in the 1880's long after the memories of Civil War sacrifices have grown dim. Containing a degree of nostalgia mixed with condescension that reflect Whitlock's long and productive absence from the small town, this lightweight story tells how the Democrats in the traditionally Republican town of Macochee finally elect their mayoral candidate by a trick. As portrayed here, this one-party town is a good one to be from, perhaps, but not one to return to, controlled as it ordinarily is by a gaggle of self-important know-nothings. Here Whitlock is more detached from his subject than in *The Happy Average*, but the narrator's attitude in the short story, despite its haze of nostalgia, is still basically one of rejection.

Whereas "Macochee's First Campaign Fund" presents only an implicit contrast between the ignoble present and the period of the Civil War, "Fowler Brunton" is much more explicit. Fowler Brunton was once an idealistic and eminently successful criminal lawyer who fought for the underdog over the years with diminishing success. As the power of the railroads waxed, the influence of Brunton waned, until finally one could observe in this relic of a better age an almost total divorce of idealism from power. All his disciples have left Macochee for the city, leaving the town to his corrupt enemies, the railroad lawyers.

In "Fowler Brunton," Whitlock's rejection of the town is more complete than in "The Orator of the Day," where he contrasts the self-seeking oratory of a young lawyer speaking in Macochee on Memorial Day with the selfless, heroic speech of the ancient Civil War veteran introducing him. Though this contrast is sharply damaging to the new age, Whitlock concedes the possibility of heroism even in the present. But the individual who will rise to meet the challenge of the town is not clearly in sight.

In "The Orator of the Day" heroic idealism is seen as a past reality and a present but remote possibility; however, the value of idealism is not questioned. But in "The Field of Honor," idealism (this time "the honor of the regiment") is presented as a heritage of Macochee that must be questioned, perhaps even repudiated in the modern age. The basic conflict of the story is between Colonel Clayton, who tells an ultimately self-defeating lie about a cowardly soldier to preserve "the honor of the regiment," and the townspeople of Macochee, who live by a much more practical set of values. This short story, perhaps Whitlock's finest, preserves a delicate balance between the two value systems represented.

"The Old House Across the Street" is the story of two Macochee sisters, quiet but fierce rivals for the love of a soldier killed during the war. After his death the sisters pass their lives in mutual recrimination and bitterness over this rivalry, ending only with the death of the one sister. This sketch is chiefly interesting as another example of the grip of the Civil War on Whitlock's imagination, and presumably on the memories and sensibilities of the town itself. The heroic note in this story, despite its references to the Civil War, is muted, however.

The two remaining Macochee stories in *The Fall Guy* are "The Question" and "The Preacher's Son." In these stories Whitlock, ignoring the possible grandeur of the remote past, returns to the mundane concerns of his own adulthood and remembered childhood. "The Question" points up the contrast between Bob Weston, already introduced as a minor character in *The Happy Average*, and his boyhood chum Jack Reynolds. Bob has married and settled down to a modest life in Macochee, while Jack has left the town, remained a bachelor, and become a sophisticated "railroad lawyer and a senator." The question of the story left unanswered at the story's end, is whether Weston, if he had his life to live over, would again settle down to an obscure country lawyer's life in Macochee. With the passage of time, the possibilities of life in Macochee have come to seem a little less drab to the narrator than they did in *The Happy Average*. Unabashedly autobiographical, "The Preacher's Son" concerns a young boy whose desire to go to the circus is finally gratified, despite his being the son of a Methodist minister opposed to such frivolities. In this instance the father, touched by his son's eagerness, makes exception to the rule and gives the boy permission to go. His day at the circus is all that his childish imagination supposed it might be, but more important than the circus itself is the story's portrayal of the family's warmth and love, qualities which may provide a clue to understanding Whitlock's intermittent nostalgia for Macochee over the years and his persistent return to the town in his imagination.

To sum up, the past appears in these stories as a time when dedication, self-sacrifice, heroism, and perhaps even true religion could be found in Macochee. The present, on the other hand, is an age in which dedication has given way to opportunism, self-sacrifice to self-indulgence, courage to egotism, and the religion of love, with an occasional exception, to institutionalized hypocrisy. For Whitlock, the end of the Golden Age of Macochee is hard to pin-point, but is invariably associated in these stories with the rise to power of the railroads and corporations in the 1880's. The railroads, especially, came to represent an irresistible and invulnerable concentration of wealth. Perpetuating and expanding their power by any means, they corrupted most men of intellect and ability, kept from power or destroyed the power of the remaining idealists, and exploited the rest of mankind.

Whitlock's second Macochee novel, *J. Hardin & Son*, recalls the first, but with a difference. Whereas Glenn Marley escapes from Macochee to find his salvation conceived chiefly in terms of worldly success, Paul Hardin stumbles on materialistic success right in his own back yard. By the end of the novel he owns a superfluity of farms and oil wells that make him the wealthiest man in Macochee. It is clear, however, that in terms of his stunted artistic impulses and his desire for personal fulfillment and love, he is as bereft of personal satisfaction as Marley would have been of material goods, had the latter chosen to stay in Macochee. In *The Happy Average*, then, the small town is judged deficient in materialistic opportunities; in *J. Hardin & Son*, Whitlock's criticism of the small town is extended to the materialistic values of American society in general, which starves the soul even when it feeds the body. Whether one conceives of success in materialistic terms or in terms of personal fulfillment, however, the town of Macochee is not the ideal place to achieve it. But Macochee is a more likely place to achieve worldly success than personal fulfillment.

It is not Whitlock's intention, though, to absolve Paul Hardin of responsibility for his failure to escape from Macochee. Paul himself recognizes his failure to act decisively and forcefully when opportunities present themselves, but instead of struggling to overcome this defect, he attempts to pass it off as the necessary condition of human life. Like none of Whitlock's earlier Macochee protagonists, he sees life as governed by fate, chance, or accident rather than by character. Evidence that Paul minimizes both human freedom and responsibility can be drawn from that imposing figure from the Golden Age of Macochee, Josiah West, Paul's childhood idol, who long since escaped from the confines of the town to become an artist of international reputation.[16] Paul, whose artistic talent is evidenced early, should have at least attempted to do the same. In *J. Hardin & Son*, Whitlock still rejects the town of his boyhood but insists on the responsibility of the individual to escape its meretricious charms, even those of the bitch goddess materialism.

Though the early Macochee stories are chiefly concerned with the private lives of its citizens (sometimes as affected by the Civil War), *The Buckeyes* extends its scope to include the cause of abolition in Ohio from 1836-1845 (the year the novel breaks off), and to the political fortunes of such historical figures as Senator Thomas Corwin, General William Harrison, Henry Clay, James Polk, and James G. Birney, abolitionist candidate for President in 1840 and 1844. The fact that Urbana was an important station on the Underground Railroad gave Whitlock the license to make Macochee an important station on the Railroad also. And the fact that General Harrison attended a mammoth political rally in Urbana in 1840 further buttresses the historicity of *The Buck-*

eyes, which portrays that rally with the utmost vividness and circumstantiality.

Whitlock's account in his published letters of the novel's conception, development and eventual abandonment is interesting, though curiously unsatisfactory in certain respects. The first evidence of his intention to return in a new novel to Macochee, the town of his imagination, appeared early in 1929 while he was still in the United States following his mother's death. (When word reached him at his home in Cannes that she was dying, he returned to Urbana to spend a few days with her before she died, and to attend her funeral.) On January 15 he writes: "Now, I think, I shall go back to novel writing. My stay in Ohio revived so many memories that I am tempted to go back to Macochee in imagination."[17]

He again mentions the new novel in a letter to Albert Bigelow Paine, Twain's biographer and editor, on Oct. 14, 1930. By this date he had focused on his grandfather and the cause of abolition as his subject. "... I woke up one morning not long since, and said to myself all of a sudden: 'Why, damn it all! there is your old grandfather Brand, who played a rather picturesque part in the early Abolition Movement in Ohio; why don't you write a book about him, or at least, around him?' "[18] By Dec. 5, 1930, in a letter to his editor Rutger B. Jewett he has narrowed the time span of the novel to "1835 or 40 to 1860—the old Abolitionists, etc., suggested by experiences of my grandfather, the same sort of thing, in a way, to be found in Tom Corwin's life," the writing of whose biography he had just projected as a possibility.[19] Already in this entry, he strikes the note that the novel doesn't go well. In his Dec. 23 letter to Jewett he repeats that note, likening his struggle to a sculptor's prodigious efforts to chip a statue from a block of marble. Whitlock's problem is complicated, he reveals, by the formidable scope of the projected novel, dealing with four generations: "I rather quail before the idea of undertaking to write a saga."[20]

Fourteen months later in a letter to Paine following a long, debilitating bout of pleurisy, he expresses the fear that he will never be able to write anything again. In this letter, and in a letter to an old friend on Oct. 31, 1932, he comes as close as he was ever to come to penetrating the mystery of his waning confidence and artistic inspiration. In both these letters he describes a single, painful encounter with Edith Wharton, whom he revered, as precipitating his abandonment of the novel on which he had labored over a period of two years and of which he had written nearly

11

100,000 words. In the second letter, after mentioning his unsettling attempts to write the novel in two different ways, neither satisfactory, he reverts to the Wharton incident again: "Then something Edith Wharton said to me one day at lunch—she is hard as nails—instilled a doubt in my mind, and in writing doubt is fatal. However, I did nearly a hundred thousand words, and then got so disgusted with the whole thing that I laid it aside in despair and I doubt if I shall take it up again. Something has happened; fiction has come to seem uninteresting and unreal compared with biography."[21] The "something" which Edith Wharton said to him is revealed in the letter previously mentioned; "I told her that I had begun a novel the day before; I was feeling rather enthusiastic and a little cocky about it, but she, with her hard realism, soon took me down. She said: 'Do you know where you are going to get off?' I told her that I knew where I might get off if necessary, but the more I kept thinking of that searching question, the more uncertain I became, and as I wrote I always had that question before my mind. . . . "[22]

According to a letter of Jan. 31, 1933 to the American dramatist John D. Barry, Whitlock was involved in another attempt to finish the novel, but he confessed to losing interest in novels generally. "Life spins better yarns than the novelists," he wrote.[23] A letter to Jewett dated July 14, 1933 reiterates his intention of continuing the novel that summer; "At least I will make a mighty effort to do so."[24] But by Nov. 12, 1933, the project has been finally abandoned in favor of his ongoing biographies of Jefferson and Jackson.[25] His last reference to the unfinished novel in the published letters is dated April 27, 1934. Here, in a letter to Barry as he is recovering from one prostate operation and awaiting another, he again recalls the fatal Wharton interview to explain his loss of confidence in the novel, adding an ironic final note to the effect that Wharton in her latest writing has contradicted the very thing she had said that dashed his confidence: "But the funniest thing of all was what she said to me two years ago which caused me to chuck the novel. She said that 'subject' was very important, and secondly, that one must have the whole thing thoroughly planned out and the end arranged before beginning. Now she says that neither of these things is of any importance, and that it doesn't matter."[26]

A month later, four days after the second operation, Whitlock died with his two biographies as well as the novel incomplete.

In its present unfinished state, the novel is divided into three books, with twenty-eight chapters in the first book, fourteen in the second, and six completed in the third. The first book begins in July, 1836, when young Blair arrives in Macochee, and ends in 1838, by which time he has had an affair with his employer's daughter Gertie Grow, become engaged to another woman, and become a lawyer in the town (pp. 45/169). The second book begins in 1840; now Blair is already a successful lawyer and family man running for the State Legislature on the Whig ticket that includes General Harrison for President and Tom Corwin for Governor. By the end of Book II, Blair has been elected to office and survived a duel with his arch enemy, Tom Nash, Gertie's husband (pp. 170-238). Book III begins in 1844 with Blair running for State Senate after having served two terms in the House. By the last page of the third, incomplete book, he is safely elected to the Senate despite the defeat of the Whig ticket headed by Blair's idol, Henry Clay. Blair's indiscretion with Gertie has come back to haunt him in the form of her child, whom Blair eventually comes to recognize as his own illegitimate son (pp. 239-263).

The plot of *The Buckeyes* can be sketched as follows. On a hot July day in 1836, Carter Blair, the novel's protagonist, arrives in Cincinnati on his way from Bourbon County, Kentucky to Macochee, Ohio, the promised land. (Carter's father is a slave owner, but the youth leaves home not from any antipathy to slavery but because his older brother's patrimony is too small for him to share in it.) In Cincinnati, Blair accidentally meets the foxy villain of the novel, young Tom Nash, son of Macochee's founder and leading citizen. Young Nash disgusts Blair by taking him to a local whorehouse. The next morning Blair departs for Lebanon on his beautiful Kentucky thoroughbred horse, Dolly D. There he meets the charismatic Whig Congressman Tom Corwin, who is to be one of the dominant influences of the young man's life. Corwin, whose home is on the western outskirts of Lebanon, is a great lawyer and politician, with an almost miraculous capacity to please the public with his oratory, especially with his flashing wit. But there is another side to Corwin, a profound, dark, and mysterious quality which the public never sees, but which Blair observes: "...the quality of the voice...revealed another Tom Corwin than the one who was always joking and making men laugh, the Tom Corwin who had thought deeply about the mystery of life, its cruelty and injustice, its brevity and futility, and so was sad at heart, and himself a kind of Prometheus, bound to a rock in this wilderness of the West." (p. 69-70).

Following his captivation by Corwin, who inspires Blair to read law, the young Kentuckian rides Dolly D. along the wilderness road to Macochee. There he presents a letter of introduction to an abolitionist friend of his father's named Ethan Grow (the surname is doubtless symbolic, in view of the man's gradually but inexorably expanding influence on the politics of Ohio). Grow gives Blair a job in his dry goods store on the town square and rents him a room in his home. Because Grow is more interested in reading abolitionist newspapers than in minding the store, he is glad to let Blair take over more and more responsibility for its daily operation. Soon Blair has an affair with Grow's crude and sensual daughter Gertie, whose character the naive Blair misreads as innocent and pure. Between working in the dry goods store and romancing Gertie, Blair reads law with a local judge. Meanwhile, Grow is bested and humiliated in a public debate on abolition by the suave, sophisticated, and conservative Colonel Nash, father of the rapscallion Tom who has returned to Macochee from Cincinnati. (Ironically, Grow's defeat is assured by the catcalls and insults of the white trash at the meeting, the bully boys of the Bottoms who "favour slavery because they like to feel that there's at least one class of human beings in a more degraded state than themselves" (p. 128).

But Blair's romance with Gertie is short-lived. Tom Nash embarks upon a whirlwind courtship of Gertie that begins at the factory pond where Blair takes Gertie skating. Nash elopes with her to Cincinnati, but not before losing a fist fight to her rejected lover Blair, and vowing to seek vengeance on him. Nash's parents are outraged and appalled at their son's marriage, for the Grows are much inferior socially to the Nashes. Gertie's family suffers proportionately, not only because the marriage is disapproved of by the Nashes, but because the Grows themselves know it has little chance of success. When Grow's business fails following the panic of 1837, he sells out to a Yankee and starts an abolitionist newspaper at great financial sacrifice to his family. Blair takes advantage of this change of management to leave the store and the Grow home.

Blair celebrates his passing the State bar exam by falling in love with Lucretia Harris, a girl from Virginia who is visiting friends in Macochee. Shortly after meeting her, he makes the mistake of lending Grow his beautiful horse to attend an Anti-Slavery Convention in Granville; at the convention, the horse's tail is bobbed by the foes of abolition, and Grow himself is pelted with eggs on the homeward journey. Following this débacle, from which Dolly D. never recovers her former beauty, Blair recoups his fortunes by marrying Lucretia. A fine member of an aristocratic, conservative family, Lucretia is a great strength to

Blair in his rapid rise to success from 1838 to 1844. She also bears him three children in their recently purchased old brick house at the corner of Miami and Walnut Streets.

As befits a candidate for office in 1840 with its log cabin and hard cider campaign for Tippecanoe and Tyler too, Blair begins his campaign for the legislature by demonstrating his pioneer skills at a turkey shoot. There he wins a set of dishes and then proceeds to do some "fancy shooting," Kentucky style—snuffing a candle out with a rifle at 40 paces. The crowd that gathers is understandably impressed by their new candidate, but the highlight of the campaign is the mammoth rally and barbecue at Colonel Nash's farm to honor the aging Presidential candidate, General Harrison. More accurately, from the narrator's viewpoint, the Whigs "had routed the poor old man out of his retirement and were dragging him about all over the country as the principal exhibit of a travelling circus" (p. 178).

At Nash's place, "great crowds of noisy men in buckeye hats or coonskin caps were trooping into the Grove, shouting and singing, in the spirit of frontier rowdyism. They had already filled the twelve long tables, and were swigging the watered cider from gourds that were handed round, and cramming their mouths with the 'salt-rising' bread and the scorched meat. The air, hazy from the dust, was filled with the rank odour of trampled ragweed, the smell of the burning flesh of barbecued beeves and sheep, and the exhalations of the sweaty, unwashed human crowd. [Such sights and smells gave Blair] a feeling that a candidate would never dare avow, an undemocratic sensation of relief that he was not to dine in that company, but was to sit at table with the quality at the big house" (p. 179). Inside, the Presidential candidate, who is supposed to prefer log cabins and hard cider to the blandishments of civilization, is sipping madeira. The dinner itself is marred for Blair only by the skulking presence of his enemy, young Tom Nash.

The barbecue and dinner are followed by a gigantic parade around the town square. Among bands and floats is a delegation bearing a banner inscribed:

The People is Oll Korrect

(from which the expression OK is supposed to have come). After the parade, Blair has the privilege of introducing the featured speaker, Tom Corwin, who as usual does himself proud with his oratory. Following the rally, the shameful word spread that Colonel Nash's grove "had suffered more from the barbecue than it had from the tornado of 1837; for this time a human whirlwind—the most destructive of all—had swept over it, breaking off the boughs of its trees, trampling its grass, strewing the grounds with débris, and rooting it up like swine" (p. 193). Careless of such liabilities of the democratic process, the Harrison-Tyler-Corwin ticket sweeps on to victory.

And that victory includes Carter Blair, despite formidable opposition from Tom Nash, who had been spreading false, malicious tales about Blair's reputation as a man "popular with the sex." In defense of his honor, Blair engages Nash in an inconclusive duel on election day. Following Blair's election, Nash slinks westward out of the town's life, permanently abandoning his wife Gertie and her child.

Blair serves one term, getting closely acquainted with the Honorable Thomas Corwin, now Governor Corwin, in the process. Though Corwin is defeated after one term, Blair is re-elected. Soon, as fortune smiles, he is able to buy a fine farm and build an addition to his house, or rather, "to build the new house to which the old was an addition" (p. 242). Then, in 1844, the Whigs run Clay for President against Polk; Blair can't believe that Clay can be defeated. By now Blair is dressing the part of a successful lawyer, getting fat, and not exercising much, though he has three horses in the stable and three children (p. 242). He is also becoming increasingly cautious and conservative in his expensive broad-cloth suit.

One day he is shocked to find that his old friend Grow has bolted the Whig party, "the party of compromise," to join the abolitionist party of James G. Birney (p. 247). Though Clay goes down to defeat in the election, Blair wins a State Senate seat with Corwin's help on the campaign trail in Ohio. Nevertheless he is becoming "disgusted with politics and all the nasty mess of [political] deceits and betrayals" (p. 253).

Though the political influence of Grow is increasing, his material plight worsens till he must swallow his pride and ask the new Senator for assistance in obtaining a clerkship in the State Senate. Blair magnanimously helps him secure his post. Now, wherever he goes, Grow takes his sober, precocious grandson with him, for Gertie and the boy are now living with her father. In the Senate, the boy is employed as a page. One day as he calls the boy to him, Senator Blair is struck by the boy's haunting resemblance to Blair's older brother Joe, from Bourbon County; this is the clinching evidence, among other bits presented in the novel, that Blair is the boy's father. Here the novel abruptly ends with Blair becoming ever more susceptible to Grow's influence as the grandfather of the Senator's illegitimate child and as the head of an increasingly powerful abolitionist movement. But whether Grow is the product of envy of his aristocratic betters, a fanatic seeking martyrdom, the prophet of a new age, or some combination of all three, he remains a controversial figure in Blair's mind right to the last page of this incomplete novel. Certainly Blair's impulse through most of the narrative is to accept the hypothesis of Grow's fanaticism at the expense of the other possibilities. So much for the unfinished plot of the 100,000 word version of the novel.

The short, 12,500 word version of the novel, which probably was conceived and at least partly written before the larger version, differs from it in point of view, chronological framework, factualness and circumstantiality. Thus, whereas the longer version is narrated principally from Carter Blair's viewpoint, the 12,500 word version is told from the point of view of Blair's grandson, also—and somewhat confusingly—named Carter Blair. The younger Blair identifies himself so closely with the older one, however, that he occasionally shifts in his imagination to his grandfather's point of view. And whereas the chronological setting of the longer version is from 1836 to 1845, the setting of the shorter one is the early 1890's, with flashbacks to the 1830's and 1850's. Young Carter Blair, who has been living with his parents in New York, comes to Macochee to celebrate with his grandfather, a lawyer, his completion of legal studies and admission to the bar at age 23. Blair arrives just as preparations are being made for his grandfather's Fourth of July reunion with the "boys" of his regiment, the Fighting Sixty-Sixth. From the early 1890's, the novel moves backwards in time by a series of conversations, narrations and reminiscences to 1836, the year when Carter comes to Ohio, and the 1850's, the heyday of abolitionism in Macochee.

Finally, the shorter version tends to be more down-to-earth than the longer one, and less dependent on fictional embroideries. Whereas in the shorter version, Carter Blair is merely accosted in Cincinnati by a streetwalker, in the longer version he is taken to a lurid whorehouse. Whereas in the short version no hint of romance develops between Blair and Gertie's counterpart, Hope, in the longer version an illicit romance blossoms forth. And whereas in the short version Grandmother Blair's maiden name is correctly given as Talbot (or Talbott), in the longer version she is assigned the fictional name of Harris. Similarly in the short fragment, the grandfather's house is located on Reynolds Street, where it actually stands; its setting and appearance are described with exact circumstantiality:

> But presently the horse, of its own accord, was drawing up before a house that Carter with the photographic memory of childhood, could recall in every minute detail, the wide brick house with the verandah standing back from the street, with a placid, self-sufficient air, remote and immune from the emergencies of life and the complications of a fevered world. Everything was familiar now; the slope of the cobbled gutter into which the surrey lurched out of the thin layer of mud with which the sprinkling-cart had overlaid the soft dust of the unpaved street; the two cast-iron hitching posts with the diminutive horse-heads on top; the unevenness in the side-walk where the roots of the elms had heaved up the bricks; the very click of the latch of the gate between the high posts; and the soft cluck of the lock when you turned the silver knob of the door, and the dimness and coolness within the wide hall and the faint, clean odour of Chinese matting... (Short MS, p. 4).

In the longer version the house is moved from its actual site to a fictional, somewhat grander setting on Miami and Walnut Streets, where the house and its setting are not so exactly portrayed.

As indicated earlier, many particulars of Blair's life are drawn from the life of Whitlock's grandfather, Joseph Carter Brand. Born on January 5, 1810 in Bourbon County, Kentucky, Brand was the son of Thomas Brand and Fanny Carter Brand. Thomas had moved to his farm in Kentucky from Augusta County, Virginia. Following their marriage in 1809, the Brands had eight children, of whom Joseph was the eldest. In 1848, when Thomas made his will, there were still two slaves in the family, John and Nancy, who were to be given to Joseph and his sisters Susan and Betsy at Thomas Brand's death. Attention is also drawn in this will to a patrimony of $1,000 already given to Joseph.

In 1830 Joseph came to Urbana, probably with the patrimony mentioned above, where he assisted his uncle, Dr. Joseph S. Carter, in a drugstore. In 1832 he moved to Mechanicsburg, a town a few miles east of Urbana, to begin merchandising with Dr. Obed Horr, a former associate of his uncle's in Urbana[27] and subsequently a well known abolitionist;[28] in the same year he married Lavinia Talbott (1813-1905), of Frederick County, Virginia. In 1833 Lavinia gave birth to the first of their nine children; the sixth of these was Mary (Mallie) Lavinia (1844-1928),[29] who following her marriage to Elias D. Whitlock of Urbana gave birth to Joseph Brand Whitlock, i.e. Brand Whitlock, on March 4, 1869.

18

In 1834 when the town of Mechanicsburg was incorporated, merchants' capital and notes were valued at $9,830 for tax purposes, of which Obed Horr had $4,000 and Joseph C. Brand $3,000. "These were the capitalists of those days."[30] In 1837 Joseph Carter Brand purchased and began farming a quarter section of land (160 acres) along Buck Creek southeast of Urbana near the Clark County line (N.E. quarter section 32, range 11 in Union Township).[31] Secretary of the local Whig party in 1838,[32] he served as Whig Representative for Champaign County in the 42nd session of the Ohio House, 1843-44.

In 1851 he moved back to Urbana, purchasing for $1,400 a modest house at 132 W. Reynolds St. which, according to local tax records, had been built in 1824 (Auditor's Office of Champaign County, Building Record Card). He subsequently enlarged this four-room house into the imposing and attractive house still standing, the house his grandson Brand so frequently visited in childhood and youth.[33] By Sept. 1, 1854, Joseph Carter Brand was inserting modest advertisements in the Urbana *Citizen and Gazette;* silks, shawls and bonnets were among the items for sale at his dry goods store. In 1856-57 he served a term in the Ohio Senate for the eleventh district,[34] and according to Whitlock, he served as a delegate to the first major convention of the Republican party in Pittsburgh, Pa., in 1856.[35]

In 1857 he was involved in the Ad White slave rescue case. Whitlock gives the following colorful account of the first incident leading to the trial in which his grandfather was a co-defendant:

> One of the accomplishments in which he [J. C. Brand] took pride, perhaps next to his ability as a horseman, was his skill with the rifle, acquired in Kentucky at the expense of squirrels in the tops of tall trees (he could snuff a candle with a rifle), and this ability he placed at the service of a negro named Ad White, who had run away from his master in the South, and was hidden in a corn-crib near Urbana when overtaken by United States marshals from Cincinnati. The negro was armed, and was defending himself, when my grandfather and his friend Ichabod Corwin, of a name tolerably well known in Ohio history, went to his assistance, and drove the marshals off by the hot fire of their rifles.[36]

Charged in Cincinnati District Court that summer with interfering with a U.S. officer in discharge of duty, he was by this time clearly associated with the cause of abolition. During the Civil War he "obtained the order for the raising of the gallant Sixty-sixth Regiment of Ohio Volunteer Infantry," serving as a quartermaster and commissary captain in the army himself. Following his appointment by President Grant as U.S. consul to Nuremberg, he spent nearly three years in Bavaria. On his return he served as mayor of Urbana for three terms (1872-74, 1874-76 and 1880-82).[37]

Whitlock recalls his grandfather during one of his terms of mayoral office as follows:

> He wore broad polished shoes, low, and fastened with buckles, and against the black of his attire his stiffly starched, immaculate white waistcoat was conspicuous. Only a few of its lower buttons of pearl were fastened; above that it was open, and from one of the buttonholes, the second from the top, his long gold watch-chain hung from its large gold hook. The black cravat was not hidden by his white beard, which he did not wear as long as many Ohio gentlemen of that day, and he was crowned by a large Panama hat, yellowed by years of summer service, and bisected by a ridge that began at the middle of the broad brim directly in front, ran back, climbed and surmounted the large high crown, and then, descending, ended its impressive career at the middle of the broad brim behind.[38]

The Urbana *Citizen & Gazette* notice of his death on Dec. 30, 1887 was captioned:

A LEADER
OF MEN FOR FORTY YEARS OF PUBLIC LIFE—
A PRINCE OF ISRAEL

His obituary concluded with the following tribute: "In his death passes away one of the strongest characters and best men of Champaign County history." He was "of a sincere, aggressive temperament and ready to stand by his convictions of right and justice if he stood alone." Thus ended the life of one who, though he may not have been the ideal figure of his grandson's imaginings, was a strong and honorable man.

Comparison of Carter Blair with his prototype Joseph Carter Brand reveals some parallels more significant than the similarity of their names, along with some differences tending to illuminate Whitlock's intentions in the novel. Both young men are from slave-owning, farm families in Bourbon County, Kentucky. Both are near the legal age of maturity when they leave Kentucky for Ohio, though the fictional character leaves home six years later than his prototype, a change Whitlock may have made with a view to compressing the considerable time span of the novel. Blair's principal assets, as befits a frontier hero, are his horse and "a little hard money." His prototype Brand was evidently in much better shape financially, probably leaving home with the

$1,000 patrimony referred to above, a substantial sum in 1830. Blair does not leave home because of any qualms about owning slaves, but from economic considerations. "His father wasn't rich. He had his Blue Grass farm and a few slaves to help him work it, but there wasn't enough for Carter and Joe both, and Joe was the elder"...(pp. 48-49). Whitlock in his autobiography is somewhat more equivocal as to his grandfather's motives for leaving Kentucky; he suggests that Brand's pity or sympathy for the slaves might have been a factor in his departure: "It may have been some such feeling as this [pity or sympathy] for the negroes that led him, when a young man in Kentucky, to renounce a patrimony of slaves and come north. It was not, to be sure, a very large patrimony, for his father was a farmer in a rather small way in Bourbon County, and owned a few slaves, but whatever the motive, he refused to own human chattels and left Bourbon County...."[39] By initially presenting the fictional character as a shade more impoverished and insensitive to the slavery issue than the grandfather may have actually been, Whitlock is able to dramatize Blair's subsequent financial success and his awakening to the cause of abolition.

Both young men as true Kentuckians pride themselves on their horsemanship and fancy shooting,[40] and both are great admirers of Tom Corwin, originally from their home county. Modeling himself on Corwin, Blair becomes a lawyer, which Brand never did, though he performed many paralegal and minor legal functions as a clerk of the court of common pleas and of the district court,[41] and as three-time mayor of Urbana presiding over the mayor's court.[42] This minor change in the fictional character perhaps reflects Whitlock's impulse to enhance the status and prestige of his protagonist.

Blair's involvement with Ethan and Gertie Grow finds no counterpart in the published records or family recollections of the Brands. It is possible that Grow himself is a composite figure based on grandfather Brand's stories about the abolitionists of Champaign County, including his business associate Obed Horr of Mechanicsburg, a known abolitionist, and of Dr. James G. Birney, referred to in the novel as the author of Ohio's famous abolitionist newspaper the *Philanthropist* and leader of the antislavery convention that Grow attends in Granville. I can find no record of any abolitionist newspaper such as Grow's *Torchlight* having been published in Urbana, nor indeed of anyone notably active there in the cause of abolition prior to the 1850's, when Urbana became an important station on the Underground Rail-

21

road.[43] (Champaign County did send a representative to the founding convention of the Ohio Anti-Slavery Society at Putnam, in 1835,[44] a time of rapid growth of the movement. And from 1836 to 1837 the number of local anti-slavery societies in Ohio is reported to have grown from 120 to 213, with 17,253 members.)[45] But it would be most surprising to find an abolitionist newspaper published as early as the 1840's in a generally conservative small town like Urbana. From 1847-1863, in fact, from the time Birney's *Philanthropist* moved from Cincinnati to Washington, D.C., the only abolitionist newspaper in Ohio was the *Anti-Slavery Bugle* published in the radicalized Quaker community of Salem southwest of Youngstown.[46] Though the origins of the fictional Grow in New England might predispose him to take an abolitionist position, his creation as the fiery abolitionist editor of Macochee in the 1830's and 40's smacks of fictional license perhaps more accurately representing the growth of abolitionism in the state at large than in a small town like Macochee-Urbana.

In the shorter fragment of *The Buckeyes* referred to above, Grow is initially called Joel Rush and identified as one of the three key influences on Blair's becoming an abolitionist (the other two being Tom Corwin and Blair's wife, whose knowledge that slavery is wrong dates back to her witnessing near her childhood home in Virginia the auction of a little black girl about her own age [MS, p. 46]). Later in this manuscript, Rush becomes Piper, with the name "Piper" sometimes being crossed out and replaced with "Grow." In this short version, Blair's acquaintance with Grow dates only from the 1850's, when Blair successfully prosecutes Grow's assailants at an anti-slavery meeting in Macochee. At this meeting Grow is pelted with eggs and his horse is cruelly "bobbed" (MS, p. 44 and cf. *The Buckeyes*, pp. 164-166). Blair takes Grow's case despite his dislike of abolitionists because he loves horses and can't bear to see them mistreated.

Grow in the shorter version lives with his wife and daughter Hope (not Gertie) on a five-acre "hardscrabble little farm at the top of the stone quarry" (MS, p. 46) along the Bluejacket Highway a mile west of Macochee. A much more colorful and realistic character than the Grow of the longer version, this one not only preaches at the Methodist church, but, because he believes in woman suffrage, makes his wife cut her hair short and wear bloomers. In addition to being an ardent Prohibitionist and teetotaller, hauling grog shop proprietors to court for the slightest infraction of the law, he is a conductor on the Underground Railroad, his home serving as one of the stations. But although he gives endless harangues on the world's evils, he is not the editor of an abolitionist newspaper, or any newspaper. Once again it appears that the ·Torchlight and the abolitionist activities of Grow as far back as the 1830's in the longer version may constitute a fictional elaboration of the narrative as originally conceived. Its purpose would be to give continuity to a tale of politics and abolitionism beginning in the 1830's, capitalizing on the Harrison campaign of 1840 in Macochee-Urbana, and culminating in the fierce abolitionism of the 1850's leading up to the Civil War.

By the end of the short fragment, probably set in 1857 or thereabouts, Blair is sufficiently sympathetic to Grow and the cause of abolition to warn him that the U.S. marshal with a posse from Cincinnati is coming to seize the slave that Grow is harboring. But Blair is still not ready to accept Grow's invitation to have dinner at a table that includes a Negro: "Sit at table and eat with a nigger! Blair instinctively [shrinks] back a pace ... " (MS, p. 48), then refuses the invitation.

In the longer version of the novel, Grow's daughter Gertie, with whom Blair has a love affair, seems little more than a device by which his eventual marriage to Lucretia Harris, from a First Family of Virginia, is made to shine more brilliantly by contrast, despite the embarrassment of Blair's illegitimate child by Gertie. In the course of the novel Lucretia becomes a representative of all the private virtues Blair finds it so difficult to maintain in public life. Lucretia, no doubt modeled on Lavinia Talbott, whom Brand married in 1832, is a petite, refined and attractive horsewoman when he courts her. In her role as wife and mother to Blair and the three children she bears him by manuscript's end, she becomes a repository of love, good taste, conservative wisdom and absolute loyalty to her husband. Though Lavinia Talbott was descended from two well-established families of Virginia, and bore nine children from 1833 to 1856, little is known of her as a person.[47] It may be assumed that she possessed at least some of the virtues attributed to her fictional, perhaps somewhat idealized counterpart Lucretia.

Blair's political career as well as his private life parallels Brand's, but with a different chronology. Whereas Blair is first a successful candidate in the 1840 campaign, Brand did not hold political office till 1843, when he served a one-year term in the Ohio House. And whereas Blair follows up his first term with a second, and the second with a successful candidacy for State Senator, Brand did not obtain political office again till 1856, when he served a regular two year term with the Ohio Senate. Whitlock's changes here focus attention on the fictional character as a successful lawyer and politician; the merchandising in which Brand engaged for many years is quickly sloughed off by his fictional counterpart.

Blair's career appears to be modeled on Brand's in one more significant respect. Like Brand, who in 1837 purchased and farmed a quarter section of land he called Pretty Prairie southeast of Urbana, Blair purchases a farm with the same name, though there is no evidence that he ever actually lives on it or farms it. In purchasing it he seems mainly intent on applying Corwin's homely wisdom that land ownership assures one's independence. Again Whitlock seems determined to elevate Blair to the landed gentry during the period of his career when his real-life counterpart was actually farming.

As befitted a prosperous merchant, Brand enlarged the four-room house he purchased in 1851 to a "modest dwelling of a dozen rooms," as Whitlock explains in *Forty Years of It:* "This gabled wing had been the original house, and additions had been built to it in two directions, with a wide hall, somewhat after the southern fashion in which so many houses in that part of Ohio were built in those days."[48] Blair the successful lawyer, like Brand the rising businessman, builds such a substantial addition to his home as to constitute a new home "to which the old was an addition" (p. 242). And though Blair by the end of the novel could not properly be called an abolitionist—as Brand probably could not in the 1840's—there are hints at the end of the manuscript, as will be shown later, that Blair may be getting ready to move slowly toward the abolitionist position that his prototype Brand accepted some years later.

Just as the protagonist and some of his associates appear to be drawn from actual characters, the town of Macochee appears to be closely modeled on Urbana. Like Urbana, whose first and only factory was for many years the woolen mill established in 1816 on East Reynolds St.,[49] with adjoining factory pond, Macochee has its "factory pond" besides its "small red-brick woolen mill established by Mr. Cowley, and the only manufacturing concern in Macochee" (p. 114). Occupied about 1912 by the Urbana tool and Die Company, itself now defunct, the woolen mill is now no more than a distant memory in Urbana.[50] And though now nothing but hummocks of earth and long weeds and grasses suggest the location of the filled-in factory pond, Mrs. Margaret English, the late Congressman Charles Brand's daughter, still

24

remembers falling through the thin ice of this pond in about 1919, when she was a girl of fifteen. Like Urbana, which had its John A. Ward to host the Harrison convention at the grove, Macochee has its Colonel Nash to do the honors, both at his home and grove. Though only a few massive oaks remain to mark the site of the grove behind the Ward house (now the Richard Rademacher home), the magnificent, old Ward house (c. 1825) still stands in Urbana at 335 College Street (see figure 7). But though the Wards has as their son the famous sculptor John Quincy Adams Ward, an older married daughter in New York who encouraged young John Q. to become a sculptor, and a younger son Edgar Melville Ward (1839-1915) who became a well known painter, it is not recorded that they had a villainous son like the Tom Nash of the novel.[51] Here, perhaps intent upon establishing a melodramatic force in opposition to the protagonist, Whitlock none too wisely exercises the liberty of the fiction writer.

Other landmarks of Macochee, such as the town Square, find their counterpart in a good many old-fashioned American towns. But one feature unique to Urbana which is also described in Whitlock's Macochee is a scene at the Square drawn by Henry Howe in 1846 and well reproduced by Middleton.[52]

Facing north from the south east corner of the Square (now Monument Square), the drawing portrays, among other buildings long gone, a building dated 1811. The building now on that site is the Citizens National Bank, established 1865. Beneath the eaves of the building adjoining the 1811 building the letters CHEAPSIDE are spelled out in bold letters. Howe in the old edition of 1847 described his engraving as follows:

> Urbana is a beautiful town, and has, in its outskirts, some elegant private residences. The engraving is a view in its central part, taken from near Reynold's store. The court-house and Methodist church are seen in the distance. The building on the left . . . was, in the late war [of 1812], Doolittle's Tavern, the headquarters of Governor Meigs. The one in front, with the date "1811" upon it . . . was then a commissary's office, and the building where Col. Richard M. Johnson was brought wounded from the battle of the Thames, and in which he remained several days under a surgeon's care.[53]

The close association of Macochee with Urbana in Whitlock's mind is evident in the following passage from *The Buckeyes*, where Blair is looking out a window of Grow's dry goods store from a vantage point almost identical to Howe's in the engraving: "And Carter went to the front of the store, and stood looking out

25

through one of the small panes of glass in the door, at the hopeless rain pelting down into the Square, and at a high-gabled building on the other side with the date 1811 on its walls, and at the row of shops with 'Cheapside' spelled out in great letters above them" (p. 112). Here, of course, Whitlock may be following Howe's engraving rather than his youthful recollections of Urbana or his grandfather's reminiscences. Regardless of the source of his inspiration, Whitlock paints a vivid and distinctive word picture of the Square in Macochee.

Throughout his novel Whitlock is generally faithful to the main events and characters of American history. Indeed his departures from historical fact are few in number and relatively insignificant, introduced deliberately, like Shakespeare's in the history plays, to achieve compression, dramatic heightening, or clarity of characterization or theme.

In the completed portion of the novel, covering the period from 1836-1845, the principal historical events portrayed involve the growing threat of the abolition cause to the Whig party viewed as the party of compromise on the slavery question. By 1840 Carter Blair, the protagonist, is carried to victory on the crest of the Whig wave, which, unbeknownst to the candidates, is about to break on the slavery issue. The leader of the Whig campaign of 1840 was of course William Henry Harrison, the first American president from Ohio. Though born in Virginia, he spent his early adult life on the Northwest frontier, obtained a distinguished military reputation at the Battles of Fallen Timbers (1794), Tippecanoe (1811), and the Thames in Canada (1813), where his forces won the decisive battle against the British in which Tecumseh was killed. In 1814 he retired from the army and began farming at North Bend, Ohio in the south west of the state. After several years of service in the House of Representatives (1817-1819) and as U.S. Senator (1825-28), he fell into obscurity. Resurrected as a living legend of the frontier in the log cabin and hard cider campaign of 1840, he ran as Whig candidate for President. Swept to victory with his running mate John Tyler (1790-1862) of "Tippecanoe and Tyler Too" fame, Harrison died of exhaustion and pneumonia in 1841, a month after his inauguration, leaving Tyler as the tenth President of the United States.

In 1840 the cause of abolition as viewed by Blair seems no more of a threat to the party than a gnat to an elephant. And even before the election of 1844, when Blair is asked where he stands on the slavery question, he is content merely to describe himself as "a Henry Clay man," meaning that he believes in emancipation "whenever it can be brought about by peaceable and orderly methods, conserving the rights of everybody without disrupting the government, disorganizing the life of the nation" (p. 247). What the Whig party in Ohio continued to ignore as long as possible, but what Whitlock brings out in his novel, was such straws in the wind as the increasingly conspicuous presence of the Ohio Anti-Slavery Society, founded in 1835, James G. Birney's influential newspaper the *Philanthropist* begun near Cincinnati in 1836, the operation of the Underground Railroad, and the formation of a national Liberty Party with Birney as its Presidential candidate both in 1840 and 1844. Whitlock's view of abolition in the early 1840's as a potentially powerful political force not yet generally recognized as such corresponds to that of Birney's twentieth century biographer Betty Fladeland: "Outside the ranks of the abolitionists themselves, the efforts of the Liberty party were drowned amid the tumult and shouting of the log-cabin and hard-cider campaign [of Harrison, Tyler, and the Whigs]; but those few who had their ears to the ground heard in it the distant rumble of mighty thunder."[54] By pointing up the defection of Whigs to the Liberty Party as a factor contributing to Henry Clay's defeat in 1844 by the Democratic nonentity Polk, Whitlock suggests that the storm heralded by that distant thunder was gathering rapidly. The correctness of his view that by 1844 the Whigs were being forced to review their stand on abolition is evident from the Liberty Party's growing strength at the polls. Whereas Birney in 1840 received 7,100 votes nationally (903 in Ohio) as the new party's Presidential candidate, in 1844 he received 62,300 (8,050 in Ohio). Since most of these votes were coming from Whigs disillusioned with their party of compromise, one can readily imagine what Whitlock portrays in his novel, the near panic of the Whig candidates as they saw fellow Whigs bolting the party for the Liberty Party and as they saw their favorite symbol of moderation and compromise, Henry Clay, going down to defeat at the hands of a cipher like Polk. The short-run consequence of the defection of these Whigs was victory for the Democrats; the longer run effect might be to give the Liberty Party the balance of power on a swing vote, and eventually, by 1856, to contribute to the formation of a new party, the Republican Party, much closer to the Liberty Party on the slavery question than either the Whig or Democratic parties had been. The record of votes cast in Ohio by the Liberty Party's gubernatorial candidates tells a similar tale of rapid growth and increasing political influence but suggests that the gathering political storm did not really break till 1853, when the new party tripled its support over a two year period, with Samuel Lewis securing 50,346 votes in 1853 as against 16,918 votes in 1851.[55]

One's sense of Whitlock's fidelity to the facts of history and to a reasonable interpretation thereof is scarcely weakened by noting a minor change he makes in the chronology of annual meetings of the Ohio Anti-Slavery Society, to which Grow evidently belongs. In the novel the Granville meeting of the Society, sparked by its leader Birney, is attended by Grow riding Blair's horse, whose mane is hacked and tail bobbed at the convention by the foes of abolition. On the journey home her rider is egged by rowdies shouting "Bobolitionist, Bobolitionist." Whitlock's account of this meeting is based on reports of the second annual meeting of the Ohio Anti-Slavery Society held in a barn near Granville, a meeting which Birney actually attended, and at which he and other delegates received the kind of rough treatment accorded the fictional Grow and his mount in the novel.[56] Whereas Whitlock assigns these events to 1838, in fact they occurred in April 1836, when Blair had not even left Kentucky for Ohio. At a slight cost to historical veracity, the novel compresses history, thereby intensifying without significantly distorting the picture presented of the times.

The highlight of the Harrison campaign in the novel is the Sept. 15, 1840 convention at Macochee. Elaborately and vividly described in 28 MS pages, Whitlock's account of this convention parallels published versions of Harrison's campaign visit to Urbana of Sept. 8, misreported in some source or sources which Whitlock apparently used as having taken place Sept. 15. Though sometimes inaccurate, as in this detail, or deliberately modified in some respects from printed reports of the actual visit, Whitlock's account of the convention is remarkably successful in capturing the wildly enthusiastic spirit of the national campaign of 1840, as described in superlatives by those who witnessed it or wrote about it. This comment by one of Harrison's twentieth century biographers is typical: "Never before was there such a campaign, and it was, indeed, to achieve heights and depths which formed a standard for all later campaigns."[57]

Highlights of the Whig rally as Whitlock portrayed it include the welcoming delegation from Macochee to meet General Harrison on the Springfield and Dayton road; a noon barbecue for the *hoi-polloi* at Colonel Nash's grove and at the same time a luncheon for the elite, including Blair and Corwin, at the Colonel's splendid Georgian house; the General's afternoon review of a long procession of bands and floats at the Square, including a genuine log-cabin made of buckeye logs and a delegation with a banner inscribed "The People is Oll Korrect"; and thereafter the speeches of ex-Governor Metcalfe of Kentucky, Blair, Harrison, and to climax all the rest, the brilliant orator Corwin. To judge by the great crowd's enthusiastic response to the procession and speakers, the rally was a huge success, assuring a Whig victory for at least thirty miles around: "And all that evening great clouds of dust rolled along the streets of Macochee as farm-waggons rattled away on their long journeys home, their occupants, many of them, full of whisky, whooping it up for Tippecanoe and Tyler too" (p. 192).

Although all available sources agree with Whitlock that a mammoth noon barbecue was held, the actual order of the day's events was somewhat different than set forth in the novel. Thus whereas in the novel the political speeches were all compressed into a long afternoon, in fact General Harrison's address was delivered at 10:00 a.m. before the barbecue, and ex-Governor Metcalfe's in the evening with other speeches.[58] And whereas Whitlock represents Blair as a first-time candidate for office in the State Legislature, his prototype Brand did not serve in the Legislature till 1843[59] and is not even reported as having been present at the rally of 1840. More damaging to the historical standing of the novel is Corwin's appearance in it as the main speaker of the rally, putting Harrison himself in the shade, when in fact Thomas Corwin did not even attend the rally. Corwin was, however, palely represented by his cousin Moses B. Corwin of Urbana, who introduced the General. Here the novelist in Whitlock, desirous of giving Corwin a continuing role in the novel, clearly takes precedence over the historian.

By way of expressing the growing condescension, mixed with contempt, that Whitlock late in life developed for popular American democracy,[60] he contrasts the legend of Harrison, assiduously cultivated and exploited by the Whigs, with the reality of Harrison himself, old, tired, and like a circus animal, scarcely able to comprehend what is happening to him:

> Like everyone else, he [Blair] was under the impression of the legend that had caught the fancy of the people, and served better than any declaration of principles or any political programme as a party platform, the legend of the rough old frontiersman and Indian fighter who lived in a log-cabin in the back country and drank hard cider. But now he was presented to a spare, long-faced, kindly old gentleman, wearing simple grey homespun and an uncomfortable high stock, sitting his white horse with the ease and grace

of a man who had spent a lifetime in the saddle, but worn out and weary, bored to death and perhaps a little bewildered by all the fuss that was being made over him. (p. 178).

When he starts to speak at the Square he is mysteriously emptied of his personality to become a "grey eidolon of a swiftly vanished epoch which, for a little while, the crude pageant that had swept by had reconstructed in the imaginations of all those people" (p. 187). As might be expected, the Whig paper of Urbana, the *Gazette* of Sept. 15, 1840, viewed Harrison as every inch a candidate, full of vitality despite his 67 years. In high-flown rhetoric replete with Shakespearean quotations, the *Gazette* describes "the glorious eighth" as a day when "hundreds of little girls, with their little hearts glowing in all the inspiration of the day," and citizens bearing "thousands of banners" have gathered to honor "Old Tip" as their Presidential candidate. Denying the charge of his enemies that Harrison is an "old dotard," the *Gazette* maintains that his frame is "healthful and vigorous," his eye "penetrating," and his two-hour speech "profound and eloquent," refuting the "vile slanders" of Democratic Senator William "Foghorn" Allen as to Harrison's conduct as commander-in-chief at the battles of Tippecanoe and the Thames. Following this combined defense and eulogy, the *Gazette* estimates the crowd at the rally as 20,000-30,000—five times Whitlock's estimate. One suspects that the truth about Harrison's alertness and vigor as a candidate must be somewhere between the partisanship represented by Allen on the one hand and the *Gazette* on the other; Whitlock, it should be noted, inclines more toward Allen's view than the *Gazette's*, but without going to an extreme. Though Harrison's twentieth century biographer James A. Green does not deal directly with the issue of Harrison's competency as a candidate, he assumes it throughout his discussion of the campaign. For example at the Dayton rally of Sept. 10, the greatest of all the rallies held for Harrison, Green gives the General credit for discussing "the issues of the campaign with the utmost frankness. He handled the accusation that he was a Federalist with skill."[61]

In describing the barbecue itself Whitlock is quite faithful to the facts as reported elsewhere, though he takes the liberty of elevating the farmer who owned the grove, John A. Ward, into "Colonel" Nash, founder and first citizen of Macochee. Ward was no ordinary farmer, though, for his father Wm. Ward actually had founded Urbana, and his son, as noted above, was a famous American sculptor. Indicting the elitism of the town and the hypocrisy of the log cabin and hard cider campaign, Whitlock contrasts the sweaty egalitarianism of the barbecue at the grove with the refined atmosphere of special privilege within Colonel Nash's house. Here a dozen prominent men were invited to dine with General Harrison, sipping madeira in preference to the hard cider which the General is supposed to enjoy but which is actually being swigged in vast quantities by those "free and equal sovereigns" in the grove.

Among the major historical figures observed at the rally and further developed elsewhere in the novel is Thomas Corwin. The historical Corwin was born in Bourbon County, Kentucky in 1794, from where in 1798 he moved with his parents to Turtle Creek, a tributary of the Little Miami River located two blocks west of the present center of Lebanon, Ohio. In the War of 1812 he served the army as a wagoner delivering supplies, from which service his political moniker "The Wagon Boy" was later derived. After schooling and legal training he was a member of the Ohio Legislature, in the U.S. House of Representatives, Governor of Ohio, U.S. Senator, Secretary of the Treasury, and Minister to Mexico under Lincoln. Swarthy and heavily built, he was best known for his keen wit and brilliant oratory.[62] At the rally, and indeed throughout the novel, two Corwins are revealed—Corwin the politician and Corwin the thinker. In his role as a politician he is a "smiling public man" and spellbinding orator "full of quips and pranks and flashes of merriment." His mastery of the crowd's emotions, whether he is making people laugh or persuading them to vote for Harrison, is complete. Thus, in the course of his speech at Macochee, when he catches the skeptical eye of the town's drunken old rip of a lawyer Giles Paten, he is able to involve Paten so cleverly and wittily in an application of the Noah story to the current political campaign that he draws "a burst of laughter as wild as anyone's" from his Democratic foe, and just possibly wins a vote for Harrison and Corwin as well (pp. 190-191).[63] Corwin's appeal to the less sophisticated members of his audience is no less profound, as Whitlock makes clear in his description of a poor farmer's response to Corwin's oratorical genius:

> His [the farmer's] tall, gaunt frame was clad in worn and threadbare garments that had long since taken on the neutral colour of the earth in which his life was passed. His coarse, unkempt hair hung lank from the hat of woven leatherwood that he wore; the skin on his lean face was tanned like leather, and from his lantern-jaws, moving incessantly as he chewed his quid of tobacco, hung a scraggy sunburnt beard. But in his blue eyes and in that tanned face, there was reflected, as in a mirror, every emotion

that Tom Corwin by his art evoked. At times his face would twitch
with pain, his lip would tremble, tears would gather in his pale,
blue eyes, and stream down his leathern face. And then a moment
afterwards he would laugh and wag his head from side to side
and say: "Ay, golly!" in the impossibility of expressing the satisfaction he felt. And when Tom Corwin soared away on one of his
loftier flights of oratory, the farmer would stand with gaping mouth
and strained expression on his face, rapt in naive amazement. And
Blair understood how these poor folk could stand there all through
the long hours of that afternoon, for this was the only pleasure,
the only distraction, the only entertainment, the only break that
ever relieved the bleak monotony and killing toil of their squalid
lives; they would remember and treasure up and talk about this
day for years to come (p.191-192).

Whitlock, in this sampling of Corwin's political oratory and account of selected responses to it is remarkably successful, I think,
in suggesting the *charisma* on which each of Corwin's biographers has remarked with amazement.

As noted above, Whitlock has endowed Corwin with a sober,
reflective, even gloomy side that is perhaps more Whitlock than
Corwin, since it finds slight support in the Corwin biographies.
As might be expected this darker side of Corwin appears only
momentarily and incompletely at the rally, though Blair is quick
to observe it as the wits in the crowd, totally indecorous, inter-
rupt Colonel Nash's introduction of the General with their crude
jokes about hard cider and "Old Tippecanoe":

> Tom Corwin had been looking on at all this horse-play and tom-
> foolery with an inscrutable air of solemnity. He looked on at it
> now through half-closed eyes, studying the crowd, that vast sweep
> of upturned, vapid faces before him, and Blair thought that he
> shook his head ever so slightly, and not so much disapprovingly
> as in sadness and despair. And presently he said, almost as much
> to himself, it seemed, as to Blair:
> "Though it make the unskillful laugh, it cannot but make the
> judicious grieve" (p. 185).

This dark side of Corwin, the side of him that despairs of
humanity in the mass, especially in its crass political manifesta-
tions, is a side that Corwin had deliberately kept hidden over
the years; indeed his political success required this deception.
For according to the theory Whitlock espouses here, popular
democracy demands that a successful candidate sacrifice the truth
as he sees it to half-truths, false optimism, jollification and spe-
cious wit of the kind that Corwin himself exhibited in its highest
form at the rally and that the Whig campaign of 1840 in general
exhibited in its lowest. Corwin has learned political wisdom over

the years, but in the process has burdened himself with a knowledge and compassion he dare not express to his constituents. As Blair somewhat romantically concludes when he first meets Corwin at his home in Lebanon, the older man has become a kind of Midwestern Prometheus of popular democracy, taking on himself the burden of suffering that his constituents are too weak to bear. So determined is young Blair to find a convenient hero on which to model himself that he fails to see the breakdown of his analogies between Prometheus and Corwin. Whereas the classical Prometheus followed his principles to save mankind, Corwin sacrifices his principles to win victories which have little likelihood of saving mankind, or any significant segment thereof. These victories do, however, provide rich compensation both in psychic and materialistic terms for the "suffering" involved in Corwin's recurrent trips to the polls. Corwin does not perhaps cut quite as noble a figure as Blair's application to him of Byron's short, lyric poem "Prometheus" (1816) would suggest:

> Titan, to whose immortal eyes
>   The sufferings of mortality,
>   Seen in their sad reality,
> Were not as things that gods despise;
> What was thy pity's recompense?
> A silent suffering and intense;
> The rock, the vulture, and the chain,
> All that the proud can feel of pain,
> The agony they do not show....
>
> Thy godlike crime was to be kind,
>   To render with thy precepts less
>   The sum of human wretchedness,
> And strengthen Man with his own mind (p. 69).

Whitlock's fascination with the character of Thomas Corwin and his inclusion of Corwin in the novel as a model for the aspirant lawyer and politician Blair is indirectly explained in Whitlock's letter of Dec. 5, 1930 to his editor, Rutger B. Jewett. In this letter Whitlock proposes writing a life of Corwin, a project that he never pursued except insofar as he incorporated Corwin's life in *The Buckeyes:*

> If I were to write anything about him I should use his life as a thread to cover the period of Ohio history between 1835 and 1860, when the Abolitionists were raising the devil with the slave hunters. It is a significant period not only in the history of Ohio but in the history of the nation, and if I had sufficient materials about Tom Corwin's life (and I have some of them) I think I could do a pretty good thing with it. My grandfather knew him well, and adored him; and I was reared on stories about Tom Corwin and

his quips and pranks and flashes of merriment. But with all this he was a scholar and a statesman, with a scorn of humbug, pretentiousness and hypocrisy; and he was a great orator and a man of dauntless courage.[64]

Like Grandfather Brand, Corwin migrated to Ohio from Bourbon County, Kentucky. Corwin came in 1798 to Lebanon as a boy of four with his family, Brand in 1830 to Urbana as a young man of 20 seeking his fortune. Though Corwin was 16 years older than Brand, they must have become good friends, as Whitlock asserts. Corwin and Brand probably met through the Urbana branch of the Corwin family, which included Moses B., Urbana's first newspaper publisher and lawyer, who introduced Harrison at the Urbana rally and with whom Brand shared business interests.[65] Another Urbana Corwin was Ichabod, a friend of Brand's involved with him in the celebrated Ad White slave-rescue case tried at Cincinnati in 1857.[66]

At the rally Blair himself is glimpsed as a young man of great promise, in the process of establishing himself as a successful lawyer and family man, about to be swept into political office by the irresistible Whig machine fueled by Tippecanoe and Tyler too. Though his success is remarkable for a man in his early twenties, Blair is willing to grant that it has been achieved in a period when Ohio is still bursting with opportunities for anyone of ambition, talent and industry. What he needs to decide, however, is whether he will continue to model himself on Corwin, who has found success as a lawyer and politician without losing compassion for mankind, or whether he will join the arch-conservative, complacent, self-indulgent establishment of Macochee represented by fine, wealthy gentlemen like Colonel Nash. There is still another option open to Blair, however—the way of his old employer Ethan Grow, who is so dedicated to the anti-slavery movement that he has been willing to sacrifice his business, comfort, family welfare, and local reputation to its insatiable demands. Indeed he has made himself so unpopular through his abolitionist newspaper the *Torchlight* that even though he is still a loyal Whig, among the most influential in town, he is not even invited to Colonel Nash's luncheon at the rally. Significantly, Blair does not even notice Grow's absence from the luncheon till he is made aware of it when Grow enters Blair's law office three or four days later. Whenever Blair is forced to think of Grow, he does so with ill-concealed loathing. However, he is forced to admit that his former employer is a man of principle, with a conscience so keen as to put to shame even Corwin,

whose compassion for humanity is so broadly diffused as to focus
on no segment of humanity in particular, least of all the slaves.
There are times, even, when Blair toys with the idea that Grow
may be not a fanatic but a prophet, not a man envious of his
betters but outraged by the injustices of the world and determined to do what he can to correct them.

By the end of the manuscript the conflict within Blair as to
which of these three paths he will finally take is unresolved.
What is clear, however, is that he has in fact, if not consciously,
been moving closer to the world of Colonel Nash. Moreover, the
difference between the worlds of Nash and Corwin seems ever
slighter with the passage of time, especially when set against
the single-minded dedication and self-sacrifice of Grow. Drawn
to the worlds of Nash and Corwin by his growing affluence and
political success, as well as by tradition and temperament, and
to Grow by his conscience, his blood kinship with Grow's grandson, and his keen political sense that Grow may indeed represent
the politics of the future, Blair is on the horns of a dilemma
that is not resolved and cannot predictably be resolved in the
novel. If we look to the subsequent history of Joseph Carter
Brand, Blair's prototype, for a clue to Whitlock's intention in
the unfinished portion of the novel, we would expect Blair
to move with very mixed feelings and motives toward support of abolition—but not nearly so far in that direction as to
make the sacrifices Grow had made. With a combination of good
will and political wisdom Blair would attempt to bridge the gulf
between the Nashes and Grows of this world by a series of com-
promises that would make him as dubious a candidate for heroism
as Corwin himself. He would be a Corwinite, but a Corwinite of
a new age, an age perhaps a shade more sensitive than Corwin's
to the need for demonstrating one's compassion by one's political
actions. To be a Corwinite in Blair's day would involve taking
calculated political risks to advance the cause of abolition, the
ultimate risk being the possible loss of political office and reputation. In the character of Blair we see the potentiality of Republicanism yet unborn as a political party in the U.S., the Republicanism
that eventually emerged in Blair's prototype, Brand, who became
a delegate to the first major Republican Convention in 1856. In
further support of this hypothetical development of Blair in the
unfinished portion of the novel we might also cite the staunch,
abolitionist character of Blair revealed in the shorter version.

Whitlock's failure to resolve the basic conflicts in the character
of his protagonist is hardly a complete surprise. In the Macochee

stories prior to *The Buckeyes,* the Golden Age of Macochee had been receding ever further into the past. Finally, in *The Buckeyes,* Whitlock is forced to grapple with the suspicion that even in pre-Civil War Macochee his talented, prosperous and privileged protagonist Blair (like Colonel Nash and Governor Corwin) may be motivated as much by political expediency as by noble idealism. Whitlock is also compelled to consider the possibility that Grow, the radical idealist and abolitionist of the novel, may be a quite unlovely fanatic, and that the *hoi polloi* of the town, including most of the voters as well as the bully boys from the bottoms, may be scarcely worth the attempt to rescue them from their mindless vulgarity, poverty and prejudice. In a word, it may not be the distribution of wealth, or the class system, or even slavery (however vile) that ultimately causes man's wretchedness on earth; it may rather be the crookedness and ugliness of human nature in general as revealed in both the body politic and its chosen leaders. Even so, the prevailing unloveliness of human nature in the mass may be redeemed by outcroppings of beauty and loveliness in individuals like Blair's wife Lucretia—and sometimes even in Blair himself, as when he magnanimously secures a Senate clerkship for his obnoxious ex-employer Grow. Unfortunately for the novel, Whitlock could not cut the Gordian knot that would resolve Blair's inner conflict either in favor of a predominately idealistic or an expedient interpretation of his nature. The result was stasis—and eventual abandonment of the novel.

More significant even than Whitlock's failure to resolve the conflict between political idealism and expediency in his protagonist is a similar conflict in his own nature, ever so closely identified with that of his protagonist. For in his later years Whitlock himself, like Blair in the novel, was torn between his reforming impulse and his incipient cynicism as a spectator of human, and particularly American, folly. The recognition of this double failure, personal as well as artistic, may have come at his traumatic luncheon encounter with Edith Wharton in the fall of 1931, an event to which he alluded almost obsessively in letters to friends.

With the laying aside of *The Buckeyes* following the Wharton encounter came a greater sense of loss to Whitlock than could be explained by his failure to complete a project on which he had labored hard over a period of nearly three years. For indeed his abandonment of the novel signaled the end of a creative though painful life-long struggle to integrate and harness the warring forces of his own nature. And with the ending of this struggle came the demise of his productive genius, replaced in his last months by the note-shuffling of the desiccated scholar striving vainly to complete his biographies of Jackson and Jefferson, characters dimly observed on the horizon of the world in which Whitlock himself had ceased to struggle. Whitlock's cessation of struggle led not to peace but to the paralysis of his powers.

That he left his last novel incomplete is unquestionably a loss; but that he could neither falsify his art to preserve his childhood vision, nor sacrifice that vision to the stark political realities of post-World War I is a qualified tribute to both Whitlock the idealist and Whitlock the realist, unhappily never harmonized. Which was the real Whitlock is a question that can never be answered, since both Whitlocks seemed equally important and equally assertive up to the last years of his life. Then the forces of death quieted the struggle that had characterized the most creative and productive years of his life leading up to *The Buckeyes*, his unfinished swan song of Macochee, Ohio.

FOOTNOTES

1. A Hero in Spite of Himself: Brand Whitlock in Art, Politics & War (New York, Alfred A. Knopf, 1969), p. 424.

2. Though I have not been able to find the exact date of this gift or series of gifts, there is in the Society's collection of Whitlockiana a red manila folder of unpublished stories and fragments with a notation over Ella B. Whitlock's signature with the date Jan. 18, 1942. Between that date and the date of her death on July 11, 1942, Mrs. Whitlock must have presented at least some of the Ohio materials to the Society. No mention of them is made in her will filed in Toledo, Ohio on July 30, 1942.

3. Macochee was the name of an Indian town 13 miles north of Urbana destroyed by Colonel Logan in 1786. According to *The Ohio Guide* (New York: Oxford University Press, 1940), p. 588, the Indian name "Mac-O-Chee" means "smiling valley."

4. The house has been the family residence of Alleen and Pauline Johnson since 1922, when it was purchased from descendants of the Brand family.

5. Brand's brothers were William Gurley, born March 19, 1880 and Francis (Frank) Elias, born June 5, 1882.

6. For a number of the above facts of Whitlock's life I am indebted to Jack Tager's *The Intellectual as Urban Reformer/Brand Whitlock and the Progressive Movement* (Cleveland: Case Western Reserve University, 1968), pp. 3, 20, 38, and David D. Anderson's *Brand Whitlock* (New York: Twayne Publishers, Inc., 1968), pp. 15-16 and elsewhere.

7. See in this regard Evan P. Middleton, ed. *History of Champaign County Ohio* (Indianapolis: B. F. Bowen & Company, 1917), I, 683-684, 753.

8. Middleton, I, 963.

9. Brand Whitlock, *Forty Years of It* (1914; rpt. New York: Greenwood Press, 1968), p. 24.

10. Allan Nevins, ed., *The Letters and Journal of Brand Whitlock* (New York: D. Appleton-Century Company, 1936), I, 510.

11. *Letters,* p. 532. The friend is Octavia Roberts from Springfield, Illinois, with whom Whitlock had long corresponded.

12. See, for example, *Letters,* p. 352 (Summer, 1924) and p. 517 (May 21, 1932). In the 1924 letter he wrote: "Democracies run to mediocrity as water runs into the gutter; and if we haven't really a democracy in America, we have a plutocracy (with the cant of democracy), and that is worse."

13. *Letters,* pp. 511, 532.

14. First comes *The Happy Average* (Indianapolis: The Bobbs-Merrill Company, 1904). The first Macochee short story, appearing in *The Gold Brick* (New York: Hurst & Company, 1910) is "Macochee's First Campaign Fund," pp. 139-164; the remaining six, in *The Fall Guy* (Indianapolis: The Bobbs-Merrill Company, 1912) are "The Field of Honor," pp. 50-95, "The Orator of the Day," pp. 120-141, "Fowler Brunton," pp. 142-168, "The Old House Across the Street," pp. 193-212, "The Preacher's Son," pp. 231-250, and "The Question," pp. 333-344. The second Macochee novel is *J. Hardin & Son* (New York: D. Appleton and Company, 1923).

15. *The Happy Average,* p. 126.

16. This sketch of Josiah West is drawn from the life of John Quincy Adams Ward (1830-1910), the once famous sculptor from Urbana.

17. *Letters,* p. 431. (Letter to Octavia Roberts.)

18. *Letters,* p. 473.

19. *Letters,* p. 476.

20. *Letters*, p. 481

21. *Letters*, p. 532. (Letter to Roberts.)

22. *Letters*, p. 511. The last sentence of this quotation begins a new paragraph in Whitlock's letter to Paine.

23. *Letters*, p. 552.

24. *Letters*, p. 557.

25. *Letters*, p. 566. (Letter to Paine.)

26. *Letters*, p. 573. Here Whitlock is referring to Wharton's *A Backward Glance* (1934), her autobiography.

27. *A Centennial Biographical History of Champaign County Ohio* (New York and Chicago: The Lewis Publishing Company, 1902), p. 629.

28. Joseph Ware, *History of Mechanicsburg, Ohio* (Columbus: F. J. Heer Printing Co., 1917), p. 40. Along with Udney (here spelled "Udnah") Hyde, Dr. Horr is listed as an early, active member of the abolition party in Mechanicsburg. As a skillful conductor of the Underground Railroad, Hyde boasted that he never lost one of the 513 slaves he helped to freedom from 1833 on. In 1857 he was involved with Joseph Carter Brand in the Ad White slave rescue case discussed later in this introduction.

29. This information comes from a genealogy of her immediate family compiled by Whitlock's mother in a letter (Whitlock MSS, Library of Congress, Box 98).

30. Ware, p. 29.

31. Champaign County Index to Deeds Q, p. 232.

32. *History of Champaign County Ohio* (Chicago: W. H. Beers & Co., 1881), p. 281.

33. *Forty Years*, pp. 20-22.

34. William A. Taylor, *Ohio Statesmen and Annals of Progress* (Columbus: The Westbote Company, 1899), II, 31. The changing times are evident in that, whereas Brand had served on the House Committee on Roads and Highways in 1843, in 1857 he reports for the Senate Committee on Railroads and Turnpikes. Ohio's growing sympathy for the cause of abolition is indicated by his Senate vote with a large majority in 1856 "to prevent the forcible abduction of free blacks and mulatto persons from the State of Ohio" and to ask Congress to repeal the Fugitive Slave Act of Sept. 18, 1850 as "repugnant to the plainest principles of Justice and humanity." On a lighter note, Brand introduced a Senate resolution on Jan. 8, 1857 that the Secretary of State be "authorized to purchase six sofas to be placed inside the bar in this Hall [the Senate Chamber], for the use of ladies as spectators, at a cost not to exceed two hundred dollars." See Taylor, I, 209-210, and *The Journal of the Senate of the State of Ohio Fifty-Second General Assembly* (Columbus: Statesman Steam Press, 1856), LII, 524, 467, 325, 421 and LIII (1857), 8 for a record of Brand's political service.

35. *Forty Years*, p. 14.

36. *Forty Years*, pp. 13-14. For a fuller account of this celebrated case, see footnote 66.

37. In addition to the sources already cited, I have obtained a good deal of information about Brand from *A Centennial Biographical History of Champaign County Ohio*, pp. 628-630, and from copies of legal documents concerning the Brand family kindly provided by Attorney Edwin English, Sr. of Urbana, whose wife is Margaret Brand English, the daughter of the late Congressman Charles Brand, cousin of Brand Whitlock.

38. *Forty Years*, p. 2. Surviving municipal council minutes from Brand's mayoralty in 1880-82 indicate that hog control, installation of telephone pole lights, purchase of gasoline, small pox control, road extension, and erection of gas lamps were among the problems faced.

39. *Forty Years*, pp. 12-13.

40. *The Buckeyes*, p. 46, 81 and *Forty Years*, p. 13.

41. *A Centennial Biographical History*, p. 630.

42. According to Auditor Blanche Rhea of Urbana, a municipal court did not replace the mayor's court of Urbana until 1946.

43. Writers' Program of the Work Projects Administration in Ohio, *Urbana and Champaign County* (Urbana, Ohio: Gaumer Publishing Company, 1942), p. 46.

44. Charles B. Galbreath, *History of Ohio* (Chicago and New York: The American Historical Society, 1925), II, 211.

45. Robert E. Chaddock, *Ohio Before 1850*, Studies in History, Economics and Public Law, 31, No. 2 (New York: Columbia University Press, 1908), p. 100, quoted from Caleb Atwater, *History of Ohio* (1838), p. 324.

46. Galbreath, p. 198.

47. She was descended from Richard Talbott (d. 1666), who in 1656 purchased Poplar Knowle plantation on West River, Anne Arundel Co., Maryland. See *The Compendium of American Genealogy*, ed. Frederick Virkus (1942; rpt. Baltimore: Genealogical Publishing Company, 1968), VII, 885. On her mother's side she was descended from William Hickman (1757-1814), a Revolutionary War patriot, according to a genealogy in the Library of Congress Whitlock MSS collection, Box 98.

48. *Forty Years*, p. 22.

49. *Urbana and Champaign County*, p. 34.

50. *Urbana and Champaign County*, p. 76.

51. *Urbana and Champaign County*, p. 134.

52. Henry Howe, *Historical Collections of Ohio* (Norwalk, Ohio: the Laning Printing Co., 1896), I, facing 374, and Middleton, following p. 952.

53. Howe, p. 373.

54. *James Gillespie Birney: Slaveholder to Abolitionist* (1955; rpt. New York: Greenwood Press, 1969), p. 189.

55. Galbreath, p. 248.

56. Fladeland, p. 134, and Francis P. Weisenburger, *The Passing of the Frontier 1825-1850* (Columbus: Ohio State Archaeological and Historical Society, 1941), III, 383.

57. Dorothy Burne Goebel, *William Henry Harrison/A Political Biography* (Indianapolis: Indiana Library and Historical Department, 1926), pp. 347-348.

58. *Western Citizen & Urbana Gazette*, Sept. 15, 1840.

59. Taylor, I. 209-210.

60. Allan Nevins, ed. *The Letters and Journal of Brand Whitlock* (New York: D. Appleton-Century Company, 1936), II, 721-722. In 1921 he wrote: "I have been homesick, in a way for Europe all my life, was so even before I ever saw Europe.... And yet there is, or was, an America that I loved: the old America of Lincoln—still the greatest and first of my heroes, and of Washington, that magnificent gentleman, soldier, statesman!—and Emerson, Longfellow, Holmes, Whittier, Lowell, Howells. But they and all they stood for, represented, or exemplified, is gone."

61. James A. Green, *William Henry Harrison/His Life and Times* (Richmond, Virginia: Garrett and Massie, Inc., 1941), p. 359.

62. Corwin's spacious home, built on Turtle Creek in 1818, is still standing, though now divided into apartments (see figure 11); a number of Corwin relics, including his desk and a silver service, are preserved in the Warren County Historical Society Museum at Lebanon, the town where he was buried following sudden paralysis and death at Washington, D.C. in 1865. My source of informa-

tion about the Corwin house and his former possessions now in the Museum is Mrs. Elva R. Adams, Director of the Museum in Lebanon. Mrs. Adams graciously provided the photo of the Corwin house, also.

63. Corwin's "Noah speech" is quoted directly from a speech he delivered on another occasion. In Corwin's Macochee speech extolling Harrison, the General is likened to one righteous man, Noah, mocked by his sons because he once drank too much. See A. P. Russell, *Thomas Corwin/A Sketch* (Cincinnati: Clarke & Co., 1882), pp. 37-42. On pp. 75-76 Whitlock quotes extensively from still another Corwin speech giving advice to a young man, printed in F. B. Pearson and J. D. Harlor, eds., *Ohio History Sketches* (Columbus: Press of Fred J. Heer, 1903), pp. 141-142. In this discourse, delivered in the early 1850's when Corwin was Secretary of the Treasury, he advises a young man seeking independence to purchase land. In the novel, this advice is put in Corwin's mouth as he addresses young Blair, who takes the older man's advice as soon as possible. Whitlock quotes from another well known speech of Corwin, the Cumberland Road speech of April 20, 1838, which Grow refers to on pp. 116-117. For the excerpt in question, see *Life and Speeches of Thomas Corwin*, ed. Josiah Morrow (Cincinnati: W. H. Anderson & Co., 1896), pp. 244-245.

64. *Letters*, pp. 475-576.

65. *Urbana and Champaign County* (1942), pp. 61, 32; Moses Corwin's newspaper was the *Farmer's Watchtower*. In Joshua Antrim, *The History of Champaign and Logan Counties* (Bellefontaine, Ohio, 1872), p. 450, the Hon. Moses B. Corwin, who died in 1872, is referred to as the son of old Ichabod Corwin, Tom Corwin's uncle, the first settler of Lebanon.

66. Whitlock's assertion that J. C. Brand and Judge Ichabod Corwin were involved in this rescue case from the beginning is not borne out by other accounts, though it may be correct.

Ad White was a runaway slave from Kentucky staying at the house of Udney Hyde near Mechanicsburg. When discovered there and approached in May, 1857 by U.S. Marshal Ben Churchill and his deputies from Cincinnati with a warrant for his arrest, White defended himself by shooting at Deputy-Marshal Elliott, who fell uninjured, the bullet having struck his gun barrel. Withdrawing amid the jeers of bystanders sympathetic to White, the posse returned to Cincinnati for warrants to arrest several, including Hyde, who had refused to assist, or interfered with, the capture. When these Mechanicsburg men were subsequently arrested by a posse of fourteen, a writ of habeas corpus was obtained from a judge in Urbana "commanding the Marshals to bring their prisoners and show by what authority they were held." The sheriff of Champaign County overtook the marshals with their prisoners just across the Champaign County line, hence out of the sheriff's jurisdiction. Meanwhile Judge Ichabod Corwin and J. C. Brand took a copy of the writ to the sheriff of adjoining Clark County in Springfield and started him off to intercept the marshals with their prisoners at South Charleston, where the sheriff's deputy was shot at several times and the sheriff himself was beaten and nearly killed, apparently by the U.S. officers. Finally these officers were arrested by the sheriff of Greene County, and the prisoners were returned to the court in Urbana, where they were released since no one could show cause why they had been arrested or should be detained.

Later that summer in Cincinnati, the cases of J. C. Brand and Udney Hyde "were selected as test cases representing the two features—that of Hyde for refusing to assist in the arrest of a fugitive slave, and that of Brand for interference with a United States officer in the discharge of duty." After the case had dragged on until all parties concerned were tired of it, White's Kentucky owner agreed to sell him for $1,000 plus all court costs, which sum was promptly paid, following which the cases were "nolled." Ad White, notified of his freedom, returned to Mechanicsburg where in 1881 he was still residing, "borne down by hard work and age, but ever cherishing the memory of those who gave him shelter and protection when fleeing from oppression and seeking his freedom." See *History of Clark County* (Chicago: W. H. Beers & Co., 1881), pp. 287-290.

Bibliography

Anderson, David D. *Brand Whitlock*. New York: Twayne Publishers, Inc., 1968.

Antrim, Joshua. *The History of Champaign and Logan Counties*. Bellefontaine, Ohio: Press Printing Co., 1872.

A Centennial Biographical History of Champaign County Ohio. New York and Chicago: The Lewis Publishing Company, 1902.

Chaddock, Robert E. *Ohio Before 1850*. Studies in History, Economics and Public Law, 31, No. 2. New York: Columbia University Press, 1908.

Crunden, Robert M. *A Hero in Spite of Himself: Brand Whitlock in Art, Politics & War*. New York: Alfred A. Knopf, 1969.

Fladeland, Betty. *James Gillespie Birney: Slaveholder to Abolitionist*. 1955; rpt. New York: Greenwood press, 1969.

Galbreath, Charles B. *History of Ohio*. 5 vols. Chicago and New York: The American Historical Society, 1925.

Goebel, Dorothy Burne. *William Henry Harrison/A Political Biography*. XIV. Indianapolis: Indiana Library and Historical Department, 1926.

Green, James A. *William Henry Harrison/His Life and Times*. Richmond, Virginia: Garrett and Massie, Inc., 1941.

History of Champaign County Ohio. Chicago: W. H. Beers & Co., 1881.

History of Champaign County Ohio. Ed. Evan P. Middleton. 2 vols. Indianapolis: B. F. Bowen & Company, 1917.

History of Clark County. Chicago: W. H. Beers & Co., 1881.

Howe, Henry. *Historical Collections of Ohio. 2 vols. Norwalk, Ohio: The Laning Printing Co.*, 1896.

The Journal of the Senate of the State of Ohio Fifty-Second General Assembly. LII and LIII. Columbus: Statesman Steam Press, 1856, 1857.

Morrow, Josiah, ed. *Life and Speeches of Thomas Corwin*. Cincinnati: W. H. Anderson & Co., 1896.

Nevins, Allan, ed. *The Letters and Journal of Brand Whitlock*. 2 vols. New York: D. Appleton-Century Company, 1936.

Pearson, F. B. and J. D. Harlor, eds. *Ohio History Sketches*. Columbus: Press of Fred J. Heer, 1903.

Russell, A. P. *Thomas Corwin/A Sketch*. Cincinnati: Clarke & Co., 1882.

Tager, Jack. *The Intellectual as Urban Reformer/Brand Whitlock and the Progressive Movement*. Cleveland: Case Western Reserve University, 1968.

Taylor, William A. *Ohio Statesmen and Annals of Progress*. 2 vols. Columbus: The Westbote Company, 1899.

Virkus, Frederick Adams, ed. *The Compendium of American Genealogy*. 7 vols. 1942; rpt. Baltimore: Genealogical Publishing Company, 1968.

Ware, Joseph. *History of Mechanicsburg, Ohio*. Columbus: F. J. Heer Printing Co., 1917.

Weisenburger, Francis P. *The Passing of the Frontier 1825-1850*. III of 6 vols. in *The History of the State of Ohio*. Ed. Carl Wittke. Columbus: Ohio State Archaeological and Historical Society, 1941.

Western Citizen & Urbana Gazette. Sept. 15, 1840.

Whitlock, Brand. *The Fall Guy*. Indianapolis: The Bobbs-Merrill Company, 1912.

—————. *Forty Years of It*. 1914; rpt. New York: Greenwood Press, 1968.

————. *The Gold Brick*. New York: Hurst & Co., 1910.

————. *The Happy Average*. Indianapolis: The Bobbs-Merrill Company, 1904.

————. *J. Hardin & Son*. New York: D. Appleton and Company, 1923.

————. MSS Collection. Library of Congress, Box 98.

Writers' Program of the Work Projects Administration in Ohio. *Urbana and Champaign County*. Urbana, Ohio: Gaumer Publishing Company, 1942.

————. *The Ohio Guide*. New York: Oxford University Press, 1940.

THE BUCKEYES

BOOK I

I

It was late in the afternoon of a torrid day in
July, 1836, that Carter Blair arrived on the
banks of the Ohio. He had been in the saddle since early morning, except for an hour at midday when he had stopped to eat,
and in the sultry heat that lay on Kentucky he was beginning to
find the way somewhat long. The heat wilted and prostrated
everything. It shimmered over the white road and was reflected
back into Carter's sunburned and perspiring face like the stifling
breath of a furnace. The bay mare he rode was glistening wet
with sweat and her flanks were lathered by the saddle-bags.
The limestone dust lay thick upon the broad leaves of the corn
and tobacco that grew in the parched fields beside the road, and
powdered the sycamore trees in the bottom where the Licking
river flowed, its waters, at that time of year, low and sluggish.
There was not a breath to be had; dazzling white domes of cloud
had been rising higher and higher and swelling in the sky, and
there was thunder in the air. Carter wondered whether he could
complete that day's stage of his journey before the storm broke.
And then, all of a sudden, round the shoulder of a bluff he caught
a glimpse of the river. He found a path that led up the side of the
bluff, and put his mare at the steep ascent; he felt her back stif-
fen and straighten under him, she dug in her toes, scrambled up,
and there it was—the Ohio.

The mare seemed to know what this moment meant as well as
he, for she stopped and stood stock-still, her delicate pointed
ears pricked sharply forward in curiosity. And Carter sat and
gazed upon the vast panorama spread out before him.

Yes, there it was, the Ohio; wide and mysterious, flowing along,
gleaming in the slanting rays of the sun, and changing with every

moment as its sinister eddies and mysterious currents wrought their tragic designs; keel-boats were plying upon its restless surface, arks, Kentucky boats and long rafts were floating acquiescently down stream. The words of the old song came to his mind:

Hi-O, away we go,
Floating down the river on the O-hi-o.

Half a mile away a steamboat moved swiftly along, up stream, her stern-paddles kicking up a disdainful train of white foam in her wake. Below him, under the bluff, the village of Covington sprawled in the mud of the bottom lands; there, across the Licking river which at that point emptied into the Ohio, lay her jealous sister town of Newport, and there, where his eyes rested at last on the other side of the river a mile or so away, stood the City—Cincinnati.

But for Carter those words "The Ohio" meant something more than the broad muddy river swirling there below him. There was something romantic and mystic about them to his young imagination, as there had been to thousands and thousands of men in those early years of the last century—Northern men from York State and the Jerseys and Connecticut, and Southern men from Kentucky and Virginia with wild dreams of riches, to say nothing of black men with still wilder dreams of freedom. "The Ohio" was that mysterious and, to Carter Blair, unknown, country lying beyond the river's sullen flood, behind those wooded hills on its farther bank. It had not been many years since the pioneers had wrested it, or wheedled it from the Indians, but now, to an imaginative young fellow with his own way to make in the world, it was the land flowing with milk and honey, an El Dorado, and he was going to seek his fortune there.

Two days before he had set out from his father's farm in Bourbon county, with all he had in the world, the mare he rode (a Kentucky thoroughbred), the clothes on his back, (though they were only Kentucky jeans), a somewhat better though rather scanty wardrobe in his saddle-bags, and a little hard money. There was, besides, in his saddle-bags, a book, *Poems of the Right Honourable Lord Byron,* recently published over the mountains at Philadelphia, the most highly prized of his possessions— after his mare, of course. He sat her with the grace of a Kentucky horseman. She was a four-year-old, a Tuckahoe of the Diomed strain.[1] (The blood of Diomed and his great son, Sir Archy, was all the fashion then.) Carter called her Dolly D., and she could singlefoot so smoothly that her rider might have thought he was in a rocking-chair. And so he had left home and set out for the Ohio, and now there it was lying before him.

He lingered there gazing in his dreamy mood at the scene, a look of simplicity in his immature, boyish face, and the glow of confident expectancy in his large blue eyes. He gazed in wonder across the wide river at the fleet of white steamboats lying along the water-front of Cincinnati, at the buildings behind and above them, and at the hills rising at the back. He lingered for a long moment and gazed, the light of his youthful dream in his countenance. Then he was aware that a subtle change was taking place in the scene before him. Twilight was gathering in the lowlands between the hills, the sky was a deepening blue, and shadows from the west were moving upon the river, darkening it portentously. And then he saw coming towards him a boat that had put out from the Ohio side, and, concluding that it was the ferry, he gathered up his rein, (he rode Dolly D. on the snaffle; she had never known a curb), turned and rode down into the town of Covington.

He was waiting at the landing in the hot, suffocating and breathless atmosphere of the river bottom, when the ferry came in. The sky to the west was filled with the blue-black clouds, which perceptibly darkened the air as though the twilight were already descending. Carter watched the unloading of the ferry; the passengers hurried ashore, followed by a train of carts and waggons, then a string of mules, and at last, when all had disembarked, a long coffle of black slaves chained in pairs and conducted by white drivers. The slaves, the bucks in ragged shirts and trousers, the wenches in slatternly calico shifts, shuffled listlessly ashore, bedraggled and fagged by the heat; their chains clicked as they moved, and as they passed they rolled up the whites of their eyes in a dumb, melancholy curiosity at the long-legged young man sitting his delicate-limbed, high-strung horse. They passed, trailing behind them an overpowering, sickening, oniony odour of negro sweat.

When they had passed Carter dismounted and led Dolly D. aboard the ferry, and the barge moved out into the broad stream. The man at the long sweep by which the craft was steered was talking with a passenger.

"Damned if I know," Carter heard him say. "From Virginia, the feller said. Takin' 'em to the auction block in Kentucky and Tennessee, I reckon. Looks as if they was goin' to be a storm."

Carter glanced up at the darkening sky where, indeed, the storm was gathering. The surface of the river was of a greasy smoothness, and from it there rose a smell of mud and fish. The air was heavy and humid, but on the water they passed now and then through currents of chilly air. Dolly D. rolled her eyes wildly about on these new and strange surroundings; now and then she shivered with nervousness, contracting her skin in sudden little tremors. Carter, standing beside her, his arm thrown over her withers, rubbed her soft nose to reassure her, and said soothingly: "There, there, my little gal, there!" whilst he watched the City on the Ohio shore slowly draw nearer and nearer.

II

It was the first time that Carter had been away from home, unless you could call going over to Frankfort to see the new State House being away from home. Going into Paris, the county seat, didn't, of course, count. And so, when he led Dolly D. down the gangplank to the floating wharf that could so amazingly accommodate itself to the varying stages of the river, he was almost as greatly bewildered by the confusion of the landing as Dolly D. Now that he found himself at last actually in this immense, impersonal city of which he had heard all his life, he felt quite visibly diminished in size and importance. He did not feel quite so big and strong and masterful as he had only three days ago, when he had bade them all good-bye, those Blairs of Bourbon County. His father, emerging for an instant from the dour Scotch indifference with which he usually treated the emotions of his children, had obviously struggled to overcome the trembling in his voice; his elder brother, Joe, had looked at him with a white, strained face; and his little sister, Fanny! The thought of Fanny wrung his heart. She had stood there by the door in the sunlight, so small, so fragile in her little slip, her eyes so big and round and full of sorrow, her tiny lip trembling, suddenly springing upon him, clutching him tightly with her thin little arms and legs, and crying out, "I don't want you to go! I don't want you to go!" He had hugged her to him, and then when he had unloosed her arms and legs and put her gently down, she had wailed, crumpled her apron to her face and run into the house. Wesley and old Laura were weeping too, and calling on the good Lo'd to bress him; even his stepmother had shown a decent regret. They were all heart-broken to see him go, but it couldn't be helped. His father wasn't rich. He had his Blue

Grass farm and a few slaves to help him work it, but there wasn't enough for Carter and Joe both, and Joe was the elder... His own throat had ached throughout all that terrible and trying scene of farewell, and it ached now again as he thought of it. They were all there now on the farm at this very minute, sitting down to supper; life in its strange, callous indifference was going on the same as ever just as though he were there; it was hard to realize; the thought was intolerable—and impossible...

"Look out thar, you goddamned, long-legged, slab-sided corn-cracker you![2] Cl'ar out o' my way! Who in hell do ye think ye are, Gineral Jackson?" A brutal voice roused him from his home-sick reverie, and made him feel more embarrassed and awkward. The confusion of the "Landing," that vast paved area, ten acres in extent, stretching along the river-front for a quarter of a mile, and back as far as Front Street, was in fact bewildering and ter-rifying. It was at the hour approaching evening when its activities were swelling to their climax. Great drays driven by burly ne-groes trundled by in all directions, trucks rumbled along over the cobble-stones, and these drivers, after the manner of teamsters everywhere were shouting and swearing at one another. The moist air that lay like a palpable cloud on the town was charged with the coming storm, and the tempers of men were worn to a frazzle by the long enervating day of heat. Carriages were rattling by, working their way through the congeries of vehicles down to the wharves, conveying passengers to the *Moselle,* the new "brag-boat" of which everyone was talking—her fame had reached even Bourbon County.[3] She lay there, meditatively letting off steam, her cabins already lighted and great torch-baskets flaring at her forward gang-way, all ready to start down the river to New Orleans.

Carter hardly knew which way to go, but he was eager to get out of all this turmoil, and Dolly D. picked her way rather du-biously over the cobble-stones to which her feet were unaccus-tomed, up to Front Street, and they found their way to the Main Street Hotel, in the street of the same name where Carter's father had put up when he went to Cincinnati. His father had told him that its prices would be high, but that the best was always the cheapest in the long run. Fortunately his stay in Cincinnati was to be short, for Carter had not set out for the Ohio without knowing where he was going; there was too much of the canni-ness of his Scotch ancestry remaining in him for that; the Blairs went ca' canny. He was going to Macochee, a town nearly a hun-dred miles north of Cincinnati, and he had letters to people there who had been originally of Kentucky. He would merely stay the night in Cincinnati and then be off for Macochee, and Dolly D. would have better going than these hard cobble-stones.

The landlord of the Main Street Hotel, Colonel Davidson, came out of the news-room scowling with irritation at having been interrupted. He was a portly, perspiring man in shirt-sleeves, with a forbidding and truculent manner, determined, in his devotion to the American principle of equality, to show that he was as good as anybody, if not a little better.

"Well, young man," he said to Carter, speaking with a mouth full of tobacco, "what d'ye want?"

"I want lodging for myself and stabling for my horse."

The Colonel looked him over, squirted out a long stream of yellow saliva on the floor, and demanded:

"What's yer name and wher're you from?"

"Carter Blair, of Bourbon County, Kentucky." (Carter pronounced his name Cyartah, and said cyounty.)

"That yer hoss out yonder?"

"Yes, sir."

" 'Bout how long do you reckon you'll stay?"

"Only tonight, sir. I'm going on in the morning."

The Colonel squirted another long stream of tobacco-juice at the floor, sucked his drooping brown moustache between his lips, wiped it with the back of his hand, said with an air of condescension, "Wull, I guess we can 'commodate you," and shouted:

"Here, nigger, show this gentleman round to the stables."

Carter had intended to ask what the charges would be, but the Colonel had returned to the news-room without giving him an opportunity, and Carter was afraid to pursue him now. He went out into the street and, leading Dolly D., followed the black boy round to the alley behind the hotel where the livery-stable stood with its sign above the door—a black horse with flowing mane and tail, trotting magnificently, with high knee action, all four feet off the ground at once. The air was oppressive in its heavy humidity, and reeked with the odours of the filthy street. Carter could scarcely get his breath. The storm that had been gathering all the afternoon was ready to burst now at any instant; thunder was rolling above the house tops, and a greenish glare of lightning flickered now and then in the darkening air. When the rolling thunder ceased for an instant, it grew preternaturally still.

The hottest place of all, of course, was the livery stable, and yet to Carter, in its familiar sights and sounds and smells, there was something homelike and reassuring. The hollow sound of

Dolly D.'s hooves on the planking as she gladly trotted into the stable; the coaches, their poles unfixed from the fore-carriage and thrust beneath its body; buggies and carts, their shafts raised on high as though in supplication, and the dim interior of the wide, low stable, the stalls with the harness suspended from its peg; the switching tails of the horses, stamping at the flies, swishing down wisps of hay from their racks and munching their feed; the negro ostlers bedding the horses down for the night; the stable smell—the sharp, ammoniac odour of manure, the hot, dusty odour of hay, the oily smell of harness—these things were all familiar. Through Carter's mind there flashed the scene in the stable at home at that very hour—old Wesley scolding the "critters": "Hyah, yo' fool hoss! Yo' all think Ah got nothin' else to do but pick up all de hay yo' was'e an' th'ow about. . . ."

An ostler unsaddled Dolly D. and wiped her wet and matted coat with a wisp of hay. Carter, bending over, lifted her feet, one after another, and felt the frogs. The proprietor of the livery-stable came up and said:

"That's a nice piece o' hoss flesh you've got there."

"Yes," said Carter, straightening up and looking at the huge man in shirt sleeves. "She's a good mare."

"Kentucky, heh—blue grass?"

"Yes. Bourbon County."

"Tuckahoe?"

"Yes. Diomed strain."

"How old?"

"Four this spring."

The man, with a professional air, spread Dolly D.'s lips apart to have a confirmatory look at her teeth, but it was too dark by this time to inspect them to any purpose. He walked round her, taking in all her points, passing his hand down her legs, feeling her shanks, pinching her posterns lightly.

"Want to trade her? I've got a—"

"Trade her!" exclaimed Carter before the man could finish his sentence. "Trade her!"

He stared at the man in stupefaction, and then with a laugh at what must be, after all, a joke, a palpable absurdity, he put his arm about Dolly's neck, and laid his cheek for an instant affectionately against hers. In the new access of home-sickness that came to him at the man's impious suggestion he felt that it would be a wrench even to leave her for the night.

He told the ostler to rinse out her mouth and not to give her to drink until she had cooled out. Then he stood by while she was rubbed down, told them to give her a feed of oats and telling the black boy to fetch his saddle-bags, he went back to the hotel just as the storm broke with a mighty crash over the town.

III

The storm raged for the hour that Carter sat at supper in the men's dining-room, the females supping in a room of their own. Carter sat at the foot of one of the two long tables, Colonel Donaldson himself, in his coat now and his hair sleeked down with oil, doing them the honour of sitting at the head of the board. The flashes of lightning spread a rosy glare in the room and the almost continuous roll of thunder filled it with the solemn boom and terrifying peals of an Ohio river thunderstorm.

The men at the two long tables ate rapidly and in silence, that is, without speaking to one another though there was a prodigious clatter of knives and forks and plates, heard even above the noise of the storm. The men gobbled their food, swigged their coffee, and, as there were no ladies present to trouble them, unbuttoned their waistcoats and trouser-bands, and were at their ease. The heat in the room was stifling, and perspiration bathed those red faces. The air grew foul as the meal progressed, and Carter was relieved when they reached the last course and a section of water-melon was set before each man. They took their slices of the fruit in both hands, plunged their faces in it, ate the red core with a sucking sound, the juice of the melons running down their cheeks and chins, spat out the black seeds into their plates or on to the table cloth, and the meal was over.

They went out into the news-room where it was almost as hot as the dining-room. The storm had ceased; there was only a distant and diminished growl of thunder now and then and a feeble flicker of lightning. But it had not cooled the air. Carter sauntered about, looked at the placards indicating the arrival and departure of steamers, and the bills offering rewards for runaway slaves. But these things did not interest him. At one end of the news-room there was a long bar before which stood men drinking mint-juleps. The room was filled with men from all parts of the country, lean, tough Yankees, and tall southerners with moustaches and goatees; they wore light nankeen trousers, long coats and wide Panama hats, and they stood in groups smoking, spitting on the already flooded floor, talking in all the various accents of the Union, and swearing like gentlemen. The air was hazy with the smoke of their cigars and filled with their loud talk, their coarse laughter, their genial, epithetical oaths. Carter recklessly bought a Conestoga segar, lighted it, and adopting the negligent attitude of the Southern aristocracy stood there smoking it, holding his segar after each puff at arm's length, with an elegant and important manner, blowing out the smoke in a long stream. He looked at the other men in the news-room and wished that he knew some of them so that he, too, might talk, as he felt inclined to do after a long day's silence on horse-back. But a timidity kept him from accosting any of them, though they seemed to have no difficulty or reluctance in addressing one another. Perhaps, however, it would be as well to keep to himself and relish this new sensation of grown-up freedom and importance, for his homesickness had vanished.

At the bar the voices were rising to a higher and noisier pitch; the laughter was wilder and more hilarious, the oaths more elaborate and picturesque. The light there seemed to gleam with a brighter intensity. He was wondering whether he should not indulge in a mint-julep himself; perhaps it would cool him off.

But just at that moment a young man came out of the bar, a young man not so tall as Carter, and apparently somewhat older than he. The young fellow had a slender, graceful figure, and he wore a blue swallow-tail coat with brass buttons, white nankeen trousers, and a cream-coloured Bolivar;[4] in fact, with his slender young figure and his fine clothes he had the air of a dashing young blade. And just at that moment their eyes met, Carter's and the young fellow's, and the young fellow came towards him with a smile on his ruddy, handsome young face. Who the deuce, Carter wondered, could this young fellow be? He had been warned, of course, against sharpers and the evil characters that prowled the City, but there was no reason for thinking that this young fellow was anything of that sort. The young fellow came towards him, and, pausing beside him, began a conversation in the free and easy familiarity of the frontier.

"Warm evening, isn't it?"

"Yes," said Carter, "it is."

"Storm didn't seem to cool the air much."

"No, it didn't, that's so."

The young fellow had a frank and open smile, and if his eye narrowed ever so slightly, Carter hardly noticed that or attached any importance to it. No doubt this pleasant stranger was as lonely as he, and only wanted someone of his own age to talk to.

Carter was glad to have someone to talk to, only he wished that he might have been better dressed; he felt embarrassed and at a disadvantage in his rough country homespun.

The young fellow, thought Carter, must have noticed his clothes, for he said:

"When did you come to town?"

"This afternoon."

"Ever been in Cincinnati before?"

"No," Carter was obliged to confess, with a certain shame.

"Expect to make much of a stay?"

"No. I'm going on to-morrow—North, to Macochee."

At this the young fellow gave a sudden start of awakened interest, alert and personal, different from his idle curiosity of a moment before.

"Macochee!" he exclaimed. "What the hell do you want to go to Macochee for? Ever been there?"

"No. Have you?"

"Have I!" The young man gave a sardonic little laugh. "Have I! Why, that's where I live, when I'm at home. I don't stay there, though, any more than I can help; I prefer Cincinnati. There's something to see, something to do."

"Then you are here for a long stay?"

"Well, as long as the old man keeps on sending me the spondulix. Know anyone in Macochee? Ever hear of Colonel Nash?"

Carter had never heard of Colonel Nash, though he felt that it had been somewhat indelicate in him to admit as much when, the next moment, the young fellow went on to say:

"He's my father. He laid out the town—I don't mean like a surveyor; I mean founded it; he was president of the land company that started it. You'll hear of him when you get to Macochee. He's the leading citizen there." The young fellow evidently had a filial pride in his father in spite of his contempt for the town which his father's commercial, rather than his engineering, genius had so miraculously conjured out of the Ohio wilderness. "My name's Tom—Tom Nash. You'll hear of me, too, when you get to Macochee. Only what you hear won't be quite so complimentary as what you'll hear of my father. May I ask what your name might be?"

"My name's Carter Blair; I come from Bourbon county, Kentucky."

"I knew you were from Kentucky. My father came from Kentucky. Macochee was settled principally by people from Kentucky. A lot o' Yankees are coming in now, though. Not that they add

1. Ella Brainerd Whitlock and Brand Whitlock at Cannes in 1933, the year before his death.

2. The original Brand house, visible on the left of the photo, was a one-and-a-half story brick structure probably built in 1824; the two-story addition on the right was built by Joseph Carter Brand a few years after his purchase of the "old" house in 1851. (Introduction, p. 1, 24.)

CORNER NORTH MAIN STREET AND SQUARE, URBANA, IN 1846
Drawn by Henry Howe.

3. This scene looking northward from the Macochee-Urbana
town square was drawn by Henry Howe in 1846. The col-
umned building is the old Champaign County Courthouse,
with the spire of the old First Methodist Church beyond. Both
these buildings have been replaced by relatively modern struc-
tures on approximately the same sites. The gabled building
marked 1811 is the site of the present Citizens National Bank.
(Introduction, pp. 25-26.)

4. A charming portrait of Brand Whitlock at about age four recalling Whitlock's revelations of his Urbana childhood in the
opening of his autobiography, *Forty Years of It*, where he
describes his close childhood relationship with his maternal
grandfather, Joseph Carter Brand.

*This photo is reproduced by courtesy of the Champaign County
Historical Society.*

5. Joseph Carter Brand, pictured here in about 1881, was the prototype of Carter Blair, the central character of *The Buck-eyes*. In 1836, when the novel opens, Blair is portrayed as a young man in his early twenties; his real-life prototype Brand was 26 in that year. (Introduction, pp. 18-24.)

6. Lavinia Talbott Brand, wife of Joseph Carter Brand. Lavinia appears as Lucretia Harris (later Lucretia Harris Blair) in the novel.

7. The Ward house, built about 1825 by Colonel William Ward, the first citizen of Urbana. The Ward farm is famous as the site of the Harrison campaign barbecue held in the grove behind the house, an event described in *The Buckeyes*.
Photo courtesy Craig Findley of The Urbana Citizen.

8. Two title pages from almanacs of 1841 focusing attention on Harrison as the central figure of the log cabin and hard cider campaign of the previous year. In the second engraved title-page, the demonic figure kneeling by the cask in a vain attempt to stop the flow of cider is Martin (Matty) Van Buren, Harrison's opponent.

These photos were supplied courtesy of the Ohio Historical Society, Columbus.

James G. Birney.

9. James G. Birney (1792-1857), abolitionist leader and Liberty
   Party candidate for President in 1840 and 1844. (Introduction,
   pp. 27-28 and *The Buckeyes*, pp. 162-167, 247.)

Courtesy Ohio Historical Society.

10. Thomas Corwin as Secretary of the Treasury (1850-1853). (Introduction, p. 31 and *The Buckeyes*, pp. 64ff.)

11. The imposing Corwin house, built in 1818 by Phineas Ross, the soon deceased brother of Sarah Ross, who married Corwin in 1822. This house was owned by Corwin till his death in 1865. Later it was acquired by the Solomon Fred family, whose members still occupy it.

anything to the delights of life in the God-forsaken town. Ever play cards? What do you say to a little game of seven-up?"

But Carter shook his head; long years ago he had heard his Uncle Jim Blair of Lexington say that he never played cards with anyone he didn't know. The remark had made an impression on Carter, and in this instance acted as a restraining influence it never would have exercised had it been made to him by way of advice. And so he shook his head and said:

"Humph-umph, it's too hot."

"It is right warm in here," Tom Nash readily admitted, taking off his tall hat and passing his hand over his forehead as though suddenly aware of the heat. "Then what do you say to a little stroll? I could show you something of the town."

It was, in fact, excessively hot in the crowded news-room and Carter had the longing and the need of a country-bred boy for a breath of fresh air. He felt, too, that he ought to see something of the city now that he was in it for the first time, and no telling when he should have another chance. And besides, he did not know how to decline.

It was almost as hot in the street outside as it was in the hotel. The storm had not cooled the atmosphere but merely charged it with a heavier and more gluey humidity. The brick sidewalk still held its heat, and from the flooded gutters and the wet roadway arose the hot and sickening effluvia of the filth that had been stirred up by the rain. They walked down the Main Street past the lighted shops. Nash, chattering on gaily and inconsequently, pointed out the two-horned church[5] and other marvels of which Carter had heard, and felt it a distinction to gaze upon at last. As they walked along Nash talked about Macochee, telling Carter what little there was to tell of the town, but promising, when he got home again, to introduce Carter to his father and, in fact, everybody else in the place. And Carter marvelled at this extraordinary coincidence which had made him acquainted on this very first evening in Ohio with so important an inhabitant of the town he was going to, and he marvelled even more at the good luck of it. He had known Nash only half an hour and yet they seemed almost by way of being friends at once. But it was not long before Macochee as a subject of conversation was exhausted and Nash began talking about women, and of his successes with them. He did this in a matter of fact way and without an air of too much boasting, but Carter, if he was impressed, nevertheless felt somewhat ill at ease, not having any experiences of his own to relate. If it had been horses or, say, rifle-shooting, he could have done better, but women—well, he didn't like to talk about women in that way. However, he entered into, or did his best to enter into Nash's interesting and amorous reminiscences, and listened and admired where he could not compete.

They were going towards the river now, and when they reached Second Street Nash said:

"Let's turn down here."

They entered the unpaved street which wore an air of less distinction than the Main Street, and was more discreetly lighted, and as they advanced Carter felt that there was something mysterious and sinister in its squalid aspect, and was uneasily conscious that they had entered the lower and more forbidding purlieu of the city. A girl, sauntering by, brushed against him, with a:

"Howdy, honey," in his ear.

He went on without replying, his heart beating a little faster at the adventure.

"Don't mind those soiled doves of the pavement," said Nash. "I'll take you to call on some nice young ladies."

Call on ladies? What ladies? Carter wondered; he wondered in a virgin innocence that was not all ignorance, for in however vague, confused and exaggerated a way, stories had come into the country-side of Bourbon county of those splendid abodes of luxury and vice to be found in the City. At the Academy where he had had his brief schooling, Carter had heard the boys dwell upon the subject with the morbid imaginings, the secret and shamed desires of adolescence; and all his life, of course, he had been familiar with the obscene profanity and bawdy talk that was the staple of conversation common to the breeders of live stock, farm-hands, grooms and ostlers and to negroes with their more primitive animal passions and florid imaginations. It was a subject of which he had heard everything and knew nothing, and now the sudden thought that at last the experience might be his, filled him with a tumultuous and troubling excitement.

"I'll take you," Nash was saying, "to the choicest place in the city, absolutely safe. Anything you want, white, creole, octoroon, quadroon, mulatto or black. Which do you prefer, light or dark meat?"

Carter felt within him a sudden and sickening revulsion. He felt the flush of shame mount to his cheeks, he felt his face flame red and his quick, hot-tempered Kentucky blood surge and whirl dizzily in his head. Nash had stopped before a doorway and raised his hand to a bell-pull; and Carter, who had liked him at first, now suddenly hated and loathed him. He longed to smash Nash's face with his fist; a moment before he would have done so, but now the door was opened, a woolly head was thrust out and a negro woman said, "Come in quick."

And before Carter knew how it had happened, or why, they had slipped into the hall. The hall was dimly lighted by a gas-jet that hung from the ceiling over the newel-post of the stairs. Once inside, Nash took command.

"Ladies in the parlour, heigh, Mammy?"

"Yes suh, deh is, and some gemlum wid dem."

But just then a portly woman past middle-age came into the hall, and Nash said:

"Good evening, Miss Annie. I've brought a young friend. I was just asking him—"

"Look here!" said Carter. "Don't you repeat that! Don't repeat it, I tell you!" He was trembling violently, his fists were clenched and he stood there, his slender form drawn up and tense, the mass of his dark hair, worn long in the Southern fashion, almost touching the gas lamp, his large eyes blazing.

Nash chose to laugh it off.

"My young friend knows what he wants, Miss Annie."

"Ah, young gentlemen are particular," said Miss Annie, "and when they're as good-looking as your friend they've got a right to be. Heigh, honey?" she said. And she could not forbear to gratify some remnant of the burnt-out fires of passion in her own breast by stroking Carter's smooth chin voluptuously. Her hand smelt of some strong perfume, and Carter did not like this sensual, patronizing familiarity, but he did not know what to say, and besides, he was still absorbed by his rage against Nash who, with every second, was growing more odious to him.

"How about the back parlor?" Nash was saying to the proprietress.

She shook her head.

"You come into my room," she said, "and I'll send Mirabelle out to him. He can go upstairs with her."

She appeared presently, this Mirabelle, a girl with bare and rather broad shoulders and long bare arms, in a skirt so short that it showed the calves of her legs. She whisked into the hall, carefully closing the door behind her, and came forward with a smile that showed her white teeth against the red of her cheeks.

"Howdy, honey!" she cried, with an air of professional gaiety, and as she caught a better view of Carter standing uncertainly against the banister, a troubled frown upon his face, she suddenly paused and exclaimed, with an unaccustomed sincerity, "My God! You *are* a pretty boy!"

She came close, and though she seemed to Carter a rather tall woman, she threw back her head and he looked down into her eyes. She laid her hands—they were large—on his shoulders and smiled. Her body exhaled the scent of musk, mingled with the odour of perspiration. Her arms were stealing about his neck; she leant against him, pressing her body against his; her lips were approaching his own, and on her breath was a strong smell of spirits.

"Come on, honey," she whispered. "Let's go upstairs!"

Carter looked down into the painted face, the shining eyes with their eager invitation, bold and unabashed. He felt confused, embarrassed and ashamed. He stood there rigidly like an unwilling but stoical victim of sacrifice, not knowing what to say, and scowled down at her. But this, he thought, this brazen painted creature, smelling of musk and sweat and liquor—this was not what he had vaguely imagined as the form in which love would come to him, the transcendent experience that was to be the initiation to life—this could not be it! He recoiled from her, but he was pressed against the banister; he raised and turned his head and averted his eyes from hers, and scowled under his mass of dark hair.

"But ain't you got a kiss for me?" she said. "Ain't you even got a word?"

She raised herself on tiptoe, caught him firmly round the neck, rubbed her cheek against his, and whispered:

"Come along, my honey dear, come upstairs—to my room. We can't stay here—someone'll come!"

Carter was overwhelmed by a great loathing; not so much for this poor, miserable creature, repulsive though she was to him— but for this place, this company, and all the squalid implications of this adventure; he loathed himself most of all, and suddenly, putting forth his strength he seized the girl's hands, unlocked their clasp from his neck, and, almost flinging her from him, he sprang toward the door, jerked it open, and incontinently fled.

Out in the hot, reeking street he ran, ran as fast as he could. Once his foot struck a soft mass, and an angry and impatient grunt told him that he had disturbed a hog lying on the brick pavement. For hogs were lying everywhere in the street, wallowing in the filthy gutters, complaining and protesting with savage, husky grunts if anyone disturbed them.

Carter did not run far; he feared to attract attention, but he went on as fast as he could, anxious to escape that street and its atmosphere, its uncleanness and bestiality. And even when he reached Main Street and breathed another and more reassuring air, and began to feel somewhat rehabilitated in his self-esteem, he hurried on, eager to get back to the hotel. But even there he felt defiled, besmirched and unclean. He was too excited to go to bed at once, and he lingered awhile in the news-room.

When at last he began to feel somewhat calmer and more collected Carter went to the large bedchamber to which he had been assigned. It had four beds in it, one in each corner; and in one of them a man was already snoring regularly and deeply. The sight of the familiar objects in his saddle-bags suddenly roused all the homesickness he had felt earlier in the evening. And what a long evening it had been! And now to the homesickness was added the humiliation, the shame, the sense of uncleanness that he could not now escape, and which somehow separated him from his kinsfolk back in Bourbon county, and made him feel unworthy of them. He undressed, and lifting the coarse mosquito nets, got into bed. His mind went back over the events of that day—his first in Ohio; he retraced them, back, back. . . . Then he had a troubled sense of some noise in the room. Two men had come in and got into the other beds and lay there, under their mosquito-nets, talking to each other with many oaths, pausing only, it seemed, to clear their throats and hawk and spit on the floor. The man in the corner snored on . . . Carter was thinking of the dark and rather ugly face of the girl at that house . . . hogs were wallowing in the gutter . . . the coffle of slaves came shuffling off the ferry . . . Hi-o, away we go, Floatin' down the river on the O-hi-o . . . Dolly D. was saying to him, with a strange smile, "Howdy, honey! Howdy honey . . . !"

IV

In his eagerness to get away from Cincinnati he made an early start the next morning, and when he had ridden past the last of the public slaughter-houses which, with their ill-smelling piles of heads and horns and hooves and hides, stretched along the Dayton road, he felt a sense of vast relief at finding himself once more in the country. He felt that his introduction to the City had not been very auspicious and he could think of the events of the previous evening only with a sense of humiliation and degradation. But he was young, and this was a new morning; he had slept like a top and eaten an enormous breakfast, and he was not long in recapturing the spirit in which he had set forth on this adventure into the new country of the Ohio. Macochee, whither he was bound, was nearly a hundred miles away, and he had planned to make Dayton that day, for the road thither, he had been told, was good, though it was not so good as the turnpikes he had been used to in Kentucky. It was evident even at that early hour that they were in for a hot day, for a soft, white, cottony haze filled the low lush-lands of the Miami Valley. To a horse with such bottom as Dolly D. the heat didn't, perhaps, matter so much. He let Dolly D. choose her own gait, but the sun beating down filled the valley with a sultry heat, and so weakened Carter's own purpose, and when early that afternoon he arrived at Lebanon he decided to give Dolly D. a rest and stay the night there. He put up at the Lebanon House,[6] kept by Colonel Mack, who was much more civil to him than Colonel Donaldson had been. Colonel Mack, eloquently praising the wonders of Warren county, obligingly told him of the numerous sights to see in the neighborhood—the settlement of Shaking Quakers at Union Village and the extensive pre-historic fortifications called Fort Ancient on the Little Miami river, six miles away. But it was too hot for excursions, especially for one as lazy as Carter found himself after the dinner at Colonel Mack's tavern. The Colonel's daughter had stood by, waving a swish of rustling paper over the table to keep off the flies. She had blue Irish eyes with long black lashes.

"You're not of these parts," she said.

"How do you know?"

"You don't talk like it."

"I'm from Kentucky."

"I guessed so. Where are you going?"

"To Macochee."

"Oh!"

The reply seemed to satisfy her curiosity. They talked on, in such desultory and banal personalities, with shy, conscious pauses in which they said nothing, but thought of the things they dared not express or seem to recognize, that is, the possibility of an intimate, passionate relationship, that was always present and always insistent between man and woman when they were alone together.

"It's a hot day," she said.

"Yes. Rain here last night?"

"Yes. But you wouldn't know it to-day."

"No, I reckon you wouldn't."

She wore a simple gown of checked gingham, like a shift. It was fresh and clean, and blotched here and there by patches of starch, glistening in certain lights from the iron. Carter had not considered her pretty at first; he had scarcely noticed her until, having set his meal before him, she came and stood by his side, rather close, and kindly kept off the persistent flies whilst he ate. Then, in this proximity, she seemed after all rather good-looking with her blue Irish eyes with the long black lashes, and the bow of bright red ribbon in her dark hair. Her arms were round and plump; her small breasts were round and hard under her shift. Yes, she was really pretty. The face of the girl in the brothel at Cincinnati came suddenly before him, with the glowing dark eyes, the broad, high cheek-bones and painted cheeks, the parted red lips, exhaling a strong odour of spirits. Why was it, he wondered, that that girl who was all panting eagerness and desire, should have filled him with loathing and repulsion, whilst this girl who was all shyness and modesty, and, of course, wholly inaccessible, should affect him as she did. It was really not nice of him to think of such things in her presence; it was lacking in respect. But, confound it, it was a nuisance to be tormented by the thought of this thing all the time, day and night, to have everything in life and nature suggest it, and remind him of it, every minute!

"Shall I get you some more biscuits?" she asked.

"Oh no, thank you; I've had enough."

The girl's mother, as he supposed her to be, thrust her untidy head just then in at the kitchen door, and said snappishly:

"Aggie, come here!"

"I've got to go now," the girl said, in a low, almost confidential tone, and with more meaning than she had put into any word she had uttered during the time she had stood there beside him. "Got everything you want?"

He supposed that her mother felt that Aggie had loitered there too long. The mother was evidently a hateful old thing. And Carter finished his meal alone, keeping off the voracious flies as best he could.

That afternoon he got Byron out of his saddle-bags and sat in a rocking-chair on the long verandah. But he sat with the book unopened on his knees. He was all alone on the verandah. In fact, there was not a soul in sight anywhere. The wide dusty street sprawled empty before him, and the heat beat down fiercely upon it, to be flung back in hot puffs in his face. Aggie, he supposed, was somewhere at the back of the house helping her mother; Colonel Mack was nowhere about. As he sat there he could think of nothing but Aggie. She was surrounded by a kind of light that set her apart and made her seem different from anybody else. He thought of her because the hot, drowsy and droning air lapped him in an element that somehow made thoughts of that kind inevitable, and filled him with desire. The little town seemed to be sunk entirely in the somnolence of that summer afternoon; he and Aggie might have had the whole world, if the world had been otherwise ordered, to themselves. During all the time that he had sat there not a person had passed by. Directly across the street there was a harness shop, with a heavy horse-collar hung out as a sign, and a set of bright new harness, with a brow-band of shining red leather and red rosettes on the bridle hung out invitingly. But no one was in sight in the shop; the saddler was nowhere to be seen. There was a grocery, too, but no one had gone in to get a drink. From somewhere far off came the musical chime of an anvil, but on the drowsy air it seemed not so much a sound of industry, a blow struck by a strong and wilful hand, as one of indolence, the stroke of a hammer that had fallen from a lazy and listless hand. The only sign of life was a cock and three hens, indolently bathing their feathers in the dust of the street; the whole town seemed to be as sound asleep as the liver-coloured hound that lay stretched on the ground before the verandah, his ribbed sides rising and falling with his breathing, his long ears twitching automatically when a fly alighted on his head.

And then, in what must have been the very hottest hour of the hot afternoon, the town was suddenly aroused by the clatter of a heavy vehicle, and a stage coach drew up before the hotel. It was the mail from Chillicothe, a heavy vehicle with high wheels, drawn by four horses and driven by a driver whose seat was on a level with that of the passengers on the seats inside. Trailing a cloud of yellow dust that trembled and vibrated on the shimmering waves of heat, it drew up with something less than its usual dash, for, after their stage that day from Greenfield, the horses were fagged. But the arrival of the coach roused everybody; Colonel Mack at once appeared, drawing on his coat, Aggie and her mother behind him; negro ostlers came from the stable, men and children came from all directions, until a curious group were gathered to watch the passengers alight.

There were but two of them, one a tall, raw-boned Western man, whose brown leathery skin looked as though it had been cured over the smoke of a hickory fire; a long, thick lock of black hair, tied with a greasy black ribbon, hung down his back like a horse-tail; he held himself very erect, and moved with an air of profound deliberation and solemn pomposity. The other man was tall, too, but much heavier than the first; his powerful figure was already inclined to the corpulence that comes sometimes with middle-age, and on alighting from the high coach he turned on the folk gathered before the hotel, a broad, fat, smooth-shaven and swarthy face with a wide humorous mouth and small eyes that twinkled with kindliness and good nature. At sight of him Carter ventured nearer in a kind of fascinated curiosity, already subjected, though unconsciously, to the spell of a great and unique personality. The people in the group were affected even more than Carter; a sudden stimulus roused them, and dropping the affected indifference of the backwoods and overcoming the lethargy induced by the heat, they pressed about him, all struggling to be the first to take his hand. Carter could see the noble head with its curly hair, bare now, and the friendly smile on the large fleshy face, and caught by the charm of it, he asked of the nearest man:

"Who is that?"

"Hell!" said the man, in a kind of indignant disgust, "don't you know who that 'ere feller is? Well, that's Tom Corwin!"

The man left the full significance of this revelation to impress Carter as it might, and joined the crowd that was pressing about the hero. But Colonel Mack, who could never forget the responsibilities of his position, was finding his way through the crowd—for by this time it was a crowd—and was saying:

"Well, Mr. Corwin! I'm mighty glad to see you home again, sir! Step right in!"

When the Colonel had wrung Tom Corwin's hand, he asked:

"And is this gentleman a friend of yours, sir?"

"Yes, sir. Let me introduce you. Senator Emory, this is my old friend, Colonel Mack."

"Not the great Senator Emory of Indiana!"[7] exclaimed the Colonel, much impressed, as he shook hands with the tall, raw-boned, smoke-cured man with the long lock of hair hanging down his back.

"Sir," replied the tall Westerner, in his best senatorial manner, and with a happy air of à propos, "Sir, I own the soft impeachment. And I am very happy to make your acquaintance."

"But you must not stop out here in this heat, gentlemen," the Colonel insisted, "you must come in and partake of refreshment."

Tom Corwin demurred; he could not remain there; he must go

to his home where Mrs. Corwin and his daughter were awaiting him. Colonel Mack understood perfectly.

"I must yield to the prior claim of your lady, sir," he said gracefully. And yet, the Congressman would consent to join them in a glass of Sangaree before going home. Tom Corwin smiled and consented. He would go in a moment to see his friend Senator Emory safely lodged for the night. He had asked the Senator to be his guest, but the Senator had declined because he was going on to Cincinnati, and the stage-coach would leave at daylight.

"But at any rate, Senator," said Tom Corwin, "you must come and break bread in my house. We have supper at six—if the neighbours have been kind enough to bring anything in."

They had gone into the hotel, followed by a few men outside who evidently felt themselves important enough for such society. Colonel Mack led his distinguished guests to the end of the news-room where a space was railed off for the bar, and asked them to sit down at a table whilst he mixed the sangarees. As they sat there Senator Emory drew his long lock of hair over his shoulder and toyed with it, whilst expressing his fears that, on such short notice, Mrs. Corwin might feel it an intrusion and a burden for him to appear at supper.

"Oh, not at all," said Tom Corwin. "The latch-string's always out, you know."

Carter stood at a respectful distance and gazed at the two statesmen, just back from the session of Congress at Washington City. Carter thought of the immense distance they had travelled, over the Alleghenies and by the National Road, rumbling along day after day in the mail-stage, from town to town, from tavern to tavern, in the gigantic, endless caravan that moved forever towards the West;—the horsemen and the coaches and the great Conestoga wains, with blue waggon-beds like boats and red running gear; and the movers' vans with canvas tilts. He had some imaginative conception of the romance there was in this mighty pageant of the urge towards the West, and felt a glow to think that he, in however small a way, was a part of it. He looked at the raw-boned Senator, with the tanned skin stretched over the bones of his thin, solemn face, as he played with his long lock of hair, and pictured him rising in the Senate and making an important speech, with Henry Clay and Webster and Calhoun sitting solemnly by and listening. But he did not look long at the Senator; even with his eccentricities he was not nearly so interesting a figure as Tom Corwin. For in Corwin there was some mysterious and magnetic quality that commanded the attention of men, and when he spoke in his rich, musical voice, they crowded round to hear, hung fascinated and entranced on his words, and felt within themselves a glow, a response, a feeling of satisfaction that remained with them long after he had gone, a feeling that they tried to communicate to others and could not, and so would give up the effort in despair and shake their heads sadly at their inability. Carter had heard of this strange power of Tom Corwin, though he had heard of it as chiefly displayed in his political speeches. He had heard his father speak of Tom Corwin, but there were two impressive facts that perhaps in his father's mind accounted more for Corwin's influence than his ability as an orator; these were, first that Tom Corwin had been born in Bourbon County, and second that he was a Whig and a follower of Henry Clay. In Kentucky all the gentlemen and all the people with property, that is, all the best people, were followers of Henry Clay; it was only the mud-sills who were for General Jackson. As Carter looked at Tom Corwin he felt himself drawn to him by a sudden and immense affection. He couldn't tell why. Tom Corwin wasn't doing anything, he wasn't saying anything; he was merely sitting there, a heavy figure that filled the large armchair, his broad, fleshy shoulders hunched up about his neck, his linen collar bound tightly in a high black stock, sticking up to his ears in two triangular points, and wilted now by perspiration and the heat, and stained like the rest of his attire by the dust of the road. He squeezed a finger into his stock as though he would like to loosen it, or remove it altogether, like Colonel Mack, who wore no collar at all. The skin of his large, smooth-shaven dark face which already, though he was barely past forty, was beginning to hang in mastiff-like jowls over his collar—the skin was shining with perspiration and his curly hair was glistening with it. What was it that made men adore him? Carter couldn't tell. All he knew was that he did adore him, and he had never spoken a word to him.

"He's our Congressman," said a voice beside him, and he turned to find Aggie standing there. "Ain't he nice? He's just got back from Washington City."

"You like him?" asked Carter.

"Like him? Of course. Everybody likes him."

"You'll make me jealous."

"Oh, not *that* way, I don't mean." She blushed violently. "Aw, you know what I mean!"

"Of course."

Colonel Mack had mixed the sangarees and set the tall glasses with the cooling drink before his guests, with one for himself.

The Colonel sat at table with them, and they raised their glasses: Tom Corwin held his up against the light and, closing one eye, looked at its transparent red and winey-colour with the droll, comic expression that made everybody laugh. The Senator wound his long lock of hair round his neck and tucked it into his bosom. They raised their glasses and took refreshing draughts.

They were a considerable while sipping their drinks, but at last Tom Corwin got up, said he must go, and, promising to call for the Senator later, started to leave the room. Seeing Aggie, however, he stopped, and said:

"Well, Miss Aggie, no need to ask how you are!"

He took her hand, smiled, and she blushed as red as the sangaree itself. And then as he was about to go, his glance fell upon Carter, and something in Carter's eyes—the sudden frank affection, the unconcealed adoration of youth for its hero—caused Tom Corwin to smile his recognition of it. His eyes twinkled with kindliness and good humour.

"You're not of Lebanon or Warren county are you, my boy?"

"No, sir," said Carter, blushing consciously at finding himself thus distinguished by the great man's notice, and, before he could go on, Colonel Mack, with the easy familiarity of the American sovereign, and his facility in furthering acquaintance, stepped up promptly and said:

"Let me introduce you, gentlemen. Congressman Corwin, Mr. Blair; Mr. Blair, Congressman Corwin. Mr. Blair is a guest of the house, and a young gentleman from Kentucky, the home of Henry Clay."

And Carter found himself actually shaking hands with Tom Corwin, and heard him say:

"From Kentucky, heigh? What part of Kentucky, if I may inquire?"

"Bourbon County, sir."

"Bourbon County! Why, I was born in Bourbon County."

"I know you were, sir." Carter had an impulse to add that Bourbon county was proud of the fact, but it seemed a rather flowery and flourishing phrase to utter, and he was too timid to attempt it. But Tom Corwin was going on:

"I came away at a somewhat earlier age than you, however. In fact, I was only four years old when I decided to move over into Ohio."

Those standing near—and they stood as near as they could get, in their eagerness not to miss a single word that fell from Tom Corwin's lips—those standing near laughed at the joke, as they laughed, inopportunely at times, at nearly everything Tom

Corwin said. There was, indeed, something inimitably droll in most of his utterances, the mysterious quality of which lay concealed, and yet communicable, in the serio-comic expression of his mobile countenance. Carter was instantly aware of it, though like an entire generation of Ohioans he was in despair whenever he tried to describe, or define or reproduce it. Just now, between himself and the elder man, he felt the bond that is instantly established between two persons from the same locality when they meet in foreign parts—a bond that increases in intimacy with the square of the distance—and Tom Corwin, in the pride a Kentuckian always retains in his native state, had many questions to ask about Bourbon county, and Carter answered them as best he could, but there were other points which Carter would have preferred to discuss with Tom Corwin alone. He was embarrassed by this gaping, grinning tavern audience, which Tom Corwin didn't seem to mind, but no doubt rather liked. If he could only have been alone with Tom Corwin who was so full of kindness and of sympathetic understanding of youth, he might have opened his heart to him and learnt, perhaps, the secret of success and fame.

But the affable Colonel Mack interrupted the Congressman, and in his loyalty to his own state he was explaining:

"Mr. Blair has come to settle in Ohio, the greatest state in the greatest country on earth."

"Are you going to settle in Lebanon—the greatest city in that state?" asked Tom Corwin.

"No, sir," said Carter, apologetically, "I'm on my way to Macochee; my father has friends there."

"Well, my young friend," said Tom Corwin, "I wish you good luck."

He was about to shake hands in farewell when his eye lighted on the book that Carter, all this while, had been hugging under his arm.

"What book have you got there, my boy?"

Carter put the book into his hand.

"Byron's poems!" exclaimed Corwin. "Do you read Byron?"

"Yes, sir," said Carter, and then added a saving "sometimes." He feared they would consider him soft and impractical if they discovered that he liked poetry. Indeed, the thought had scarcely passed through his head before Colonel Mack pronounced judgment:

"A young feller won't have much time to read poetry if he expects to get along in Ohio, will he?"

"Probably not," said Tom Corwin sententiously, and in a dry tone. He was slowly turning over the leaves of the book, his eye running down the pages, the expression of his face changing with each line he read. He read on and on, with now and then a smile of amused appreciation, now and then a sympathetic nod of the head: in oblivious distraction, as though he had forgotten where he was. He read on, bit after bit, and presently, without lifting his eyes from the page, he said in an aside:

"Mack, I wish you'd get your man to hitch up a buggy for me. It's too hot to walk out to Turtle Creek."

And then he said:

"Listen to this, Emory."

The Senator bowed gravely as though yielding to a question. The others standing about crowded up, craned their necks and cocked their ears. And Tom Corwin began to read:

> Titan, to whose immortal eyes
>   The sufferings of mortality,
>   Seen in their sad reality,
> Were not as things that gods despise;
> What was thy pity's recompense?
> A silent suffering and intense;
> The rock, the vulture, and the chain,
> All that the proud can feel of pain,
> The agony they do not show.

He read on, in the lower register of his mellow voice, and everyone in the country bar-room listened in a deep silence. Senator Emory, playing with his long lock of hair, nodded his head now and then with senatorial solemnity, as though he, of course, understood. Perhaps he did, and perhaps some of those tavern idlers standing about understood. As for Carter, he was not so sure he understood, and he was rather distressed by the fact. The poem was one that he had never read. Nevertheless, if he was not moved to instant appreciation by the words, he was thrilled by the peculiar rich timbre of the voice in which they were now read out; the mere physical effect of those deep, musical vibrations was stimulating. The idlers must have felt some such impression as well, for they listened with a certain eagerness. And Corwin read on:

> Thy godlike crime was to be kind,
>   To render with thy precepts less
>   The sum of human wretchedness,
> And strengthen Man with his own mind.

Carter became vaguely aware of another emotion; the quality of the voice, matching the human pity and compassion of the poem, revealed another Tom Corwin than the one who was always joking and making men laugh, the Tom Corwin who had thought deeply about the mystery of life, its cruelty and injustice, its brevity and futility, and so was sad at heart, and himself a kind of Prometheus, bound to a rock in this wilderness of the West.

When he had read the poem to the end, the jovial smile did not return to the dark and sensitive face; he was serious, almost sad. He gave the book back to Carter, saying as he did so:

"Come round and see me when you have the time."

And then, asking the Colonel if his buggy was ready, he told Senator Emory that he would send for him at six, and strode out of the bar-room, followed by the ever curious, ever fascinated crowd.

V

As Carter sat on the verandah of the tavern in the cool of the evening, he heard the strains of a band. The long summer twilight had faded into a soft darkness, and in the wide, dusty street dim figures of men and boys trooped by, and the little town, after the long hot day, seemed to have been awakened by an unusual and pleasant excitement. He could hear laughter and lively conversation, and presently he heard a passing man say to his companion:

"Yes, they're going out to Turtle Creek to serenade Tom Corwin."

Aggie, having heard the band, came out on the verandah at that moment and stood beside Carter.

"I thought I heard the band," she said.

"Yes," said Carter. "Listen! there—don't you hear it? They say it's going out to serenade Mr. Corwin. Let's go and see it—what do you say?"

"Oh, I'd just love to! It's an elegant band!"

"Is it far—Mr. Corwin's house, I mean?"

"No, only a quarter of a mile—just out to the edge of town, beside Turtle Creek."

"Let's go!"

They jumped down from the verandah and excitedly followed the crowd. The heat of the day still lingered in the air; the little town was dark, even in the quarter where the few shops were, and the lights of their oil lamps burned dimly at the centre of glowing yellow balls of dust shuffled up by the crowd. Here and there in the crowd a man carried a lantern that cast long shadows of his legs on the ground, opening and shutting like scissors as he walked.

Carter and Aggie hurried along, increasing their pace as the distant music sounded louder. They passed small frame dwellings whose occupants sitting on the doorsteps made blurs in the darkness, and before long they passed dark fields, and came to the Western edge of the town where, beside Turtle Creek, as the narrow tributary of the Miami river was called, stood the residence of Tom Corwin. It was, as seen dimly in the darkness, a large square house of two stories, standing in wooded grounds of its own. The band had ventured within the white picket-fence that surrounded the grounds, and at that moment the musicians had their heads together in consultation; they were talking in low tones, evidently trying to decide which of their pieces they would play next. Some of the crowd, either more privileged or more forward than the rest, had gone inside the grounds with the band, but Carter and Aggie stood outside with the majority and looked over the picket fence. There was to Carter's imagination, a certain mystery in the scene—the unlighted, silent house, the dark trees, the dusky forms of the bandmen, the dim glow of the few lanterns, and the crowd strung along the picket-fence, silent too, except for a phrase now and then spoken in a low tone. Above the blur of shrubs and bushes inside the grounds fire-flies were flashing their phosphorescent lamps, tiny sparks that winked and then went out in the purple darkness; the warm air was heavy with the sweet odour of honeysuckle. The bandmen, however, had reached a decision; a voice said: "Number twelve." There was a premonitory grunt in the deep throat of the tuba, the leader trilled a note on his cornet, and said: "Ready!" and the band began to play:

"Home, Sweet Home!"

The sentimental strains of the tune and all its implications brought a sudden ache to Carter's throat, and renewed the homesick pang that, every now and then since he had left Bourbon County came to his breast. Tom Corwin was from Bourbon County, too, and that thought was a bond and a consolation—but Bourbon County was no longer home to Tom Corwin, nor, indeed, to him. This was home to Tom Corwin, and what more could one ask than to have a home like this, a large house, a wide mansion in its own ample grounds in the quiet edges of a town, and to have one's friends and neighbours welcome one home as they were

71

welcoming Tom Corwin home now? Aggie drew close to his side, and he found and held her hand, finding a comfort and a thrill in its warm, moist clasp. They did not speak.

And then, when the band had done playing, the windows of the house, one by one, leapt into light, until they were all bright, upstairs and down. There was a stir on the verandah; figures were moving there, and presently there was the portly figure of Tom Corwin, detached from the rest, standing on the edge of the verandah.

A shout went up from the crowd:

"Hurrah for Tom Corwin!"
"Hurrah for the Waggon Boy!"

Tom Corwin raised his hand for silence and began to speak. He spoke in a rather low, intimate tone, and those on the edges of the crowd could hardly hear. The members of the band had gone up close to the verandah, and some of those outside now ventured into the grounds, Carter and Aggie with the rest. It was merely a homely little speech of thanks to friends and neighbours, that Corwin delivered. The crowd listened, one moment in silence, the next in laughter. Carter strained his ears to catch every word. He was strangely moved. He had not, of course, heard many speeches in his life. Once to be sure, he had gone with his father and brother, Joe, to hear Henry Clay make a political speech at Paris; it was a long speech, lasting an hour or more, and though it had caused queer little shivers to run up and down his back at times, it had not, if the truth must be told, caused him quite so much rapture as it had his father, who had stood there in that enormous crowd for two hours, his face transformed by the emotions he made no attempt to hide. But this speech was different; the soft darkness of the summer evening, the fire-flies sparkling in the purple shrubbery, the scent of the honeysuckle, the intimate presence of Aggie by his side, the blurred figures on the verandah and the form of Tom Corwin standing on the topmost step, the light of the hall behind him, and the sound of his voice—all this stamped the scene on his imagination with some new and deep significance, and caught him in the spell of a romantic charm.

The speech was over before he knew it; there was a sudden clapping of hands, laughter, three cheers, and boys, with shouts and shrill whistles, chasing one another round and round in horse-play. And then the band struck up another tune, and when the tune was finished, the musicians went stumping up the steps of the verandah.

"They have been invited into the parlour to partake of refreshments," explained Aggie, in her knowledge of the local custom. "Cake and wine, I reckon."

They walked back to the tavern, he and Aggie, with arms intertwined and hands clasped, sauntering as slowly as they could in order that the crowd might get ahead of them. They did not speak for a while, and then Aggie, looking up into his face, asked:

"What are you going to do? I mean, what are you going to be? What business are you going to take up when you get to Macochee?"

"I'm thinking of taking up the law and becoming a lawyer."

He spoke as though it had been a long settled ambition, and did not tell her that it was a purpose, perhaps nothing more than a velleity, formed within the last few hours of that very day. Nor did he let her into the secret of that sudden and elaborate development which the ambition had undergone during that last quarter of an hour when he had dramatized himself, not only as a lawyer, but as an eloquent and witty Member of Congress, arriving home after the House had arisen for the long vacation, and that evening, from the verandah of his mansion in the edge of the town, making a little speech to thank his faithful supporters, his devoted friends and kind neighbours for turning out in such numbers to serenade him and welcome him home.

"It must be nice to be a lawyer," said Aggie. "I've always said I'd marry a lawyer."

They sauntered along so slowly that the noisy crowd soon passed them and left them in the darkness of the wide and sparsely built street. The houses at that point were few, with many vacant lots of land between, and as they strolled, always more and more slowly, his arm about her now, they came to a grove, a remaining bit of the original forest. They stopped in the thick shadows of the oak-trees. Aggie looked up into his face; he put his arms about her and drew her close and kissed her on the mouth. It was the first time in his life that he had ever kissed a girl. His head swam a little. He felt like sobbing; then he felt like laughing. Then an immense happiness pervaded him. They kissed again and again, until their kisses became one long kiss. The street was quite deserted now. The town was still; the immense silence of night had settled down upon it.

"It's late," Aggie whispered. "I must be going home."

They sighed together in longing and despair. They kissed again, and then went on to the tavern, Carter bending solicitously, tenderly, protectingly over her, his whole being flooded with wave on wave of sentimental emotion.

And when he went to bed in that hot upper room of the tavern, he lay tossing in a fever of desire, made all the more tormenting by the fact that in her room under that very roof, and perhaps not so very far away, Aggie lay in her own bed with her virgin pure dreams.

VI

He had intended to be off the first thing in the morning, but Tom Corwin had asked him to come to his law office, and to Carter a request from Tom Corwin was a command. But what did Tom Corwin want of him? He put the question to Aggie, who, when he sat down at the breakfast-table, came and hovered solicitously about him. She was not, perhaps, in her checked gingham dress and blue apron, with her sleeves rolled up her red arms, and seen thus in the unsparing light of a hot summer morning—she was not, perhaps, quite the fairy-like, ethereal being she had seemed the night before in the soft, summer darkness of Turtle Creek, and yet some of the aching tenderness of those poignant, blissful moments remained, and Carter was glad to have her near. He was thinking, however, more of Tom Corwin this morning than of Aggie—and what could Tom Corwin want of him?

"Maybe," she said, "he wants you to come and work in his office. Maybe he needs a young lawyer to help him."

"But I'm not a lawyer, yet," Carter had to confess.

"Oh well," the girl replied, "you soon will be. You will go, won't you? You will stay over another day for a chance like that?"

Carter pushed back his chair from the table, thrust out his long legs before him, and scowled a little.

"You would stay over one more day for that, wouldn't you?" she pleaded.

But Carter shook his head stubbornly. His plan had been made, and he couldn't change it now. He had made up his mind. He would go and see Tom Corwin, of course, and that would make him late in starting, but he must go to-day. The girl's face fell.

Tom Corwin, it seemed, kept late hours. He sat up talking until all hours of the night and did not get down to his office until late in the morning. It was one of the bad habits, no doubt, acquired at Washington City, and Lebanon hardly approved of it, though as a privileged character, Tom Corwin was pardoned for it. It was, therefore, fully nine o'clock when Carter found him at his law-office, a small frame building of two rooms. The great man was sitting in a large rocking-chair between two open windows, one in either wall and directly opposite each other, so that they gave a strong draught of air, refreshing to a heavy, corpulent man on such a warm morning. He sat very low in his comfortable chair, his heavy shoulders hunched up to his large head on its short neck, and whilst smoking his cigar, talked to a group of three or four admirers, who hung on his words in delighted attention. He was telling some story of the new President, Van Buren, the Red Fox of Kinderhook.[8] His face was glowing with the interest he found in his own story and his pleasure in telling it; he illustrated it with gestures of his hands which could be almost as eloquent as the expressions of his face. He did not notice Carter's entrance, or if he did, he made no sign, but went on with his story, and whilst waiting, Carter glanced around the room with its few law-books on a set of shelves and its plain deal table littered with dusty papers. The place had the neglected and unused air of the office that serves more as a background for a political career than a scene of legal study.

But presently, having finished his funny story about the Red Fox of Kinderhook, Tom Corwin espied Carter and raising himself somewhat in his chair, said:

"Well, young man, and what can I do for you?"

Carter, with a feeling that Tom Corwin had forgotten him, and a slight sense of disillusion in consequence, approached and said:

"You asked me to come and see you this morning, sir."

"Oh, so I did!" And then, saying to the men who were with him: "Excuse me, gentlemen, a few minutes. I've got an important appointment with this young gentleman," he got up and led Carter into the room at the back of the building, where they could be alone. The room wore an even more neglected and dusty air than the larger room they had left, besides an odour of disuse of which the strongest and most pungent element was the smell of the large open fireplace in which still lay the ashes and the charred back-log of its long extinguished fire. Tom Corwin threw up a window and let in the air, then sank into another large armchair before the fireplace, flecked the ashes of his cigar on the hearth, and was ready to talk again.

"Let's see, you're on your way to Macochee, aren't you?"

"Yes, sir."

"And what do you propose to do when you get there?"

"My father has a friend there who will give me a job."

"A job?"

"Yes, sir, in his store."

"What kind of store?"

"A dry goods store."

Tom Corwin's gaze wandered, as though with a sudden want of interest. He continued his cross-examination, however, a few minutes longer, and then said, as though announcing his conclusions:

"Well, my young friend, you, of course, know your own business best. But Ohio is a new country. Its soil hasn't even been scratched yet. It is teeming with boundless possibilities. Don't work for another man; you will be his slave. Go and buy 160 acres of land, or, if you haven't got the money to buy it, squat on it; get you an axe and a mattock; put up a log cabin for a habitation, and raise a little corn and potatoes; keep your conscience clear and live like a free-man—your own master, with no one to give you orders, and without dependence upon anybody. Do that, and you will be honoured, respected, influential and rich. Don't work for anybody else; you sink at once all independence. But if you own an acre of land it is your kingdom, and your cabin is your castle. You are a sovereign, and you will feel it in every throbbing of your pulse, and every day of your life will assure me of your thanks for having thus advised you."

Carter did not speak for a moment. He looked at Tom Corwin, feeling that these words of excellent elderly advice were intended to announce the end of the interview. He felt that he ought to get up and go, but he ventured to say:

"But that isn't what you did, sir."

Tom Corwin shot at him so sharp a glance and with such a sudden show of interest, that he had, for an instant, a horrible fear that he had been impertinent, but this fear vanished when Tom Corwin laughed, and said:

"You're right, my boy, I didn't. And do you want to know why?"

"Yes, sir."

"Well, I'll tell you if you will promise not to give me away." He flung the end of his finished cigar into the fire-place, and then, leaning forward out of his armchair, and placing his hands on his fat knees, his arms akimbo, he said, fixing on his face the most irresistibly comical of its most serious and solemn expressions:

"Because farm labour is the hardest in the world, and I'm the laziest white man alive!" He sat looking at Carter with that serio-comic expression, and Carter was embarrassed; he didn't know whether to laugh or not, and was relieved when Tom Corwin, his expression changing to one of self-commiseration, went on:

"Oh, I know all about it! I tried it on my father's farm here in Warren County, and the happiest day of my life was when I broke my leg and so couldn't work any more—for a while—at that sort of work, at least."

And he fell to talking of his youth, of his meagre schooling—a few terms at a school kept by Francis Dunlevy at Lebanon, and a few terms later at another school kept by an English Baptist clergyman, the Rev. Jacob Grigg; of his experiences in the War of 1812, when he drove a waggon filled with supplies for the army of General Harrison at his camp on the Maumee; of his interest—and his triumphs—in the debating society at Lebanon; of his reading law under Judge Joshua Collett.[9]

"I want—I mean I should like to be a lawyer," Carter found the courage at last to confess. And he hastened to add: "That is, if I had sufficient education. I'm afraid I don't know enough."

"Don't let that deter you; any more than it has many another at the bar. What schooling have you had?"

Carter told him of the few terms he had attended a school kept by Mr. Burroughs in Bourbon County, but he did not tell him of the unfortunate end of that experience. He was still too young and the experience was too recent for it to have acquired that glamour of the past, the charm of the long ago, which in the memories of the old transmutes all youth's disappointments into pleasures and all its defeats into victories. And so he forbore to describe to Tom Corwin the little scene that had occurred one afternoon when the school was dismissed for the day. The boys were obliged, on leaving, to pause, each one, in the doorway, turn round and make a bow to the master, and say "Good afternoon, sir." But the master had been unjust that day to Carter; the master had a favourite, and Carter and this favourite had both broken one of the rules. The master had punished Carter and let the favourite go scot free. That evening, on leaving, Carter had paused in the doorway, made his bow, and said:

"Mr. Burroughs is a damn rascal."

After that he had been sent for a while to an Academy in Paris, but not for long—he had got, as he explained to Tom Corwin, only as far as Virgil—the fifth book of the *AEneid*.

But Tom Corwin saw no reason why Carter should not take up the law if he felt that way inclined; after all, it was not what one learnt at school; it was what one learnt in life. And there was reading, the most delightful pleasure of all. And so the conversation, or the monologue meandered on, and before long he had got back to Byron. It was not often that Tom Corwin found in Lebanon at least an auditor who was content to listen whilst he talked about books. And so he talked on about Byron, Burns, Shelley, Shakespeare, Dante, whilst the morning slipped away, and an ever increasing body of men, local politicians, Whig office-holders or office-seekers, town idlers and possibly clients waited in the next room or on the doorstep outside to discuss more serious matters with their Congressman just home from Washington City. Carter had never heard anyone talk in that way before; it was all rather bewildering, he could not understand much of it. The men that he had known talked of nothing but cotton and hogs and dollars, like those men in the news-room of the hotel at Cincinnati; when they wandered from those standard subjects it was to discuss politics, or to talk bawdy, to make rude and ribald jests and obscene stories pointed with nastiness, at which in barn-yard and bar-room they guffawed coarsely and mirthlessly. Carter had heard many of these stories; and they had a disheartening way of clinging tenaciously to his memory, whilst purer products of the human imagination vanished almost instantly from the mind. He had not read a great deal; there wasn't much in a new country to read and little incentive to read what there was. In his home there were Shakespeare and Burns, and of course the Bible. His father read Burns and the novels of Sir Walter Scott, and Carter shared his Scotch liking for these, to him, all-sufficient favourites. And then one day he had got the copy of Byron, and fell at once under the modern spell of the poet who had stamped his generation, and introduced its young men to the emotional delight of a romantic melancholy and disillusion with life. His vast influence and popularity, like that of *The Sorrows of Werther,* had spread so wide that it penetrated even the wilderness of the West, and gave to many a young fellow like Carter a catharsis for the emotional longings of youth, which in that region was to be found only in the debaucheries of the camp-meeting and the groggery.

And now Tom Corwin opened to Carter's imagination a new world, a world of such illimitable vistas that he was at first frightened, almost appalled, and felt that in that world there was no place for him. The thought of all the studies he must master before he could ever become a lawyer, and all the books he must read before he could see what Tom Corwin saw in that world, filled him with something like despair. How was he ever to achieve such an ambition, that is, how was he ever to become another Tom Corwin?

Oddly enough, the achievement so perfectly realized in Tom Corwin himself, did not seem to have made Tom Corwin happy or contented. He was always joking, always making men laugh; he could mimic anyone he had ever seen perfectly, do him to the very life; he had the face of a comedian, an actor; it was so mobile that he could convey his thoughts by its sensitive expression, or, if he chose, conceal them altogether behind its blank and impenetrable mask. Men would listen to one of his political speeches and laugh so that their sides would be sore for days. But as Carter looked at him now, he thought that he had never seen a face so sad, with a sadness deeper and more real than the sorrow that Byron was perhaps, too fond of displaying to the world. Carter did not know what caused such a profound sadness, but he supposed that he should have to cultivate that too, if he was ever to be like Tom Corwin. . . .

"Prometheus," Tom Corwin was saying, "Prometheus, of whom we read in your Byron yesterday, is the symbol of man. When he stole the divine fire he offended the gods, and was chained to the rocks in revenge. The divine fire was consciousness, imagination, the power to think, but the power to think, alas, is not sufficient to enable us to find the answer to life's persistent question, to solve the mystery of life's pain and sorrow and injustice, to discover its meaning and its purpose. It enables us to ask the question, but refuses the answer. To think is to be sad, and all thought is suffering. We are, each in his way, little Prometheuses."

Then suddenly he stopped, and emerging from this strange and sombre mood, he said:

"But see here, my boy; you mustn't pay too much attention to what I say. If there's anything more dastardly in an old man than to destroy the sublime confidence of youth, I don't know what it is. And anyhow, I must go and see what those American sovereigns outside there want. Byron, you know, isn't the only poet to write about old Prometheus. Shelley wrote about him too. Ever read Shelley? Well, you will, some day. Shelley wrote about Prometheus; let's see, how's this it goes now? Oh, yes—listen:

> "To suffer woes which hope thinks infinite:
> To forgive wrongs darker than death or night,
>   To defy Power which seems omnipotent;
> To love and bear; to hope till hope creates
> From its own wreck the thing it contemplates;
>   Neither to change, nor falter, nor repent;
> This, like thy glory, Titan, is to be
> Good, great, and joyous, beautiful and free;
> This is alone Life, Joy, Empire and Victory."[10]

79

He recited the lines and then he rose. Carter stood up. And Tom Corwin laid his hand on Carter's shoulder and looked into his eyes with that smile of his, and said:

"My boy, I expect to hear great things of you some day. You won't forget me, will you? You'll come to see me the next time you're in Lebanon, won't you? Maybe you'll write me—" And then, drawing his mouth down in a rueful expression, he added: "Only don't bear me a grudge if I don't answer your letter. I shall fully intend to, but if you could see the letters out there on my table, all unanswered! Well, good-bye, God bless you—and good luck!"

VII

Carter came away from Tom Corwin's law office with a feeling of high elation, but slightly bewildered too, as though intoxicated by some strong, delicious wine. The vision that he had seen whilst Tom Corwin talked was not wholly clear to him, but he was conscious of new aspirations, somewhat vague, perhaps, but nevertheless high and noble, and if he was to achieve the resolves he formed, he felt that he had no time to lose. He stopped at the inn no longer than was necessary to saddle Dolly D. and to bid good-bye to Aggie. He had rather dreaded that experience; good-byes in any circumstances were hard, and in the present case he felt that he was treating Aggie somewhat cruelly. However, the ordeal was made less difficult for him because Colonel Mack was present, with a great deal to say and much advice to offer, and some information to impart about the road; so that Carter and Aggie were compelled to trust to eloquent glances to express the emotions they felt in this parting. He might have stayed the night, since so many of the morning hours of the present day had gone; the Colonel thought that he ought to do so, but since he was decided, he had better take the new road to Xenia instead of the old road to Dayton, for his route to Macochee would thus be shorter and more direct.

Carter had not ridden many miles up the Little Miami before he remembered that the longest way round is the shortest way home. The old road by which he had come from Cincinnati was a turnpike, or as good as a turnpike, and led through a pleasant farming-land, well tilled and prosperous. But the new road was corduroy, and led much of the way through virgin forest, vast, illimitable, everlasting, which, beyond the fringe of civilisation along the river, covered the whole of that part of Ohio. Its trees, black walnut, beech, Balm of Gilead, sycamore, and oaks of magnificent growth, twenty feet in girth, towered eighty feet above his head; but the sycamores, or cotton-trees, the giants of the wood, reared their heads above them all. There was a thick undergrowth of spice-bushes,[11] as impenetrable as the cane-brakes of Kentucky. The forest stood as it had stood when the Indians roamed it; a few of them indeed roamed it still; it was as it had been when Daniel Boone and Simon Kenton had passed through it on their mysterious and romantic errands; stood as it had stood for ages, its fallen logs rotting and crumbling into dust to fertilize the soil for their successors. The pioneers had been hewing and hacking their way in it for half a century, and still, after one had left the borders of the Ohio and its tributary streams, the Muskingum, the Scioto and the Miami, the traveller might ride for days and scarcely see a trace of their herculean and exhausting labours. He might come now and then upon a woodman's hut or a clearing, a new settlement, even a town, but still the forest was everywhere, and a rod or two away it had obliterated all these scratchings of the hand of man, all traces of the beginnings of civilisation, and he would ride for hours through its gloomy and primeval silence.

Carter was no stranger to the wood, but it was the wood of Kentucky that he knew, the wood that had been cleared of its undergrowth, and was more free and spacious, and filled with light and air. He had wandered in those woods many a day, shooting squirrels with his rifle, and often at night with hounds hunting racoons. Carter was a crack shot with a rifle; he could bring down a squirrel from the top of the tallest tree—shoot it right through the eye—and he would have considered it unsportsmanlike to shoot a squirrel with any weapon other than a rifle. One day in the autumn he had shot a squirrel in the top of a beech-tree; the squirrel had tumbled down, but did not reach the ground. On examination he had discovered that the tree was hollow, and finding a large hole in the trunk on a level with the earth, he thrust in his hand to draw out his quarry. He felt something soft and cold and clammy, and withdrew his hand to find a large copperhead snake coiled about it.

A rattlesnake before striking would have given warning, for the rattlesnake was a gentleman. But the copperhead, as Carter knew, was not a gentleman but a mud-sill, and his bite venomous and often fatal. Luckily, however, the copperhead on this occasion was torpid, having no doubt turned in for the winter; and Carter had shaken it off his arm to the ground and killed it before it could harm him.

Oddly enough, however, he saw no wild creatures in the forest, though it was teeming with wild life and full of game; the only animals he saw were hogs, and he came upon a drove of a thousand, being driven to the Eastern market beyond the Alleghenies where, he was told, they fetched $6 or $8 apiece. They were driven slowly, so slowly that they seemed to make no progress at all, feeding meanwhile on acorns, mast, and chestnuts. The drove moved slowly through the forest, rooting and grunting as it advanced; the drovers, wild, dishevelled, shaggy men, had ample leisure to stop and chat with Carter and ask him the news of the world outside the forest. Whilst they were talking a boar caught and killed a black snake, catching it on his tusks and then, with a shake of his head, tossing it high in the air above his tufted back.

And these were the only living things he saw for hours, and until he came to a small clearing in the wood. It was, indeed, hardly a clearing as yet; a small space in the forest had been opened to the sky, and in the midst of it a double log-cabin stood, a thin, blue wreath of smoke, winding from the squat chimney built of sticks and clay. In the space about the cabin stood the stumps of trees already felled by the settler, and about them, in the edge of the forest, other trees that had been marked for destruction by girdling them. They stood lifting their dead, hopeless branches to the sky, and all about them and about the stumps, grew the young sickly stalks of Indian corn, the only crop, except potatoes, that had been planted. In the yard before the cabin, pigs and chickens foraged in the filth and as Carter rode past a thin, bronzed woman, sinewy and slatternly, with a group of sickly, yellow, aguey children clinging about the skirts of her calico shift, came out from the cabin and gazed after him with large, wistful eyes, out of the appalling loneliness, the dreary, hopeless monotony, and the cruel and killing toil of her pioneer life....

And this was the Ohio, and this was the forest, the symbol of the obstacles that he must surmount before he could become a lawyer, and wear a coat of rich, black broadcloth, and a ruffled shirt and a silken velvet waistcoat, and live in a wide mansion and be admired and loved and serenaded by his neighbours. He rode for two days through the forest, staying the night at an inn where one basin in the kitchen, the same towel and same water-glass were used in common by all the lodgers—and then he came suddenly to the Grand Prairie, and in a plain that rolled away westward from the foot of a range of handsome hills, he saw the grey roofs of a town. Half an hour later he rode into Macochee and drew rein before the Dennison House.

VIII

The morning after his arrival in Macochee, Carter went to present the letter he bore from his father to Mr. Grow, who kept a dry-goods store that faced on the Public Square. He found the merchant alone, sitting at a small desk at the back of the long narrow room, reading a newspaper by the dim light that straggled through the small and dingy panes of glass in a window that gave on to an alley. At Carter's entrance, Mr. Grow looked up somewhat impatiently, as though he resented the interruption. He looked up, slid his steel-bowed spectacles down his nose, and peered over them into the dimness of the long room, but did not rise or show any alacrity, or even, indeed, any interest in the appearance of a possible customer.

Carter walked the full length of the store between the counters that were stacked at intervals with bolts of calico and cotton goods, that smelt strongly of sizing; behind them on the shelves were bolts of other stuffs sticking out at an angle, and pasteboard boxes of buttons with a sample of their contents gleaming on the end of the box, the slender stock of merchandize being spread out in a way to make the best show. When Carter had come up to the desk and asked if he was speaking to Mr. Grow, Mr. Grow said:

"That's my name, young man. What do you want?"

Carter gave him the letter and Mr. Grow, pushing up his spectacles, began to read it. He read a few lines which apparently had the effect of mollifying him, for he kicked a chair into the space before his desk and told Carter to sit down. Then he read on, and whilst he did so, Carter studied him.

He was a serious, grim-looking man, was Mr. Grow, with a thin, dark straggling beard, and a long blue, shaven upper lip, and he wore black clothes which, in that subdued light, did not look so shabby as Carter afterwards observed them to be. He stole a glance at the newspaper Mr. Grow had laid aside, and read the title: *The Liberator*.[12] He was, for an instant, somewhat shocked; had he got into a nest of Abolitionists?

Mr. Grow had finished his perusal of the letter, removed his spectacles, and now sat meditating, tapping the letter with the spectacles.

"Hm, yes," he said. "Yes." He thought a moment, and then asked: "How is your father?"

"He's very well, sir."

"Glad to hear it. Fine man your father; good man, too, in his way and according to his lights. Pity he's a slave-holder."

This estimate of his father, so warming to Carter's heart in its praise at first and then almost instantly chilling in its qualifying disparagement, was rather difficult to deal with. And then there was the way in which Mr. Grow applied the phrase "slave-holder," it was almost like an offensive epithet. He had never thought of old Wesley and Laura and the two or three others as slaves; they were, well, more like servants, you might almost say members of the family and, in their way, friends.

"But you've left Kentucky," Mr. Grow was going on, before Carter could make any defence of his father, "and come to the free state of Ohio and you have done right. Your father did me a great favour once; I've never forgotten it. Hm yes; let's see." Mr. Grow began to stroke his beard thoughtfully. "You don't know much about this business, I suppose?"

"No, sir; nothing at all."

"No, of course not. You see times are hard and business is poor, and I see no chance for improvement now that Little Van is in. Still, I ought to have someone to help me—" he looked longingly at *The Liberator* lying there still unread—"and you might learn. If now, you'd work for your board and lodging, and two, or say, three dollars a week—when business picks up, why, we might fix it up some way like that. I'll speak to my wife at noon. Drop in this afternoon and see me."

Mr. Grow picked up his newspaper and put on his spectacles. And it was upon these vague, indefinite and somewhat elastic terms that Carter went to work for Ethan Grow as a clerk in a dry-goods store, and began that career in Ohio on which he had fixed such high and ambitious hopes.

IX

Ethan Grow, as Carter soon noted by his accent, was not a Southern man, even if he had come to Ohio from Kentucky; nor was he, strictly speaking, a Yankee, though he came from somewhere back East. He did not, for the first few months of Carter's acquaintance with him, vouchsafe where; he was a silent, reticent man, and evidently had the Western frontier feeling that a man's antecedents were of no importance, or else nobody's business but his own. He had gone out to Kentucky and had known Carter's father there, but what the favour that Carter's father had done him, Carter never knew. He often wondered, then and afterwards; he rather feared to ask Mr. Grow and finally it became too late to ask his father, so that this favour, which had meant so much in his life, was lost like so many myriads of other trifles that had once made up his father's life—lost for ever in the void in which all life smiles at last. At any rate, Grow had not prospered in Kentucky; things had gone against him, and after successive failures in agriculture and in merchandizing, he had given up the struggle to make a living in that state. Though not precisely, perhaps, of a sort and of a condition to be classified with the poor whites, he had all the envy and dislike they felt for the slave-holding aristocracy, and by that process of self-flattery, or that need of self-respect which among the unsuccessful so easily transmutes prejudices into principles, and envy into righteous wrath, he had become an Abolitionist. Then he had pulled up his stakes and come over into Ohio, resolved for the future, as he put it, to breathe only free air. But as air was the only necessity of life that was free, even in Ohio, he was compelled to try a number of experiments before he found himself proprietor of a dry-goods store in Macochee and could get on his feet, that is if a man who made nothing beyond a mere living could be said to be on his feet. In that respect he was no worse off than most of the merchants of Macochee. There was little money in circulation; most of the men of business there could remember a time, not long past, when coon-skins had been the medium of exchange. High prices prevailed and business was done on credit. Few made both ends meet. When Carter went to work for Grow, he knew, of course, nothing about the dry-goods business, and Grow himself knew very little more. He seemed, indeed, to endure his occupation as a regrettable necessity in his life, the duties of which he discharged as well, in his empirical way, as he could. He was a somewhat melancholy, but withal not unkindly man who would rather not have had his reading and meditations on philosophical, political and theological subjects interrupted by customers, but when they came he would readily extend them credit in any amount and for any length of time. There was, however, in his manner, a nuance, a certain touch of patronage; he acted as though, in selling them his goods, he was doing them a favour; and, in many instances, as matters turned out, so he was. He kept his accounts in the vaguest and most casual manner. They were a great trial to him, almost as great a trial as the rush of business on Saturday when the farmers came into town. Another of his peculiarities was that he did not like to unroll the bolts of material on his counters. The legend "No trouble to show goods" did not greet the customer with its affable reassurance from his walls. To him it was a trouble, a distinct and positive trouble to show goods. He would not, he told Carter, have them tumbled about, and all wrinkled and "mussed"; he said it riled him; a customer ought to know what he, or rather she, wanted, before she came in; she ought to ask for it at once, take it, and go. It was reported to Carter that Grow had once said to a lady who could not make up her mind: "You don't want a damn thing and you had better clear out, the sooner the better." The story may have been true—except the oath, which was probably apocryphal, for Ethan Grow was a Methodist and never swore except when it was necessary. In fact, he measured up to the frontier pattern of the ideal man, for he did not drink, smoke or chew.

A man, however, of such an idiosyncratic make-up could not have found, perhaps, a worse person to help him in his business than Carter Blair. In giving Carter his original instructions, telling him what would be expected of him, the first thing that Grow mentioned was the accounts, and having mentioned them Grow had sighed, as though already a great load had been lifted from his mind. Besides keeping the accounts Carter was to open up the store in the morning, sweep out, and wait till Grow should come before going back to the house for his breakfast. Then he was to be there all day, waiting on customers, doing whatever there was to do, to lock up at night and then post the accounts— above all, the accounts.

In addition to these multifarious duties at the store there was Dolly D. Carter could not afford the expense of boarding her out at the livery-stable; and in consequence he asked Grow if he might not keep her in the empty stable at the back of Grow's house. As there was no reasonable excuse for denying this request, Grow mumbled some sort of not very gracious assent, though as he had no horse of his own and could not afford the luxury of one—he laid a special and invidious emphasis on the word "luxury"—he thought that Carter would do better to sell her than to let her stand there in the stable eating her head off.

But that was a suggestion which Carter could not entertain for an instant; how was a man to get along without a horse? No one had ever heard of such a thing!

On the evening of the day that, acting on Grow's consent, Carter had ridden Dolly D. round from Ferny's livery-stable and installed her in Grow's empty stable, Grow returned to the subject and again proferred his wise advice; and Carter made the same argument in reply. How was a man to get about without a horse to ride?

"It's plain to be seen, young man," said Grow, "that you are from Kentucky."

They were seated at supper in the small dining-room of Grow's cottage—Grow, his wife, his daughter Gertrude, and Carter. Mrs. Grow had just set the meal on the table, and Grow had just asked a blessing on what he termed "these slight temporalities," and then, sitting sidewise to the table with one long leg flung over the other, had begun to read the newspaper he held in one hand whilst he fed himself with the other, not seeming to care very much which of the temporalities he conveyed to his mouth. He had a way, as Carter learnt, of reading whilst he ate, bestowing on his family as on the purely physical process of nourishing his body, of feeding what he called the inner man, only the scraps of his attention, reserving the more powerful part of his intelligence for the reforms he had in hand. With his somewhat slighting reference to Carter's provenance, he let the subject of Dolly D. drop and was soon lost in the more absorbing topic of the wrongs of slavery as disclosed by William Lloyd Garrison. But Mrs. Grow took the matter up more tactfully as she intimated by her ruddy smile, and said:

"Wouldn't it be nice if you could get a harness and a buggy, then you could hitch up and we could *all* take a ride."

There was, in the stress she laid on the word *all* an intimation of a certain selfishness on Carter's part, but he did not notice it, for Mrs. Grow's suggestion was almost as shocking as that advanced by her husband; indeed, it was even more shocking. A gentleman might sell his riding-horse, many did so, and quite excusably. But to harness a riding-horse to a buggy! The idea was preposterous and contrary to nature; it left him for a moment quite speechless.

He glanced at Grow, but he was lost in the clouds of another world. He looked at Gertrude and she smiled at him; a smile that was precisely like that of her mother to whom she bore a resemblance that had often startled Carter, and, if the truth must be told, repelled him.

"Yes," said Gertrude, her eyes shining in her broad high-cheeked face, "it would be lovely! We could take long buggy-rides these warm nights!"

"Gertie," said Mrs. Grow, in sudden, sharp reproof, "don't make such suggestions! They ben't nice, coming from a young lady!"

Gertrude's dark eyes flashed a look of resentment at her mother for this disloyal desertion.

"You know you just said yourself, Ma, it would be nice."

"I said," retorted Mrs. Grow, witheringly, "that it would be nice if we could *all* take a ride, like."

Carter felt that he ought to intervene with something conciliatory, but the best he could do was to say:

"But you can't put a saddle-horse to a buggy! They aren't broken to harness. We keep them for riding—in Kentucky."

"Young man," said Mrs. Grow, "your ideas air a mighty sight too high."

Perhaps they were, but to sustain them at such a level Carter was willing to rise an hour or so earlier every morning and to groom Dolly D. and, unless he had overslept himself, to take her for a canter in the cool, sweet air of dawn, and at times in the short twilight after the store was closed. On Sunday mornings he could go for a longer ride, in the hills to the east of Macochee, or down the Marmon Valley. As he rode along he wondered if the day would ever come when he could own a farm in that snug and fertile region, with white fences and long-legged colts, descendants of Dolly D. grazing contentedly in the green pastures. Not that he had any intention of becoming a farmer, not at all; he would be a lawyer, swaying juries by his eloquence in famous murder trials, and delighting vast audiences on the stump in political campaigns; the farm would be but an elegant appanage to his career at the bar; he would live, of course, in a fine mansion in a grove at the edge of the town, and when he came back from some long and patriotic absence—from Washington City, for instance—the people would have the band over to serenade him; the band would play "Home, Sweet Home," and he would make a touching little speech from the verandah. Then, when the time came for him to decline re-election and retire from Congress, he could pass his declining years on his farm, and be known as the Sage of the Marmon Valley. At these engaging prospects his heart would beat high with hope and swell with ambition.

But with all he had to do at the store, and considering Dolly D's insatiable need of exercise—if she stood a day in the stable she got so nervous that she nearly kicked her stall down and

Mrs. Grow complained that the noise kept her awake at nights—
with all these hindrances he wondered when he was ever to find
the time to study law. There was, of course, the classic example,
which added such lustre to so many of the statesmen of the
Republic, the pine-knot at midnight; but pine-knots were not
practicable in a small frame-house like Grow's; you had to have
a log-cabin and a fire-place if you wanted to study by the light
of a pine-knot. The best he could do at present would be to
study by the light of a candle in his little room upstairs.

His position in the dry-goods store gave him the opportunity
of seeing many of the substantial and consequential citizens
of Macochee, and, in the free and easy manner of the West, of
making their acquaintance; it was in this way that he came to
know Judge Amos Diller, who had sat for a while on the bench
of the Court of Common Pleas, and was now practising at the bar.
Judge Diller came into the store occasionally, with his wife, and
when he did, Carter observed that Mrs. Diller did not make her
purchases with the extravagance she used when she came alone;
they kept an account at Grow's and had everything "charged;"
but when the Judge came he restrained his wife and damped her
enthusiasm. The Judge often came alone, not to buy anything but
to discuss political questions with Grow, and especially political
questions that ranged in the higher altitudes of the altruistic and
ideal; that is, questions with a moral and ultimate, rather than a
purely utilitarian and immediate incidence and effect, questions
like the abolition of slavery and the prohibition of intoxicating
liquors, but especially abolition; they were both Abolitionists,
and it was clear to Carter that he had indeed got into a nest of
them. However, Judge Diller was a lawyer, and the best in the
county, and when Carter found the courage to ask him one day
if he might read law under him, Judge Diller said, speaking with
the nasal twang, the Yankee accent, and a kind of dry, mordant
humour peculiar to him—he was a native of Massachusetts:

"Well neow, young man, do you consider yourself smaa't
enough to study lawr?"

Carter, somewhat embarrassed, said that he trusted he was.

"And you calc'late that you'll go right straight through with it?"

"Yes, sir."

"The law, my young friend," he observed with an air of originality, "is a jealous mistress."

"I know that, sir."

The Judge, stroking his long, lean jaws reflectively, looked at
Carter critically, as though he could tell from the green tree what
he would be in the dry, and presently agreed.

Thus Carter began to read law, and on the evening when he went up to his room, lit his candle and opened the first volume of Blackstone's *Commentaries on the Laws of England,* and began to read how important it was that noblemen, gentlemen and educated persons generally should be acquainted with the laws of the land, he felt that the date marked an epoch in his life.

Grow's house in Locust Street was hardly more than a mere cottage; it had only a storey and a half, and had a shingled roof; Carter's room had a low ceiling, he could easily touch it with his hand when he stood up; and on those hot and breathless August nights, a candle attracted such swarms of flies and mosquitoes and moth-millers, that he could not keep his mind on Blackstone. No use to try to study in the scorching heat of an Ohio summer! He tried the expedient of taking his book to the store and reading there behind the counter. But Grow soon put a stop to that practice; for how was he to read *The Liberator* and this new paper just published by James G. Birney, *The Philanthropist,*[13] how was he to get any reading done at all, in fact, if Carter were to read too?

However, there was no need of haste. Life lay before him opening a long vista of spacious years; they stretched on before him interminably; they had no visible, indeed, no imaginable end; there was time enough to do everything he had ever hoped to do, everything he had ever dreamt of doing. Besides, there was another thing that made it hard for him to concentrate his attention on the law, and that was Gertie Grow.

X

He had not, at first, paid very much attention to Gertie. For one thing she looked too much like her mother, or perhaps it would be more accurate to say that her mother looked too much like her; that is, Mrs. Grow was a kind of warning caricature of her own daughter, showing to what favour the girl would come at last. As they sat at table so close together, the mother and daughter, or as side by side they bent over the dish-pans in the kitchen afterwards or sat in their rocking-chairs on the "porch" in the cool of the evening, Carter would behold Gertie, not as she was but as she was destined to become in a few short years. He lived, during those early days, not in the stark reality of the frontier settlement that Macochee then was, but in that other imagined and pre-figured world in which a few years hence he was to be so important, so highly honoured and so happy. And the beings that were to people the world with him must be susceptible of a growth, a development, and an ultimate flowering as satisfying and as wonderful as his own. It was plain enough to anybody, with Mrs. Grow there as a warning model, it was plain enough just what Gertie would be, what she would look like when that great day of hope's fruition should dawn; it was all too implacably certain that Gertie was not fashioned for the world in which Carter destined himself to shine. The broad face, the high cheek-bones, the dark eyes, the black eyebrows that met across the nose—these traits which, in the case of Gertie, were all redeemed by the charm and freshness of her youth and a certain wistful eagerness in her expression, were, in the case of Mrs. Grow, exaggerated by premature age and the monotonous drudgery of keeping a household without means, into a dark scowl of habitual and querulous discontent. Whatever freshness her cheeks might once have known had long since faded, and left them sere and withered. The mouth which, in Gertie, could turn up so prettily at the corners, whenever she smiled at Carter, was in Mrs. Grow's face, always drooping and set in a kind of inveterate hostility—not towards Carter, of whom she seemed rather fond, but against life which, in a gratuitous irony, had offered her all these and no doubt many more indignities.

They were never alone together, Gertie and Carter, and, living as they did in the sordid intimacy of a small house of six rooms, four below and two above, Carter accepted Gertie as a part of the domestic economy; in the hard, realistic atmosphere of that frugal household he could invest her figure with no aureole of romance. They sat at the table, Grow aloof, detached, absorbed in his newspapers, his theories of reform; Mrs. Grow and Gertie repeating the trivial personalities and petty gossip of the little town; Mrs. Grow was not so well educated or so well read as her husband; she had, indeed, read nothing at all, and her interests were confined within the narrow limits of her provincial life; her husband had a contempt for her intelligence and treated her with a certain sardonic tolerance, as an inferior. She never had a red cent she could call her own; (Carter would have liked to turn over to her the weekly sum he paid for his board, if Grow had ever paid him his wages, which he never did with any sort of regularity.) She spoke, too, in general, with the accent and in the vernacular of the backwoods.

"Ain't ary one o' you ever goin' to come to yer supper?" she would complain when Grow, in his shirt sleeves, would linger on the back-porch where there was a better light to read by, and Gertie, at the last minute, would fly upstairs to knot a red ribbon in her hair, and Carter would continue to primp before his glass by way of preparing to go "up town" that evening. The contrast between Mrs. Grow's uncultured speech and the clear, careful and educated precision of her husband's, was marked. Gertie, when she addressed Carter, spoke consciously with her father's care and manner; but when she was not listening to herself she lapsed into the easier accents of her mother.

However, Carter and Gertie were young, and since Nature exclusively absorbed by her one insane preoccupation of assuring the reproduction of the species, always takes advantage of fortuitous propinquity, this indifference could not last indefinitely, and after an incident that occurred one afternoon, Carter began to look at Gertie with other eyes and from another point of view. He was crossing the Square one afternoon on his way to the Post Office, when he stopped to talk to an elderly man whose acquaintance he had somehow made named Giles Paten, a drunken old rip who, from a capable lawyer, had degenerated into a pettifogger and somehow made a meagre living practising in a small way before Justices of the Peace. Carter liked him, as did everybody who knew him, for nobody knew him except the ungodly portions of the community. Carter was standing there talking to him when Gertie Grow happened to pass by. Carter spoke to her casually, and then when she had passed, remembering that he had something to say to her, he excused himself from Paten a moment and ran after her, calling out:

"Oh, Miss Gertie, wait a minute!"

She stopped, smiled, and he told her not to wait supper for him that evening; he might be late, for he was going to see Judge Diller and be examined by him, to see what progress he was making in his law studies.

"All right, Carter," said Gertie, smiling again. "Come whenever you get ready; I'll keep something hot for you just the same."

Carter rejoined Paten, but the old man did not continue the ribald story he had been telling; he had stood gazing at Gertie and at the scene, this casual, careless encounter between Carter and her, and his rheumy old eyes had widened and gleamed in the hopeless envy age has of youth.

"My God!" he exclaimed, when Carter rejoined him, his eyes still following the trim figure of Gertie as she walked briskly on towards her father's store, switching her skirts provokingly this way and that, "My God! Can you go up and speak to one of 'em that a-way, casual like! My God, boy! You don't appreciate your blessings. Why, I'd give everything I ever had or was, or hope to be, here and in eternity, to stop and speak to a young gal that a-way and have her smile at me the way she did at you! And you come back calmly and talk to an old codger like me! Why, if I was you, by this time I'd have her climbin' a stone wall back'ards, I would!"

Carter turned and gazed an instant after Gertie; he noticed, perhaps, not for the first time but now more particularly, that she had a rather trim figure, and as she lifted her skirt, she showed a neat ankle.

"I've been standing on the corner," said Paten with a confidential air, "for the last forty years watching these pieces of calico go by, and I want to tell you that they get prettier all the time."

Carter glanced at Paten; the old man was still rolling a blood-shot, lickerish eye after the disappearing girl. There was, to Carter, something disgusting in the old fellow.

XI

And yet Carter could not help liking Paten; there was something in him that Carter could not define, something human, a queer combination of wisdom and folly and profligacy, shrewdness and humour, kindly, tolerant, good-natured and rollicking. He was generous, generous in his judgments of the faults of men, at least their more amiable faults, and generous, too, with his purse when it had anything in it; when it was empty—as it generally was—he expected the world to be as generous with him, and when the world wasn't generous—as it generally wasn't—he damned it roundly with picturesque and original profanity. He had, from the first moment of their casual and accidental meeting, taken a liking to Carter, a compliment which Carter perhaps did not properly appreciate. There would be no use in pretending that Giles Paten bore a good reputation in Macochee; Grow had early warned Carter against him, saying that he was a man of no moral principle who led a loose, outrageous life, and set a dreadful example to the young. Judge Diller had proferred the same advice. "He is a disgrace to the baah, sir," Judge Diller had said, "a disgrace to the baah." Mrs. Grow said that it was a sin, the way he drank, a sin and a shame. And yet, in spite of all this, in spite of all reason and logic, Carter liked him and found amusement and pleasure, and perhaps a certain profit in his company. For old Paten had read enormously; he was as thoroughly saturated with declamatory poetry as he was with alcohol, and his brain always at the boiling point, kept it in such a state of readily available fluidity that it was oozing forth all the time. He knew Shakespeare and Burns by heart, and spouted them forth on all occasions. Whenever it was known that he was to appear in a case at law, half the men of Macochee, in that love of oratory which distinguished the early Americans, because oratory, pulpit or forensic, was the only kind of public amusement offered for their distraction—half the men of Macochee would crowd the court-room of the Court of Common Pleas, or, as was more apt to be the case in Carter's day, the office of a Justice of the Peace, to roar with delight at his sarcasm and buffoonery, or thrill at his flowery and ornate eloquence. In some ways to be with Giles Paten was almost a liberal education.

Paten had long since established his headquarters in the back room of a grocery and grog-shop kept by Joe Tappan; it was said that, when he was a member of the legislature, he had written many a statute on the top of a whisky-barrel there, whilst seated on a wine-keg. It was there that he was generally to be found, especially on Saturday nights; for on that evening he held high-jinks with a number of his cronies. These symposiums had been discontinued during the heated term, but now at the approach of the cooler weather they were resumed, and it was at one of them that Carter made the acquaintance of several of the choicest spirits of Macochee. Or so, at least, they considered and proclaimed themselves. Their numbers varied; on the evening that Carter was introduced there were present either six or eight; Carter could never be quite sure afterwards, for their red convivial faces floated uncertainly and indistinctly in his confused memory as they sat in the golden haze of candlelight and pipe-smoke of that back room with its odour of stale spirits. Among them was Fowler Brunton, a young man somewhat older than Carter and already admitted to the bar; Carter had made his acquaintance shortly after coming to Macochee and they were by way of making fast friends. Like Carter, Brunton had his own way to make in the world, and if he were in advance, to the extent at least of being admitted to the bar, he had not so far outstripped Carter that he could not sympathize with his difficulties and his perplexities. It was he who introduced Carter to the group that assembled at Joe Tappan's and overcame Carter's sense of inferiority and disadvantage due to his clothes and his lack of money, his fears of cutting a poor figure, and, in the language of the pioneers, of not being able to hold up his end. He sat at the great round table in the small room at the back of Tappan's grog-shop, embarrassed and subdued, trying to conceal the excitement that fluttered at his heart at finding himself in this brilliant company, and fearful of drinking too much. The proceedings were rather tame at first; perhaps it was because he had expected too much, or perhaps, as Fowler Brunton whispered to him, it was because Giles Paten, for some reason, was late in putting in an appearance, though that did not cause those who were there to postpone their potions until Paten should arrive. One of these early arrivals was Joe Wales, Deputy Clerk of the Courts, a serious-looking, red-faced man with a drooping yellow moustache: another was Hiram Winship, editor of *The Macochee Weekly Democrat*. Winship was already in his cups, and Carter could not take his eyes off him; he was a small, thin man, in shabby black clothes, a frayed neckcloth and the generally untidy appearance of the needy journalist. His hands were permanently begrimed with printer's ink, for he not only wrote all of his newspaper, but set up most of it at the composing-case himself, and his scalp under the matted tresses of his thin and greying hair was almost as grimy as his hands. Winship's most striking feature, however, was his nose. It was long and at the end spread into a large, corrugated, bulbous, plum-coloured growth. His small black eyes gleaming on either side of it seemed unnaturally bright. His newspaper was the local organ of the Democratic party and supported President Van Buren, and on this evening he was disturbed by a recent rumour that it was proposed to establish a new Whig paper in Macochee and support the cause of abolition; and he was fulminating against the abolitionists, or bobolitionists as he contemptuously called them, as a miserable, despicable, hypocritical, psalm-singing lot of fanatics who were always meddling in other people's business.

But Winship's diatribe was interrupted by the entrance of a young man who was hailed by a shout of boisterous welcome.

"Well, well, stranger," said the usually calm Wales, "come right in and make yourself to home."

And Winship cried:

"Damned if here isn't the prodigal son, tired of the husks of the City! Did the old gentleman kill the fatted calf?"

And Carter looked up to see Tom Nash standing in the doorway in a fawn-coloured surtout, a whimsical, rather foxy smile on his thin young face. And there came to Carter that sense of suspicion and dislike which he had felt when, for the first time, he and Tom Nash had met at Cincinnati that evening not so many months before, and he suddenly felt embarrassed and humiliated as he recalled the unpropitious encounter. He wondered if Tom Nash would remember him; he hoped that he would not, and had an impulse to turn away and evade, or at least postpone, the recognition he feared. For, he said to himself, Tom Nash, the most dashing and evidently, from the reception he had just received, the most popular young dog in Macochee, could easily by a word make him appear ridiculous among these new friends and companions. Brunton, he noticed, had not been quite so effusive in his welcome of Nash as the others had been, and there was some encouragement in this fact, but it was Brunton who now introduced him.

"Mr. Nash," Brunton was saying, "make you acquainted with Mr. Blair."

Nash laughed and held out his hand with a jaunty readiness that was reassuring, but instantly added:

"Mr. Blair and I have met before, in the City."

Carter wondered if it was his imagination that caused him to ascribe an ulterior meaning to the phrase, but Nash said no more, though as their eyes met for an instant and Carter detected the sly expression in Nash's glance, he knew that they should never be friends. Nash turned away, took off his surtout, and took his seat on the other side of the table, and whatever embarrassment the moment may have held was overcome by the arrival of Paten, Giles Paten.

The sudden appearance of Giles Paten, indeed, changed the atmosphere of the room. Paten suddenly appeared in the doorway which his bulk almost filled, and he stood there for an impressive moment; huge, corpulent, his velvet waistcoat rounded over his paunch, his long brown broadcloth coat with its velvet collar sprinkled with dandruff, and as Winship caught sight of him he cried:

"There he is at last, the devil in the likeness of an old fat man, that tun of a man, that grey iniquity, that father ruffian, that vanity in years!"[14]

Paten glanced round the group to make sure of his audience, and then addressing Winship, replied:

"Do thou amend thy face, and I'll amend my life: thou art our admiral, thou bearest the lantern in the poop, but 'tis in the nose of thee; thou art the Knight of the Burning Lamp. I have maintained that salamander of yours with fire any time this two and thirty years; God reward me for it!"

This banter in Shakespearean metaphor went on until Paten had taken his place at the table and called for sack. "Come, sing me a bawdy song; make me merry," he cried, and for want of sack, and doubtless in preference to it, tossed off a tot of Bourbon whisky. He talked on for a while in the archaic style that passed well enough for Shakespearean when it did not consist of direct quotations from that source; Paten could do that, Fowler Brunton explained to Carter, almost indefinitely, and then as the bottle went round they began to recite poetry and to sing songs, bawdy and otherwise. Carter could remember afterwards that Tom Nash had told of his adventures in the City, and Carter's heart was in his mouth when he began. But Nash mercifully spared him all reference to that one notable evening; he boasted rather of his conquests, and told some nasty stories. Then Joe Wales recited "Holy Willie's Prayer," which was vastly enjoyed as satirizing certain respectable citizens of Macochee; Paten recited Hamlet's soliloquy as Falstaff would have given it, which, considering the state he was in, was easier than to have given it as Hamlet would have done. He promised to render Falstaff's Honour speech as Hamlet would have done it, but he never got to that, or if he did, Carter did not hear it. Brunton recited Byron's "Farewell to Tom Moore," and Carter regretted that he had not done this himself, for he knew the poem by heart and felt that he could have given it with much more feeling than Brunton gave it, though Winship protested against its being given at all, because Tom Moore on his visit to America in 1804, had insulted Mr. Jefferson; Winship denounced Tom Moore roundly as a contemptible little dandy, and kept on mumbling to himself about the outrage long after the others had told him to shut up.[15] Later, Carter thought that Winship had wept, and confided to him that he could not endure the thought of anyone, especially a foreigner, insulting Mr. Jefferson. They were singing at the moment, Paten singing the first line in a hoarse, alcoholic voice, the others joining in the chorus:

(Paten)   Oh, the little black bull came down the mountain
(Chorus)   Hoosen Johnny, Hoosen Johnny!
(Paten)   Oh, the little black bull came down the mountain, Long time ago.
(Chorus)   Long time ago,
           Long time ago,
           Oh, the little black bull came down the mountain
               Long time ago.[16]

Carter sat low down in his chair, his long legs stretched out under the table; he slowly turned his small tumbler of whisky round and round; carefully lifted it up and set it down, making wet circles on the smooth, shining walnut surface of the table. The room was filled with a haze of golden candlelight with thin, gracefully undulating strata of tobacco smoke through which the faces of his companions smiled upon him, happy and contented, all save Winship's perhaps; Winship, though his husky bass voice joined in the chorus, was still oppressed by sorrow, thinking of the indignity offered to Mr. Jefferson by Thomas Moore. Carter himself felt happy and contented; a warm, genial sense of well-being pervaded him. The sense of inferiority he had felt, especially when he glanced at Tom Nash, had now quite vanished. He had all at once an assurance of his own dignity and importance in a world that had suddenly revealed itself to him as friendly, appreciative, sympathetic, glowing with friendship, filled with whole-hearted, honest fellows. He felt now certain that he would achieve great things in it; he would sway courts and juries and vast crowds by his eloquence, as Tom Corwin did; his mind seemed all at once to have become astonishingly clear; it teemed with brilliant epigrams, great truths, and the loftiest ideas. He must express them; dazzle and confound this congenial company, and so impress himself upon them; he would do it as soon as the song ended, for the song was roaring on:

> He whetted his horn on a white-oak sapling,
> Hoosen Johnny, Hoosen Johnny!

Scenes drifted before his mind; charming scenes of home, of Bourbon county in spring; he could see his father, Joe and little Fanny; his heart swelled with affection for them; he must tell his friends about them, and about a bull his father used to own; he could see his father now, leading it carefully and with difficulty, but fearlessly, out to the pasture beside the Lexington turnpike; everybody was afraid of the bull except his father; he led it by a thick ash-stick fastened to the ring in its nose.

The song had come to its uproarious end, and the company were all applauding themselves; Carter had intended, when the song ended, to divulge to them that profound and important philosophical truth which had been so clearly revealed to him a while ago, but now, for some reason, he could not for the life of him think of it; though his mind was still preternaturally clear, and as it were blazing inside his head with a brilliant light, the great philosophical truth had suddenly grown vague, and floated away tantalizingly; one moment he was just on the point of seizing it; then it floated off again, out of reach. And so he sat there and smiled complacently, rather importantly, nodding his head sagely in agreement and approval to everything that was said, in that warm, flattering atmosphere of mutual understanding and good fellowship. They had begun to sing again, this time a hymn:

Blest be the tie that binds.

The familiar words and the familiar tune almost moved him to tears.

We share our mutual woes,
Our mutual burdens bear;
And often for each other flows
The sympathizing tear.

Carter was never able to recall the great and burning truth, it had flashed like a meteor across his mind, blazed and gone out. It was a pity that it must be lost, and lost for ever. The world was surely in need of these great, blasting truths. But there was nothing that he could do about it now. His mind was not so clear as it had been an hour ago; it was growing rather muddled.... He must sit very still, very craftily pretend to toss off his glass, but not do so; spit it out, if necessary behind his chair and continue to smile in that wise, impressive manner. They were talking now about—What were they talking about? Women, of course; women and girls in Macochee, and what kind of reputations they had, and how far they would go, and that sort of thing. They mentioned a number of names that meant nothing to Carter, for he knew no girls in Macochee except Gertie Grow. But pretty soon Gertie's name came up; old Paten was telling what he said that day when Carter had spoken to her in the Square—telling it with certain improvements and embellishments of his own.

The company laughed, and Carter found himself suddenly the centre and focus of interest. His mind, however, was so confused and hazy that he could not grasp the meaning of their glances or their words, for they seemed to be talking, all of them at once. But through the haze of tobacco smoke, so like the haze in his brain, he suddenly detected in the eye of Tom Nash a knowing and significant glance, as though between them there were some discreditable secret to which they two alone were privy. Just what Nash's glance meant, Carter was not sure, but he was sure that Nash was thinking and reminding him of the girl at Cincinnati, and somehow mocking him; he had surely shown himself on that occasion no such gay dog as Nash so obviously admired.

Nash continued to look at him with that mocking, supercilious smile on his foxy face, and the smile enraged Carter. They were making a quiz of him,[17] all of them. And then the next thing, Nash said something, Carter was not sure what, but he heard him mention Gertie's name.

Carter's quick temper flared up; he got to his feet; the glow of the candles had become suddenly red like Nash's face. Carter banged his fist down upon the table, and shouted:

"No, by God! You can't say that! You can't insult a lady—"

"Oh, don't fly off the handle, Kentucky," said Wales. "Take it easy."

"No, by God," shouted Carter, "if anybody says she isn't pure as the—as the—"

"Driven snow," said Paten.

"Then," Carter shouted, "I say he's a damn liar!"

"Well, my boy," said Winship calmly, "who said she wasn't?"

"I say he's a damn liar!" Carter shouted.

Fowler Brunton was tugging at his coat.

"Sit down," said Brunton, "sit down. Don't make a fool of yourself."

He had no recollection of what happened after that. The next thing he knew he was walking out Locust street with Fowler Brunton walking beside him, steadying him now and then. The town was dark and still and all asleep in those small hours of the morning. The cool air of the autumn night was grateful to his face. Now and then he would stop and enter again upon the long, endless explanation to Brunton, and Brunton would pay no attention, but say, "Oh, come on now, Carter, you're all right." And Brunton would urge him on, and their feet would resound on the hard, worn earth of the footpath inside the road. They came at last to the small house, all dark and silent now, where the Grows lived. Brunton opened the gate and closed it softly behind him when Carter had gone in.

"All right now, are you?" Brunton whispered. "Well, good-night."

Carter stumbled slightly on the steps of the little porch, but got up and reached the door. He had no key, but doubtless the door was never locked, anyhow. He laid his hand on the knob, and then, at this light touch, it opened, and there in the thick darkness of the hall stood Gertie. He knew her by her voice when she whispered:

"Sh! Don't make a noise! They're asleep. They won't know. I waited up to let you in. Sit down here on the stairs. There now!"

She had steadied him as he sat down. And now she crouched before him and drew off his boots.

"Come on now," she said. She helped him to mount the stairs and went with him to the door of his little room and left him there.

XII

When Carter awoke the sun was shining in at his window. He lay an instant in that interval between sleeping and waking when consciousness is still benumbed, that moment before memory, identity and personality return to take possession once more of the mind and body of the sleeper. Then, as he remembered, as he came to himself and became once more that conscious ego which was Carter Blair, it all came back,—the little room at Joe Tappan's, the barrels of whisky against the wall, the glow of candlelight, and the ruddy faces swimming in that hazy atmosphere; the rhythm of "Hoosen, Johnny," thumping with tireless iteration through his tired brain; himself standing up at the table, drunk, making a fool of himself; yes, drunk and making a fool of himself. He groaned, and turned over and hid his face in his pillows.

It was deathly still in the house; not a sound anywhere. He wondered what time it was. He got up, went to his window and looked out; it was deathly still in the town; the wide street below, just beyond the white palings of the low fence, sprawled yellow in the glittering sunlight of fall. Not a breath of air was stirring; the broad yellow leaves fallen from the buckeye trees that grew along the edge of the sidewalk, lay there crisp and dusty and motionless, just as they had lain when they had rustled to the unsteady shuffle of his feet a few hours before. The Sabbath stillness lay on the town, dense, heavy and oppressive.

He should, by rights, from all that he had ever heard of drinking-bouts, have felt a vast and annihilating weariness, and his head should have been swollen and throbbing with pain. But he did not feel weary in the least; his head did not feel swollen; he had no headache. He could not complain of feeling half dead; on the contrary, he felt uncommonly alive, and after he had filled his basin with water from his jug and bathed his face and doused it over his broad muscular shoulders, strong arms and his great chest, he felt not only astonishingly, if somewhat disappointingly, fit and well, but he could glory with pride in his lithe white body glowing with the bounding, ruddy health of youth. Besides, he was as hungry as a wolf. In fact, had it not been for that mortifying memory of having made a fool of himself, he might have looked back upon the evening at Joe Tappan's as a most delightful experience, and a successful initiation into a larger life.

And then suddenly he thought of something, and he swore at himself for his treachery: he thought of Dolly D. He hurriedly finished his toilet, and hastened, half-dressed, downstairs. No one was about. In the dining-room he glanced at the Seth Thomas clock, ticking solemnly on its shelf; it was half past eleven. He ran through the kitchen, and there on the steps of the little porch sat Gertie, gazing out on the small kitchen-garden, with its withered stalks of sweet corn and its blasted vines. She turned at the sound of his footfall and glanced over her shoulder with a smile.

"Oh, there you are, Carter. Had your sleep out?"

At sight of her pleasant, kindly, smiling face, he must have blushed and stammered:

"Yes, like an idiot; and there's poor Dolly going all this while without her feed!"

There was bitter self-reproach in his voice, a withering self-contempt; it showed in his face, his lip curled, and his eyebrows knit in a dark scowl as he stood looking down into Gertie's upturned, smiling face.

"Miss Gertie," he said solemnly, "that's the very worst thing a man can do—to neglect his horse; to let his horse go hungry. It's the unpardonable sin!"

"But I fed her," said Gertie, "and gave her to drink."

"You!"

"Yes."

Carter stepped away to the well, and, drawing up the dripping bucket by its chain, he filled the long-necked yellow gourd that lay on the coping of the well, and drank a deep draught of the clear, cold water. Then, dipping the gourd into the bucket a second time, he raised it half-way to his lips, and looking at her over the edge of it, said:

"You're too good to me, Miss Gertie. I don't deserve it. Besides, that's a man's job, not a woman's; it's outside work. But I'm ever so much obliged."

He covered his sudden confusion by raising the gourd to his lips and tipping it up until it hid his face, while he gulped down the water.

102

"But it's nothing, Carter, to give a horse a feed of oats and a bucket of water."

"That isn't all; you were good to me last night."

"Cain't a body do a little thing like that?"

"Did they hear!" he asked. "Your father and mother?"

"Nary a sound," she said.

"They've gone to meeting?"

"Yes. And you'd better come in and get a bite o'breakfast. I saved it hot for you on the hearth."

"It's hardly any use now. It's nearly dinner-time. Might as well wait till then."

"Well, just as you like. We're going to have fried chicken."

"Is the preacher coming to dinner?"

"No; you needn't be afeared."

He sat down on the step beside her. She tucked the long, voluminous skirts of her home-woven linsey-woolsey gown, and the blue-and-white-checked apron that covered it as closely round her legs as she could, and made a place beside her. The wide, full skirts were pleated into the waist of her tightly fitting bodice; she wore a white kerchief, crossed on her full breast. And as Carter looked at her he discovered all of a sudden that Gertie was beautiful. Some mysterious and enchanting change had taken place in her—or perhaps the change had taken place in him. Whichever it was, she no longer bore that deterrent resemblance to her mother; she had suddenly been transfigured by a beauty that he had never perceived before, and had become tempting and desirable. He gazed into her face and, as he did so, she was covered with confusion; her cheeks flamed red, and she turned her face away. He bent nearer to her and his arm, as of its own volition, slipped round her waist. His lips approached and sought her own; he clasped her in his arms; beneath all the heavy folds of her skirt he could feel her sturdy legs.

"Don't Carter," she insisted; "don't! You mustn't!" She waited a moment and then in a whisper she said: "Not out here! They'll see—the neighbours. You know what they are!"

There was, in the whispered words and especially in the implications of her phrase "Not out here!" not a refusal, but a postponement and a promise that inflamed his desire.

"Besides," she added, "I must go in and begin to get things ready for dinner; the folks will be back any minute now."

He released her, and they went indoors. She got out a clean white table-cloth, shook out its folds, and with a movement of her arms that to Carter was one of exquisite grace, she flung it over the dining-table; it billowed a second over it and then settled to its place, and, leaning over the table, Gertie adjusted it with nicety, smoothing out its white and glistening folds with the palms of her hands. And, employed thus efficiently in household duties—inside work, that is, woman's work—she was irresistible, and Carter seized her again in his arms and strained her to him. She gazed at him, her eyes glowing in the dim light of the room, her lips parted.

"Just one," she said, as though, while willing to be kind, she had no intention of compromising herself by an exaggerated generosity. "Just one, mind." And she held up her lips to be kissed.

"And now," she said with a practical air, "I must get to my work."

"I'll help you set the table," he said.

"But that's inside work; that's not a man's work," she reminded him.

He caught her again and kissed her. Then they began to set the table. He was more of a hindrance than a help, but the pretence of aiding her served well enough; they were constantly together, their hands or their bodies were constantly touching: he kissed her on the cheek, on the neck, on the lips, and they were standing locked in a long embrace, mouth on mouth, when they heard Grow's step on the front porch, and Gertie pushed Carter from her and fled to the kitchen. And he hurried out to the stable, gave Dolly D. her dinner and even made a pretence of grooming her, though it was only a lick and a promise.

XIII

After that for days and days Carter had never a chance to be alone with Gertie, and he began to have a feeling that he should never have a chance again. He couldn't tell why, but so it was; whenever he was at the house either Grow or his wife was present, and usually both of them were there. Not, apparently, by any sort of connivance or prudent purpose; it merely happened that way. Neither of the parents knew or even suspected the passion that had so suddenly sprung up between the two young people living in the intimacy of their small house; Grow was absorbed in his great scheme of liberating the slaves; he ranged at a higher and to the younger

ones, inaccessible altitude of the spirit, whilst they were confined to what Grow no doubt would have considered, if he ever
thought of it at all, the lower levels of the body. Grow read *The
Liberator* or *The Humanitarian*,[18] either to himself or aloud to his
family, and if he ever condescended to discuss the personal aspect of the question, it was to tell Carter that it was a shame that
his father owned slaves, and to express astonishment at his failure to set them free; sometimes he urged Carter to come out and
join the abolitionists. Mrs. Grow was a woman of no imagination,
or if she had ever had any it had been completely deadened by
household cares and labours, and the constant problem of making
both ends meet. And she kept Gertie always at household tasks,
scarcely letting her out of her sight.

Carter found a little comfort in the knowledge that it was no
fault of Gertie's that they could never be alone together; she
seemed to be as distressed as he by the constant obstacles that
mocked and inflamed their desire. They would exchange glances
of hopeless adoration and sigh in their longing; they might touch
each other an instant in passing, or even now and then snatch a
kiss, but that was all. The two elder folk, dwelling with them in
that narrow house, by their presence balked that passion with
which the house by this time fairly throbbed, though they were
all unconscious of it.

The effect of all this on Carter was marked and deplorable. He
went about in a kind of suppressed excitement, a moody and
taciturn rage. He avoided his few friends, and saw nothing of
Fowler Brunton; he did not go to the symposium at Joe Tappan's
when Saturday night came round; and he failed to attend the
meeting of the debating society where he had thought to master
the rudiments of the art of oratory. Even when alone in his room
he could not strike a posture before his glass, and practise those
speeches that later were to command the applause of listening
senates. It told, too, on his studies. When he went to recite to
Judge Diller and review his reading for that week, he cut such a
poor figure that the Judge exclaimed in pained amazement,
"Well, I want to know!" and reminded him again that the law
was a jealous mistress.

Yes, to be sure. But how was a fellow to keep his mind on ad-
vowsons and contingent remainders, and the Rule in Shelley's
case, when he could hear another mistress, alive and pulsing
with passion, with red lips and ruddy cheeks and warm, round
limbs, undressing and getting ready for bed in the very next
room?

But, in the following week when Wednesday evening came, and Grow and his wife prepared to go to the prayer-meeting, Gertie, who was always required to accompany them, said that she guessed she wouldn't go; she said she had a headache. At this her mother looked at her critically for a moment, and then said:

"Well now, child, you do look peaked like; I've noticed it for some little time. I'll have to give you a doset of sulphur and molasses to-morrow."

"You going, Blair?" asked Grow, standing in the doorway with his broad-brimmed, low-crowned felt hat on. (He was always asking Carter to go to church, and Carter was always wriggling out of it, usually on the ground that he was an Episcopalian and there was no Episcopal church in Macochee.) But now he advanced an excuse more likely to appear valid in Grow's judgment than that one, when he said:

"I reckon I'd better go up to the store and finish posting the books."

And he got his hat and made as if to go at once, then remembering something he had left in his room, he went to fetch it. He waited there until he heard Mr. and Mrs. Grow close the gate behind them and go on down the street; then he waited a while longer in a kind of fear, or perhaps embarrassment; a sudden excitement had seized him and, when he went down the stairs, he went with his heart in his mouth.

Gertie had gone into the small parlour that opened off the narrow hall, a musty, unused room, set round with ugly walnut furniture, upholstered in haircloth. She was reclining on a small sofa in the almost complete darkness that filled the room, and at Carter's entrance she made a place for him at her side.

"Is your head better, Miss Gertie?" he asked, solicitously.

"Goose!" she said, and laughed and sat up straight. "And why, Carter," she irrelevantly continued, "why do you call me 'Miss'? Why don't you just call me Gertie, like everybody else?"

"We always say 'Miss' to young females in Kentucky," he explained.

"I love to hear you talk," she went on, as though the explanation were satisfactory. "It sounds so different, so pretty. Your voice is so soft. You pronounce words so—oh, well, so funny. 'Is yo' haid bettah?' " She tried to repeat his question with his Southern accent. "But I can't say it like you do," she despaired. "Anyhow, it's better now." And she leant with her head on his shoulder, and he drew her into his arms and kissed her lips with the kiss of passion.

"How long it seems since that Sunday morning!" she said.

And between the lengthened kisses that would compensate and make up the arrears of those lost days of denial, they tried to describe for each other the pangs and the pains of that cruel frustration.

The frustration, however, was not at an end. Either the time spent in those oblivious prelusive delights flew more rapidly than they imagined, or else the extemporaneous petitions offered at the prayer-meeting that evening were not of such fervent length as usual, for they were startled by the click of the gate-latch and almost caught unaware by the return of Mr. and Mrs. Grow. With a bound Carter was up the stairs and in his room.

He undressed and went to bed in the dark, and long after he had heard the others retire he lay tossing in the hot fever of his frustrated desire. He lay and listened, all his senses preternaturally acute with excitement. How long he lay he had no notion. He heard all those sounds that are proper to a country town at night. A passing boy rattled a stick noisily along the palings of the fence; a brisk pedestrian went striding importantly along, keeping step to the stirring measures of a martial air he was shrilly whistling, with a provincial pride in his empty and irritating accomplishment. A couple of spooning lovers strolled by, rustling the autumn leaves with their lagging feet, to pause, no doubt, at some house further down the street and hang over the front gate. They passed, and the town was still. The house was still. Gertie, no doubt, had long since gone to sleep; no sound came from her room. Up through the hall, from the far chamber beyond the dining-room, he could hear the regular snoring of Grow, dreaming no doubt of emancipated slaves. Carter had forgotten to draw the curtains at his window, and now the moonlight came into his room. And suddenly, in its radiance, he saw a white figure, the figure of Gertie in her shift, her hair about her shoulders; she stole on tiptoe across the floor, and slipped into his bed.

XIV

After that Carter's life seemed to flow on more smoothly. A new equilibrium had been established between his mental and his physical existence; whereas once they had been in constant antagonism they were now in harmony and set to the same rhythm. He had never felt so fit, never so full of exuberant health and bounding vitality. His mind was no longer haunted by fears and morbid fancies and vague, unsatisfied longings, no longer clouded by vapours that caused him to imagine all sorts of slights and neglects, and to feel himself awkward and inferior; he was no longer subject to moods of loneliness and homesickness, or to those whimsical and pouting spells of sullen taciturnity which back there in Bourbon County used to be attributed to some dark inheritance from his Scotch ancestry. He was now good-natured and even-tempered, full of self-confidence and secret, manly pride. He worked by day in the store, and spent the evening in his room over his studies, his mind being no longer distracted. Thus he made notable progress in his law studies, and Judge Diller complimented him highly, spoke to Grow in praise of him, and held him up to Fowler Brunton as an example of regular habits which Fowler Brunton might well afford to emulate and follow.

"Why don't you ever come round to Joe Tappan's any more of a Saturday night?" Fowler Brunton asked him one morning when they chanced to meet in the square. "We all miss you."

"Well," Carter replied, with a slightly superior smile, hugging his delicious secret to his breast and knowing how they would all envy him if they only knew! "Well, I'm too busy with my studies. I want to be admitted in the spring and get out of that store and begin my practice at the bar."

My practice at the bar! How grand the words sounded! And indeed the realization of this ambition was drawing near. He had finished Blackstone and Chitty's Pleadings, and was now deep in Starkey on Evidence. Only Tidd's Practice and Espinasse's Nisi Prius remained to be mastered, and then he would be as much of a lawyer as Fowler Brunton, or in fact, anybody.[19] Fowler Brunton and he, indeed, had discussed a partnership, but lately, so rapid and satisfactory had been his advancement, Judge Diller had hinted at the possibility of an association with him, and if that opportunity really should offer, why of course, he was made. There was nothing like the law to get a man on in Ohio. The country was new, and its inhabitants having brought with them from the older States "back east", a sense of injury and grudge, were apt to be touchy and quarrelsome and ready to take offence; and since they were free and independent sovereigns and equal to anybody on earth, they were always fearful that their rights were being invaded, and this made them litigious. There were constant differences over boundaries, and questions of disputed land titles to settle. There was a good deal of crime, too, committed, not by professional criminals, but by citizens able to fee lawyers for their defence. Besides these advantages, the lawyers, as was natural and proper in a republic, traditionally dominated the realm of politics, and had a monopoly of public office.

Thus the future seemed as bright as the present and, in short, Carter had never been so happy and contented as he was in the regular life of that winter.

Everyone remarked the improvement in his appearance, and was at a loss to account for it. He was filling out, as people said, growing stouter and heavier.

"Carter," Mrs. Grow observed one day before the autumn had passed, "You are putting on flesh. You don't look so scrawny like as you used to."

"And no wonder," said Gertie. "Just look at the way he eats!" Her dark eyes sparkled with merriment.

"Well," said Mrs. Grow, "I al'ays said he had got a healthy, relishing appetite. It does a body good to see the way he eats his victuals. He never leaves a bite on his plate."

"I hope you don't begrudge me them, ma'am," said Carter.

"Law no! I like to see a platter licked clean. What a body leaves on their plate, you know, is a sacrifice to Satan." Mrs. Grow held the opinion, prevalent in Ohio, that fat people were in better health than thin.

They all laughed, and Carter and Gertie exchanged a glance that may have had encouragement for Mrs. Grow.

"He'll have to let out his clothes," Gertie went on. And giggled again; they could giggle at anything.

His clothes, indeed, were becoming uncomfortably tight: he should have to get new ones. When he stood up before his glass to make a speech, he himself noticed that his cheeks had lost the lean look they had when first he came to Macochee; they were becoming round and smooth and rosy. His thick long hair, falling beside them, no longer imparted the slightly Byronic air they once had so generously lent his features. But, by way of compensation, he felt that before long—in a year or two, perhaps—he might expect to develop a portly figure like Colonel Nash, and even sport a round paunch which, under a velvet waistcoat below which dangled a fob and seal, was the envied symbol of prosperity, respectability, wisdom and importance.

Mrs. Grow had grown very fond of him, and treated him now not so much as a mere boarder as a son, or at least as a son-in-law, potential or prospective. By various and rather too transparent little expedients, she contrived to leave the two young people alone together, in the hope that they might soon come to know their own minds, and that this simple and innocent friendship between them might ripen into love.

Carter soon perceived an awakening interest in his future welfare on the part of Grow, who generally paid no more attention to him than to the other members of his household. For a while in the beginning of their acquaintance, Grow had tried to convert Carter to his own extreme views on the slavery question, but Carter could not feign much interest in the problem, his mind being so full of other things. He was a Whig, and took his political views from Henry Clay and Tom Corwin, and in any event, in the innate conservatism of youth, he distrusted anything unconventional, shrank from the queer and the bizarre, and looked upon Abolitionists as outlandish people to be shunned and avoided. He suffered a kind of vicarious shame for Grow, which Grow would not feel for himself, and tried to hide Grow's odd views from customers who came into the store, a practical service in most cases, especially in a community so largely imbued with Southern sentiment as Macochee was in that day.

Politically, Grow had long since given him up as a hopeless case. But now Grow showed a new interest in him.

"What do you calculate to do, Blair, after you're admitted to the bar?" he asked one dull, cold, rainy morning in December, abruptly laying aside his everlasting abolition paper and backing up to the tall iron stove and parting his long coat-tails to warm himself. Outside the rain pelted down into the empty square, flecking its broad, dun expanse with puddles. The store was empty of customers, for no one was stirring abroad on such a morning. "Going to begin practice all at once, or wait a little while till you feel more sure of yourself?"

"I want to get into a practice as soon as I can, sir."

Grow made no reply at once. He stood there, dangling the tails of his coat, his lean face framed by an unkempt mass of grey hair, his chin sunk deep in his high stock and neckcloth, and looked at Carter over his spectacles, which he had allowed to slip far down his nose when he laid aside *The Liberator*. His small, sharp eyes, under their shaggy brows, burning always with a fanatical intensity, were suddenly fixed on Carter with a sudden and somewhat perturbing interest. Carter had never felt wholly at his ease in Grow's presence; few people could feel at ease in his presence for that matter, for Grow in any company was an accusing presence, with his severe, habitual scowling expression that too

110

frankly disapproved of the world in which he lived, and announced his grim determination either to set it right, or shatter it to bits. And he seemed always ready to begin with, if not on, the person before him, especially if that person dissented from Grow's opinion on any subject. He was not much over forty, but to Carter he seemed very old.

"I don't know," Grow went on presently, with a want of confident assurance unusual to him, "I don't know as you're just exactly cut out for a lawyer. I don't know as you're exactly cute enough. A lawyer'll take any side of an argument, either side of a case. That's why they get on so well in politics; they know how to straddle a question, and be on both sides of a question at once. That's what's the trouble with our country; our public men all dodge the issue of human slavery; they won't come out on it. I'd a thought, now, that you would prefer some honest business; I cal'lated you might want to go into partnership with me, like here in the store. I've been thinking, it's kind o' borne in upon me that I'd ought to start a paper, an anti-slavery paper here, and do something for the cause, and if I had a partner I'd not be bound down so tight, I'd feel more free to attend to it."

Grow paused, and seemed to hesitate, as before some delicate question he hardly knew how to broach. Carter wondered what was coming next. He had been slightly vexed by Grow's reflections on lawyers and their noble profession. Tom Corwin and Judge Diller, for instance; they were not dishonest men. He thought of this, but he didn't say it. He knew that if he did he would only bring down on his head a long tirade about the slavery question, in which Grow would become personal and offensive, and ask him why his own father did not see the light and set his niggers free. And Carter did not wish to argue with him, for he could never argue without getting angry; in discussion he lacked presence of mind; he was hot-headed and apt to fly out, not having yet learnt to sweat his temper.[20] And besides, he was too well satisfied with what as a budding lawyer himself he called the *status quo;* he wished things, for the present, to stay just as they were.

"Now there's my daughter, Gertie," Grow went on, or began.

And Carter's heart stood still. What was coming now? Grow was looking at him with those cold, steely little eyes of his. Did he know? Did he suspect?

"I thought, mebby, you and she being such good friends—but pshaw now! What am I saying!" And Grow, suddenly finding himself hopelessly entangled in his own tactlessness, dandled his

111

coat tails over his arms a moment, and then went back to his desk. And Carter went to the front of the store, and stood looking out through one of the small panes of glass in the door, at the hopeless rain pelting down into the Square, and at a high-gabled building on the other side with the date 1811 on its walls, and at the row of shops with "Cheapside" spelled out in great letters above them.

XV

This too apparent readiness on the part of Mr. and Mrs. Grow to welcome Carter into the family as a son-in-law was the only constraint that troubled his satisfaction in that happy winter, and he did not allow that to trouble him very much. At the slightest effort at pressure he would have rebelled; he had no intention whatever of adopting the mercer's calling, or that of any merchant whatever. Land-owning, or a profession, or both; these were the only occupations possible to one of his old-fashioned views and prejudices. Even to a new and crude community like Macochee, though it had commercial buildings erected as long before as 1811, the settlers had brought with them the distinctions that survived in the older communities beyond the mountains to the East, those conventions of older civilisations, that determined the relations of the population and decreed that those who worked with their hands should occupy a lower status in the social order. The denial did not extend to merchandising, of course, as it did in Europe, and yet—and yet—well, Carter Blair had all the aristocratic notions of the South, even if he was poor; and perhaps they were more important to him on that very account.

And just as he had no intention of becoming a merchant, so, for the present at least, he had no intention of marrying. Gertie expected no such thing of him; they had never even mentioned such a possibility. Gertie had given herself to him because she was kind, and could not bear to see him suffer, and because she found the same gratification in their passion as he. She made no demands on him, expected nothing, asked nothing; she did not even resent his sensitive reluctance to appear anywhere in public with her. There were not, to be sure, many places in Macochee where they might have appeared publicly together. There was, of course, the Methodist church, the plain frame structure that stood in the severity of its fresh white paint in the main street a few rods north of the Court House, and Grow and his wife never set forth to go there of a Sunday morning that Mrs. Grow did not pause a moment, and in the new prestige given to her presence by her great poke-bonnet, her plum-coloured dress with the wide, voluminous, flowing skirts, and her velvet mantle, fold her mitted hands and say:

"Be'nt ye goin' with us to meeting, Carter?"

But Carter would thank her and shake his head.

"Better come," she would plead. "We'll do you good."

And then Grow would say, impatiently, knowing it was no use: "Hurr' on, hurr' on!"

And Mrs. Grow and Gertie, in their bonnets, would gather up their skirts and follow Grow, for Gertie went to church with great regularity that winter, having no longer any need to pretend a headache in order to stop at home.

Carter had been reared as an Episcopalian, though at that period he fancied himself, like most lawyers of his day, especially the more interesting and picturesque among them, a free-thinker. But that was not the real reason for his refusal to go to church. The real reason was that he did not think it becoming to go to church with a girl who was his—well, with Gertie, in fact. There were certain things a fellow simply could not do: he might do a lot of things of which his conscience did not approve, but he must respect the proprieties. Then, there was an occasional lecture at the Lyceum; but Gertie was not interested in lectures, and there were the meetings of the debating society at the Mechanics' Institute[21] to which he went from a sense of duty; Judge Diller had advised him to do so and to take part in the debates.

"It will accustom you to think on your feet, and teach you to keep your temper in an argument," the Judge had said. And surely he needed some such aids.

And so Carter went to the Mechanics' Institute, and even ventured to take part now and then in the debates, but he never asked Gertie to go, and doubtless she would not have cared to go if he had, unless it had been to be seen with him.

She would have liked to go to the occasional dances, but Grow, in his evangelical strictness—his moral code was that of the primitive Methodist—looked upon dancing as highly immoral and forbade her indulgence in it, and Carter felt that he was compensating her rather handsomely and loyally by not going to dances himself.

The only times they appeared together in public that winter was when they went skating on the "factory pond," thickly frozen over by the hard frost that succeeded the January thaw. (For some inscrutable metaphysical reason, skating had been omitted from the Methodist canon on the deadly sins.) They could not be so very conspicuous there, or to Carter not seem so conspicuous, because everybody in Macochee seemed to be there, skimming over the smooth ice on their great Dutch skates, or gathered round the fires kindled on the bank, and looking on whilst they warmed their mittened hands, and stamped their feet on the frozen, snowy ground. Everybody went skating during that fortnight, even the rowdies who came up out of the Bottoms and sought a pleasure of their own by interfering with the pleasure of others.

It was during the hard times of 1837, and business being slack in the store, Grow would let Carter have the afternoon off, or a part of it at least. Skating was an accomplishment that Carter had had little opportunity of acquiring in the mild winters of Kentucky, and he could not take much satisfaction in the figure he cut on the ice, and as Gertie skated well, she skated with other men oftener than with him, or else dashed away by herself, skimming round and round the pond in the rhythmic order into which the skaters naturally fell.

One afternoon when she had left him thus, Carter stood on the snow and watched her; he thought her uncommonly pretty as with lithe grace she glided along in her red wollen dress, her tippet flying over her shoulder, and her small head in its fur turban, inclined to one side, her cheeks red in the frosty air, her eyes shining with excitement in the exhilaration of the sport. Now and then he would lose her in the throng; and he would watch eagerly until she came skimming lightly back into view again, and as she passed he would greet her with his eyes; she would smile and a glance would flash between them, a glance that recognized the secret between them, and he would feel a sudden glow of pride at the thought of his possession of her.

But he could not stand there long in that stinging cold; he must move about and get his blood into circulation; he tried a few figures at the upper end of the pond where it narrowed near the factory, the small red-brick woollen mill established by Mr. Cowley, and the only manufacturing concern in Macochee. That end of the pond was devoted to beginners, and was largely occupied by small boys who were either too inexperienced or else too timid to venture out on the larger pond, and Carter felt that it

114

was rather undignified to be seen among them. Now and then the ruffians from the Bottoms would dash in, trip them up, and tumble them over; the little boys on their clumsy skates would scramble to the bank and stand there, some of them crying with terror and the cold. Now and then a bully, a leader among the boys from the Bottoms, would dash among the skaters on the larger pond, swinging his arms wildly, cutting figure-eights and fancy flub-dubs, skating backwards with uncouth movements of his great buttocks, and bumping into everybody. Carter felt an impulse to give the fellow a thrashing, but his mind was suddenly turned from that desire, to another and more personal concern. For now, swaying along in perfect rhythm with long glides together, holding each other's hands crossed before them, he saw Gertie and Tom Nash. Nash was dressed in a tight blue surtout with brass buttons, and a high stock; he wore buff trousers tightly fitted to his slender legs, and fastened beneath his boots by straps. He skated divinely, and as they swept along their eyes, Gertie's and his, saw nothing but each other's eyes. They swept past him without noticing him, though they passed so close that Carter could see a flake of the snow that floated now and then in the sharp air fall on Gertie's long black lashes and rest an instant there. She was looking up into Nash's face with a smile of perfect happiness. They passed and passed again. The long stream of happy skaters flowed round and round, the keen, curled-up runners of their skates cutting the surface of the ice into a thin powder, their bodies all swaying in graceful unison; their laughter and their cries of joy filled the wintry air. Carter moved away from the spot where he had stood unnoticed; he lost sight of Gertie and Nash and hardly dared search among the crowd to find them again. Then he saw them on the shore beside one of the fires whose wavering flames were red in the early twilight; the blue smoke went up to the low grey wintry sky; the pungent odour of burning hickory was faint upon the frosty air. The western sky was glowing red where the sun had gone down, and beyond the ugly hulk of the factory building a cluster of beech-trees spread the exquisite delicate tracery of their black leafless branches against the cold sky.

Gertie was sitting by the fire; and Nash was on his knees before her unfastening the straps of her skates. She leant over towards him with a smile, and Nash, ceasing an instant to fumble with stiff fingers at the frozen buckles, looked up and smiled too. Their ruddy, happy faces were close together, and the smile on Gertie's face was one that Carter well knew. He looked an instant and then turned and went home alone.

XVI

As Carter walked homeward alone through the sparsely built-up streets of the town in the gloom of the early twilight, thinking of the tender little scene he had just witnessed and nursing his sense of grievance, he was conscious of no jealous rage. His resentment of Gertie's momentary lapse into unfaithfulness to him went no deeper than his feeling for her, which was not one of serious or lasting devotion. But there was the burning pain of the wound to his pride, and the embarrassment he dreaded when he should meet Tom Nash again.

When he reached home he went at once to the stable to feed and water Dolly D. and bed her down for the night, and when he went back to the house Gertie had not yet come home. She did not come home, indeed, until after dark, and there were reproaches for her from both her parents when she somewhat breathlessly took her seat at the supper-table across from Carter. They did not speak, she and Carter, or once look up at each other, and Mrs. Grow, with a knitted brow of concern, observed this sudden coolness between them far more closely than she had ever observed more suspicious signs of a warm passion between them.

Grow, not so sensitive to atmosphere, was wholly oblivious, and the silence was so agreeable and so auspicious that he took advantage of it to read out to his family, and especially to Carter who, he said, would be especially interested, the peroration of the great speech that Tom Corwin had just delivered in Congress on the Cumberland Road, closing with its well-deserved tribute to the great state of Ohio which he urged certain honourable but, it appeared, ignorant gentlemen of the East and South, to visit. Drawing the candle close to his plate, Grow read out:

"They might see there, in the very spot where but yesterday the wild beasts of the wilderness seized their prey by night and made their covert lair by day, on that same spot to-day stands the common school-house, filled alike with the children of the rich and poor—those children who are to be the future voters, officers and statesmen of the Republic. Over that vast region, so lately red with the blood of savage war, the seed-fields of knowledge are planted, and a smiling harvest of civilization springs up. And there, too, may be seen what a Christian statesman might well admire. The schoolmaster is not alone. That holy religion which is at last the only sure basis of permanent social or political improvement, has

116

there its voices crying in the wilderness. Upon the almost burning embers of the war-fire, round which some barbarous chief but yesterday recounted to his listening tribe, with horrid exultation, his deeds of savage heroism, to-day is built a temple dedicated to that religion which announces 'peace on earth and goodwill toward men.' Yes, Sir, all over that land, side by side with the humble school-house, stand those

'Steeple-towers,
And spires whose silent finger points to Heaven'."

Grow finished reading, and, as though he had made the speech himself, waited for applause.

"Well, I must say," said Mrs. Grow, "I don't see anything so very funny in that."

Grow glared at his wife over his spectacles with scornful severity.

"Funny!" he snorted. "Why, woman, whoever said it was funny?"

"But I thought Tom Corwin was always funny," explained Mrs. Grow, with a touching innocence.

"Funny!" exclaimed Grow again, indignantly, and, getting up from the supper-table in disgust, he left the room. Mrs. Grow got up, too, presently, and went to the kitchen to fetch some more coffee, of which beverage she consumed enormous quantities, usually sitting at table after the others had left to gratify her intemperate taste.

And in the moment of her absence Gertie shot a look of anger out of her black eyes at Carter across the table, and said:

"What'd you want to treat me that away for? Go off and leave me like you did?"

"Why did you treat me as you did?"

"Me! What did I do?"

Carter looked at her sharply an instant, and then with only a single ironical "Humph!" he, too, got up and left the table, took his candle and went up to his own room. He shut the door and drew the blind at the window, the single window which looked down upon the small front yard and the wide street. Usually by the simple, almost symbolic act of drawing this green blind, Carter could shut out the narrow little provincial, almost frontier world of Macochee, and find himself in a large, free, magnificent world peopled by the great and imposing figures of the future, thronging round him, enthralled by his eloquence, his logic, his satire and his wit, as those distinguished Representatives in Congress had sat enthralled there at Washington City only the other day while Tom Corwin in his mellow tones had unrolled the

117

periods that old Grow in his husky, harsh voice had read out to them at the supper table. For that small chamber with its four bare whitewashed walls, its walnut bed, its wash-hand-stand with jug and basin, its short strip of rag-carpet on the floor, its deal table and pine chair, had been by turns and could be made by fancy's whim, Senate and law court, platform and stump; there grave statesmen had listened to the lofty eloquence of patriotism; judges had been forced to nod assent to irresistible logic; juries had been swayed by pathetic appeals, and vast audiences in hot, crowded halls, or covering acres in the open air, had been moved now to laughter, now to tears. That little barren room had been the scene whereon he had rehearsed all his future triumphs, and by a mere effort of the will, when he was alone in it, this silent, reticent, timid boy could summon all those vast throngs, and in its cosy, warm and silent seclusion find an anodyne (as Tom Corwin would have said) for all the ills and slights of the present.

But this evening the magic would not work. None of those flattering and consoling presences would appear when he beckoned. He sat at his table, with his candle and Coke on Lyttleton open before him, and tried to read, but the hard lines were more obdurately incomprehensible than ever. He rested his elbows on the table, and with his head in his hands tried to study, but he could not. For that small room was no longer the future where everything was perfect; it was the present where everything had suddenly gone awry, and it was invaded and dominated by a figure, a single figure, which in throbbing life and passion, put to rout all those hosts of phantoms. He could see her, her flesh warm and rosy in the soft glow of candlelight, or feel her body, soft and palpitating in his arms. And then he could see her cheeks red in the frosty air, her eyes flashing, her lips parted in a smile, not now for him but for Tom Nash, rich, handsome, well-dressed, dashing Tom Nash. He had assured himself when he came away from the factory pond that he didn't care, but now he discovered that he did care, most desperately care; his whole being was swiftly invaded by a longing for her and by a furious, jealous hatred of Tom Nash. He clutched his long hair in his fists and groaned aloud. Why had he turned away from her, there in the dining-room, in the cruel way he had? Worse, why had he left her to come home alone from the factory-pond? And worst of all, why had he attached such tragic importance to her skating with another man who could skate better than he could? What an ass he had made of himself!

He could not read Coke on Lyttleton;[22] there was no balm

118

there for wounded hearts. What about Byron? The book was there before him on the table, with his half-dozen other books, against the bare, bland wall.... But no; there was no solace there, either. Sad poetry was only for happy hours.... Had Gertie come upstairs yet? Old Grow, of course, would be reading, most likely in the kitchen, for it was warmer there than elsewhere in the house these cold nights. Mrs. Grow and Gertie must have cleared away and done up the dishes by this time. Then Mrs. Grow, always tired, would go to bed.... Was that Gertie now coming up the stairs? He had heard a noise; something had creaked. No; it was a branch of the maple tree in the corner of the front yard, snapping in the cold. Gertie could come up the stairs without making any more noise than a cat; she was light of foot anyhow—how gracefully she could skate!—and besides, that winter they had both learnt to slip about the house, even in the dark and dead of night, as noiselessly and stealthily as cats.

And then all of a sudden he heard the latch of his door click ever so lightly; his heart leapt into his mouth; he pushed Byron away and bent over Coke on Lyttleton again. The door opened; she crossed the room on tiptoe; he felt her hands steal over his eyes; she leant over him; he could feel her warm body, scent her odour, and she said:

"Guess who it is!"

He gave a little laugh, a laugh of relief, of happiness, of love, and her arms stole about him, she laid her cheek against his, and said:

"You ain't really mad at me, are you Carter? Say you ain't! And say it wasn't really very nice of you to let me come home all that way in the dark and cold alone!"

She pushed back Coke on Lyttleton and came around and flung herself into his arms and they were reconciled, though now that fatal doubt and painful suspicion had planted themselves in his mind, Carter did wonder whether there was not something vicarious in her embraces that night.

XVII

Gertie did not go skating again. As if for Carter's reassurance the cold snap did not last; a spell of thawing weather set in, and the ice on the factory-pond was soon dissolved into those unromantic waters that were discol-

oured and polluted by the dyes and waste products of the wool-
len-mill. The incident that for a moment had troubled Carter's
trust in Gertie was soon forgotten, or nearly forgotten; perhaps
a slightly disillusioning trace of it remained in Carter's mind,
but that was all, and he could pretend to himself not to see
it, and things went on as before. Spring was coming, and Carter
was studying as hard as he could in order to be ready for examination when the Supreme Court came to hold its annual term in
Macochee. As a consequence he could not devote quite so much
attention to Gertie; the law, his other and more jealous mistress,
claimed all his time. He would go nowhere, not even to a joint-
debate at the Mechanics' Institute on the subject of slavery, to
which Grow, somewhat too impetuously, had challenged Colonel
Nash. Grow, Carter feared, was somewhat hurt by his refusal to
attend, though too proud to say so. But Carter had already heard
Grow on that subject so many times that he felt that he was
thoroughly acquainted with his views on it; besides, he was
somewhat embarrassed by his relation to Grow; if he went to
hear him he could hardly escape the imputation of being one of
Grow's partisans. Colonel Nash would no doubt present the more
conventional and respectable point of view, that of a reasonable
compromise for the present, with perhaps an ultimate solution in
gradual and compensated emancipation, and Carter did not like
to be identified with the radical and extreme, unconstitutional
and revolutionary methods that Grow was sure to advocate.

On the evening of the debate Grow was in such a highly nervous state that he could scarcely eat a bite of supper. He sat at the
table, nervously leafing over in his trembling hands a sheaf of
rustling papers on which for days he had been busily transcribing
the points in his argument, fruits of so much reading of Garrison's firebrand of a paper. Mrs. Grow was even more nervous
than her husband, and looked at him across the table with a face
that was drawn by anxiety.

"Do eat something, Grow," she said. "You will need all your
strength."

But Grow only shook his head impatiently and scowled at the
sheets that rustled in his nervous hands.

"Then do drink another cup of coffee!"

Grow, though he had already drunk two cups, consented and
passed up his cup.

"Here's a cup just the way you like it," she said: "with the
bead[23] on."

Carter felt a great sympathy for Grow—almost a pity. There
was something pathetic about him sitting there, racked by nerv-

ous apprehension, suffering tortures, and about to face the richest, the most consequential and most redoubtable opponent in Macochee. For this formidable encounter Grow, as Carter noticed, had done what he could to smarten his appearance; he had blackened and polished his boots (except the tops) and his wife had forced him to stand still while she washed his ears; he had had his shaggy hair and beard trimmed; he had shaved his long upper lip, and now, serious and shorn and generally tidied up, he awaited the ordeal. He had partially dressed; he had put on a clean white shirt, immaculate from his wife's iron; but he had deferred putting on his neck-cloth until after supper. Carter could see his Adam's apple incessantly rising and falling in his lean throat as he swallowed in his nervousness. He tilted up his cup, drained its last drop, shuffled his notes together, and went to his room to finish his dressing. Mrs. Grow announced that she would let the supper dishes go till morning, and went to put on her plum-coloured dress. After a while they reappeared, Grow and his wife, he solemn in his long-tailed coat and tall beaver hat; she in her enormous poke-bonnet. Grow's nervousness had communicated itself to his wife; her countenance was ravaged by anxiety and her hands trembled as she tried to draw on her black silk mitts. Gertie fluttered about her, plucking out the folds in her skirts, while in the impatience of the reformer, Grow irritably exclaimed:

"Hur' on! Hur' on!"

And they set out for the Mechanics' Institute.

For a long while Carter bent over his table, trying to study. But something in the air that evening made it hard for him to concentrate his attention on the abstract principles of the legal code. The soft air of spring came in through his open window, and it seemed to be charged with some peculiar and disquieting quality, the disturbing influence of the restless life of the small town, its conflicts of interest and passion which imperiously claimed precedence over the dull and lifeless formulas of Coke. Now that spring had come the town was noisier than in winter; people were abroad, shouts of laughter came to his ears; cries, and the shrill whistles of boys who roamed the streets at evening. He wondered what had become of Gertie. He thought that he had heard her come upstairs and shut herself up in her room, but he was not sure. He wondered if she could have slipped out of the house and gone somewhere. Then he thought about the debate, and wondered how it was going on. Somehow or other he seemed to feel the various shocks of its conflicting ideas, as though the atmosphere were charged with them, electrically.

How was old Grow getting on? Was Colonel Nash proving too much for him? Colonel Nash, of course, had everything on his side, and besides, he was in the right. No one with the least sense could have any patience with those wild and crazy and dangerous notions of Grow; there was no sense in them; they were revolutionary, unconstitutional and seditious; they would undermine the basic principles of law and order. And yet he could not help feeling a certain sympathy for Grow; it may have been foolish of him to get into this dispute with Colonel Nash; it must certainly hurt his business, and get all the best people down on him; but he had not lacked courage at any rate—he would say that for old Grow. After all, old Grow was the under dog. . . . However, this was not studying law; he must be firm with himself. He resolutely determined to shut out Macochee and its debates on modern issues, and go back to Coke on Lyttleton and ancient times. . . . Then suddenly he heard a distant sound. Were they to have a thunder shower this early in spring? But no, there it was again, a kind of sharp rattle; it must be applause, floating out on the air through the open windows of the Mechanics' Institute. . . .

No use to try to study. He closed his book and went out. As he passed the door of Gertie's room he paused and knocked timidly. No answer. He went downstairs and called out:

"Miss Gertie!"

But his voice echoed hollowly through the empty house. He got his hat and started down town.

It was a soft, balmy night of spring. The windows of some of the dwellings in that sparsely built quarter of the town were alight, and a few couples were out strolling, taking advantage of the warm night. He walked up Main Street, crossed the empty Square and on to Melodian Hall, where the Lyceum lectures were delivered, and the Mechanics' Institute held its debates. Long before he reached it Carter could hear the sounds that told of the interest the debate had aroused—a voice raised to the oratorical pitch; bursts of applause and the sharp rattle of clapping hands. The windows of the hall were all open and alight, and even before he mounted the steps in the dim, lighted stairway that led to the hall above, he knew that the place was packed.

Colonel Nash was speaking when Carter arrived. Carter, standing at the back, just inside the door, could see him on the low platform above the heads of the audience that held nearly everybody he knew—Judge Diller, Giles Paten, the Methodist and

Baptist pastors, Winship, Wales, and Fowler Brunton. They were seated, however, well towards the front, among the more important people of the town, whilst, in the rear seats and in the spaces about the door were gathered a number of young rowdies from the Bottoms looking on the scene with truculent and cynical expressions on their sallow faces. They stood about in slouchy and provocative attitudes, insolently voiding their tobacco on the floor, and applauding with an exaggerated enthusiasm and with loud and uncouth noises every other period of Colonel Nash's speech. Colonel Nash, in his suave manner observing scrupulously all the parliamentary proprieties, treating his opponent with elaborate courtesy and speaking in almost mellifluous tones, was rounding out his conciliatory argument in favour of patient and constitutional methods in dealing with the vexed problem. Colonel Nash was a fine figure of a man as he stood on the platform with his white hair, his classical and rosy features, the blue swallow-tail coat with the high collar and the ruffled shirt-front to which he clung; he was as dignified and impressive as one of the signers of the Declaration of Independence, or a member of the Constitutional Convention. He was a sound Whig, the personal friend of Henry Clay, and he stood there before them all as the embodiment of all the fundamental principles of conservatism and vested rights, the friend of progress and the enemy of change.

Grow, who had had the opening and was soon to have the close of the debate, was sitting on a splint-bottomed chair at the back of the platform under the framed portraits of Washington and Jefferson that hung on the wall; his gaze was fixed on the floor, he was scowling irritably, his hair, which had been so neatly brushed when he left home that evening, was rumpled, and he increased its disorder by constantly running his nervous fingers through it. His trousers had crept up the wrinkled and rusty legs of his boots, and he looked almost ridiculous. Beside the handsome, ruddy, rotund Colonel Nash, immaculate, conventional and correct, the lean, ill-favoured Grow, so obviously poor and unsuccessful, presented a mean and ungainly appearance even in his Sunday blacks. Why, Carter wondered, why had Grow ever rushed so blindly and so stubbornly into this impossible situation!

Colonel Nash, with a patronizing compliment for his opponent, concluded his speech amidst applause that the rowdies from the Bottoms would not allow to come to an end. But when the audience grew impatient with them they desisted, and Grow slowly rose, drank a whole tumbler of water at a draught, and stood before them to speak. He stood there a moment, his dark brows knit in a scowl, his trousers half way up to his knees, and glared at his audience. Then, clearing his throat, he began in a husky voice. But he hadn't uttered a dozen words when the storm broke upon him. The roughs gathered at the back of the hall set up a howl and some of them started down the aisle, shouting:

"Pull him down! Pull him down! Pull the abolitionist down!"

Grow's adherents in the audience, though they were not many, raised an opposition shout, but this had no other effect than to add to the uproar and confusion. The entire audience was on its feet, the men shouting angrily, the women white-faced and trembling with fear. Carter caught a glimpse of Mrs. Grow, her hands clasped tragically against the bonnet-strings at her chin, and he had an impulse to go to her and reassure and, if needs be, protect her, but she had been seated in one of the front seats, and in the press of disorderly men there was no way to get so far. The Rev. Mr. Croker, the Baptist minister, who had been chosen to preside over the meeting, stood behind the table on the platform, rapping the table with his knuckles; but he was pale, neutral and ineffectual and no one paid attention to him. Grow stood in his place holding his ground; his lips moved; but he could not make himself heard in the tumult. Then a peculiar light came into his eye, a gleam of that fanaticism which was latent in him, and had only wanted some such incident as this to bring it out; he drew himself up, stood for an instant like an inspired and prophetic figure of wrath, and then, folding his arms across his breast, he looked down on his tormentors, a sarcastic and contemptuous smile on his dark, lean face, and perhaps not altogether unhappy.

Carter feared for a critical moment or two that Grow was in danger of being man-handled, and he kept as close as he could to the leader of the lads from the Bottoms—that bully whom he had seen skating backwards on the factory-pond—intending, if a real mélée should develop, to tackle him the first thing. He was so angry and indignant, and had grown so excited that he could hardly control himself as it was, and felt a primitive and savage impulse to aim a blow at the sallow and hateful face of a creature he would have loathed and despised in any circumstances.

But just then something happened which instantly changed the atmosphere. Colonel Nash arose and intervened. He proceeded to the edge of the platform and, with a word to the effaced clergyman who was presiding and a most courteous gesture of apology to Grow, he stood there, majestic in his frills and ruffles, his imposing waistcoat, his fob with its seals and breloques dangling below his small but most respectable paunch, and raised his white hand with the authority of the first citizen of Macochee. He motioned to those in the front rows to take their seats and they obeyed. Those behind them sat down; the roughs, for a moment, were overawed, and in the stillness that fell the Colonel said:

"I should like to appeal to all those within sound of my voice to maintain that order and decorum which should characterize an assembly of this kind. The reputation not only of our fair city, but of our great and glorious State of Ohio, is for the moment the object of our solicitude and care, and I for one, speaking as an humble citizen, should be distressed if word were to go abroad that we were lacking in that reverence for law and order and devotion to the great American principle of the right of free speech and American love of justice and fairplay which is the distinguishing characteristic of our great and independent nation. I ask you, therefore, to listen to my honourable and distinguished opponent with the same polite and careful attention that you have shown me. And I say to certain elements that have unexpectedly honoured us with their presence this evening, that, while they are welcome so long as they conduct themselves with the manners of gentlemen, the moment they indulge in any further demonstrations such as those that have already disgraced our meeting this evening, I shall appeal to the Chair to instruct the Serjeant-at-Arms to clear the hall."

There was a brisk clapping of respectable hands and cries of: "Good! Good!"

Carter wondered who, or where, the Serjeant-at-Arms was; or how, if called upon, he would clear the hall. He had never seen the Serjeant-at-Arms at any previous meeting of the debating society. Perhaps a special one had been named for this debate which, in its interest and importance, so far transcended any debate the Society had thus far held. It was of such importance that neither the Mayor nor the City Marshal had ventured to be present, no doubt fearing that they might be called upon to take sides themselves in some such strained situation as had arisen. Or perhaps it was merely force of habit that led the Colonel, remembering his service in the State Senate and his devotion to parliamentary rules, to suggest the parliamentary method of dealing with disturbance. At any rate, the method worked. The house quieted down, and poor Grow was allowed to proceed, which he did in his nervousness for a quarter of an hour, finding it impossible to use up the twenty minutes allotted him for the close. As he sat down Colonel Nash, with courtly politeness, felicitated Grow warmly on his effort. But there was no doubt who had won the debate.

Carter indeed did not wait until it was all over; he saw Grow lamely conclude, and he saw the Colonel gallantly congratulate him, but he felt so sorry for poor Grow that he could not bear to encounter him just then; he felt that it would be kinder and more delicate on his part to go away, and perhaps never let Grow know that he had attended the debate at all. And so, sensitively, he stole away and walked home in the darkness, alone, lost in his thoughts; thinking of this debate and wondering whence came this strange power that some men exercised on the human crowd.

He was going along Locust Street, his head down, lost in these speculations; he had almost reached the Grow house, when, for some reason, he looked up. And there in the darkness, at the gate, he saw two figures, a man and a woman, locked in each other's arms and immobile in a long, passionate kiss. And his heart for an instant stopped beating. He looked again; no, there could be no doubt of it; they were Gertie and Tom Nash.

XVIII

Carter stopped, and for an instant stood stock-still. At his footfall the couple, adopting a careless and indifferent attitude, sauntered nonchalantly away down the street. He felt a sickening sense of humiliation and the pain of wounded pride; he had an instinctive desire not to be seen by them in the rather ridiculous light in which he would appear in their company after what he had witnessed. He turned in at the gate to enter the house. He thought he heard Gertie say, "It's Mr. Blair," or something of the sort, and then he heard Nash laugh, a loud, insulting and contemptuous laugh. Carter could not mistake the intention of that laugh and, in an access of primitive rage, he strode after the couple. As he drew near Gertie turned round and said in a sweetened tone:

"Oh, it's you, Carter!" And then in the most matter-of-fact way she asked: "Is the meeting out?"

He made no reply, but, rushing forward, he seized Nash by the shoulder, turned him violently round and said:

"Look here, Nash; what do you mean?"

"What do I mean? What do I mean by what?"

"By that laugh, as you very well know!"

"That laugh?" Nash laughed again in that insulting and contemptuous way.

And then Carter in a blind rage struck him a blow in the face. Nash tottered an instant, recovered his equilibrium, then lunged out in defence of himself at Carter. Carter was about to strike him again when Gertie pushed him aside, and thrust herself between them.

"You mustn't!" she said, in a low voice. "You mustn't! For God's sake behave yourselves! You mustn't fight here!"

The two young men, breathing heavily, their fists clenched, stood glaring at each other in the savage, primitive hatred of male animals fighting over a female, and Gertie stood between them, pleading with them in hoarse whispers to desist.

"Quit it, I say!" she kept repeating; "quit it! You'll rouse the whole neighbourhood—and I can't have that! And then, my father and mother, they will be home any minute, now! Quit it, I say!"

"Blair," said Nash, when he had caught his breath, "Blair, God damn you, I'll pay you out for this!"

"Whenever you like, Nash," said Carter, "I'm at your disposition."

He thought that he could detect, even in the darkness that made Nash's face an indistinct blur, the sarcastic expression with which he said:

"You don't understand. What I mean is that I'll give you a cowhiding. One only fights duels with gentlemen!"

Carter for an instant could scarcely believe his ears. The words stung his face like nettles; he went hot all over, and almost gently setting Gertie aside, he sprang on Nash, seized him by the throat and slowly, remorselessly, almost calmly, began to choke him. Nash tried to resist, but his strength was not equal to Carter's. Carter choked him, and Nash sank slowly, and as Carter gradually forced him to his knees he said, in a low, even voice:

"Take that back, Nash! Take that back! Take that back!"

Gertie stood by, weeping softly, wringing her hands and moaning:

"Oh! Oh! Oh!"

And Carter kept on forcing Nash, and saying:

"Take that back, Nash! Take that back! On your knees! On your knees!"

At last Nash nodded, and Carter released him. And Nash said: "I take it back, Blair."

127

He got to his feet slowly and leant against the fence, still struggling for breath. And Gertie, weeping still, went to him, and taking her handkerchief pressed it to his cheek where, as Carter now realized, he had drawn blood by the blow of his fist. And suddenly he felt half ashamed; here he was letting his temper get the better of him again, and turning him into a brute and a savage.

"I wouldn't stop here very long if I were you," he said quite calmly. "Mr. and Mrs. Grow will be coming home soon."

In fact, at that moment he heard a sound that brought back to him with a strange effect of something that had happened long ago, the incidents of the earlier hours of that evening—the ironical cheers, the jeers and shouts of the crowd that was hooting Grow on his way home.

XIX

If Carter had found it difficult to live in the same house with Gertie and keep up outward appearances when he was her lover, he found it far more difficult now when they were no longer even friends. They had scarcely spoken since that night of the fight with Nash; indeed, they had not spoken at all except when they met at table and were obliged to keep up the old pretence which now concealed, as they fancied, another and totally different feeling between them. But at that they did not succeed very well; the atmosphere of the house was heavy with constraint and charged with some troubling quality. Grow, perhaps, did not feel it, or if he did, he did not notice it. Ever since the disastrous debate with Colonel Nash he had been moody and silent, brooding over none of them knew what, whether the shame and humiliation of his defeat, or some new scheme for future victory. Only once did he mention the debate to Carter, and then merely to refer to the ruffians from the Bottoms in saying:

"They favour slavery because they like to feel that there's at least one class of human beings in a more degraded state than themselves."

With this reflection he dropped the subject, and they passed those several days together in the store in absolute silence and almost alone, for very few customers appeared though it was the spring season when the minds of women were turning naturally to new clothes.

But Mrs. Grow was more percipient than her husband, perhaps more sensitive to atmospheres; and then, her mind was concerned with the things of this world, while his was concerned with things not of this world. Carter frequently detected her glancing first at him and then at Gertie, in anxious wonder and concern. He felt sorry for her, and because he felt sorry for her he grew to be rather fond of her; there was something so very touching about her.

And now, as Carter saw her worried and concerned by the mysterious change in his attitude towards Gertie, and could see, or could think he saw, some new trouble stalking her and marking her down for its prey, he felt sorrier for her than ever.

Most of the time, however, he felt sorry for himself. The first effect of the revelation at the gate that evening had been to plunge him into one of those black and sullen tempers that made him go days without speaking to anyone; but after a while, on reading his Byron, he had taken refuge in a kind of callow and romantic melancholy not altogether unpleasant. He cultivated the cynical manner of the misogynist, and in short was never going to have anything to do with women again. He deplored his loss of temper on that fatal night, and regretted that he had not treated Gertie and Nash with a lofty and withering contempt and gone away. Nash would grow tired of her soon enough, and that would serve her right. In fact, he realized now that he himself had been growing tired of her; what was she, after all? Certainly not the kind of girl a fellow would wish to marry; a light baggage, that was what she was! And it wasn't dignified for him to stay on longer in this house; he must go away. But that wasn't so easy as it sounded; if he went away he would have to give some reason to Grow and to Mrs. Grow, and he durst not give them the real reason; that was impossible. And it would be hard to concoct any reason that would seem plausible unless he were to leave Macochee for good, and he didn't like to do that. He couldn't explain it, but already he had begun to take root in Macochee.

One day, however, as they sat at dinner, something having been said about Carter's forthcoming examination for admission to the bar, he thought in a flash that it might be a favourable moment to prepare their minds for the impending change, and ventured to say, though not so delicately as he felt he should have put it:

"You'll be looking out for another clerk in the store, eh, Mr. Grow?"

"What say?" said Grow, casting a glance over his spectacles.

"I was just saying that you would be looking out for some one to take my place as soon as I am admitted."

"Oh!" said Grow, as if that were of no importance, and turned to his newspaper.

But Mrs. Grow, at Carter's remark, had given a sudden start, and now she turned to Carter with a face of almost pained concern, and said:

"You don't mean to say you're going to leave us, Carter? Why, you've come to be just like one of the family."

"Yes, but you know, Mrs. Grow," replied Carter, trying to smile, "I've got to begin some time—"

"But I didn't know you cal'ated to begin at oncet. Tschk! Tschk!"

He could see that the thought troubled her, and he hadn't the heart to pursue the subject further.

That evening he was sitting on the steps of the front porch just before supper when Gertie, leaving her mother at work in the kitchen, came out and sat down beside him. She sat as close to him as she could get, just as though nothing had happened. If the slight contact with her body for an instant thrilled him, he nevertheless drew away from her with a rather marked aversion.

"Carter," she began, "I must have a word with you."

"Well?"

"Please don't say anything just now about going away."

"Why not?"

"If you knew how it troubles Mother! She's so fond of you!"

"Now see here, Miss Gertie, I can't stay here any longer. It's impossible. You ought to see that."

"Yes, but I don't want you to go now."

"Why should you care?"

"Well, because it would upset Pa and Ma, and for a little while I don't want them to think—"

"What are you driving at?"

She hesitated a moment, and then with some embarrassment she faltered:

"Carter, Mr. Nash has asked me to marry him."

"Well, I wish you joy, but what's that got to do with me?"

"But the folks don't know it—yet."

"Why don't you tell them, then? Or better still, why doesn't Nash tell them, and ask your father for your hand?"

"But you see, Carter—it's really hard to explain—but you see—the Nashs are a fine family and very rich—"

"Yes, you're making a fine match!"

"It isn't that—but Mr. Nash doesn't know yet whether his folks will approve. His father you know and his mother are very proud—and he's got to bring them round."

"Oh, come off, Gertie! What are you giving me? Tom Nash hasn't got the least—" He did not finish his phrase; it was too cruel. But Gertie apprehended it.

"But honestly, Carter; it's the truth, honestly!" She laid her hand confidingly on his arm, and her voice was lowered to a whisper when she said: "Carter, he does want to marry me—and he's going to—you'll see. And if you went away now—he'd suspect, well—you know."

He looked at her a moment, and then said:

"You mean he doesn't—know?"

"Not a thing! He doesn't even suspect."

He looked her in the eyes and he saw that she was sincere. He gave a little laugh, which he trusted was sufficiently sardonic, and then said:

"Well, I hope you will be happy."

"And you, Carter," she answered. "I hope you will."

He gave again that sardonic laugh, and said:

"Happy? Me?"

"Yes, you. You'll find some nice girl some day, and marry her."

"Oh no, thank you! No marriage for me!" He looked away, solemnly, waited impressively, and then recited in a sad tone:

> " 'No more, no more, oh, never more on me
> The freshness of the heart can fall like dew.' "[24]

Gertie looked at him a moment with naive admiration, and then said:

"Carter, I think that's perfectly lovely! Did you make it up yourself?"

XX

The necessity, however, for Carter to continue to act a part in that household did not last very long. It was only two or three days later that, on going downstairs one morning he felt instantly that something had gone wrong, and on entering the dining-room he saw that Mrs. Grow had been crying. Grow was already at his breakfast of bacon and corn-pone. Gertie was not there.

"Where's Miss Gertrude?" Carter asked, in an impulse he regretted even as he yielded to it, for he realized that he knew, essentially, all that need be known—doubtless more than they knew. For when he blurted out his question Mrs. Grow burst into tears again, gathered up her apron, and fled sobbing to the kitchen. Grow sat there in silence, filling his mouth with corn-pone, taking a noisy sup of coffee on top of it, and never saying a word. But Carter, who knew all of Grow's moods by this time, saw that he was deeply moved and, naturally in such a case, would not trust himself to speak. Carter felt embarrassed and confused; this family trouble imposed on him at least a reticence, and, without another word, he stepped out on the back porch.

Dolly D. must have heard his step for she began to whinny, and, glad of the insistence of a common task, he drew a bucket of water at the well and went to the stable . . . .

When he got back to the house Grow was just finishing his breakfast. He drained the final drop of coffee from his cup, wiped his lips with his hand, got up from the table, and, as though Carter had asked his question that very minute, instead of a quarter of an hour before, he said:

"She's run off with young Nash." And, as though he could trust himself to say no more, he added: "The woman'll tell you," and abruptly left the room.

Mrs. Grow came in with a platter of newly fried bacon and hot corn-pone, and said:

"I guess you'll want your breakfas' anyhow."

She sat down at table and poured out another cup of coffee for herself; she was always ready for another cup of coffee, on the theory that "A body's got to keep their strength up."

Carter had never seen her so forlorn, so woe-begone and dragged down. She had ceased weeping, but her eyes were red and swollen, and likely to weep again at any moment, and her hair fell unkempt on her neck in the untidy abandon of despair.

"Yes, she's gone!" she sighed.

"When did she go?"

"Last night some time. I don't jus' exac'ly know what time. I heerd her stirrin' in the night, but I didn' pay no attention; you know how she could steal about o' night, making' no more noise nor a cat. It must 'a' been then that she slipped out; I wasn't hardly wide awake but jus' dozin' like. This mornin' I found a note from her; she'd stuck it'n under the door of our bedroom. Le's see, yes, I've got it."

She pulled up her apron and fumbled in the pocket of her dress. "Yes, here 'tis." She handed a folded sheet across the table to Carter, and he read:

"Dear Ma:
    "I've gone away with Mr. Nash to get married in Cincinnati. He thinks it's better that way than to be married here. I'll write you at Cin. as soon as we are married. Don't worry.
                "Your loving dau.
                        G."

He glanced at the note and handed it back to Mrs. Grow without a word.

"What do you think of that, now?" she appealed to him. "Ain't it awful? Did you ever dream of such a thing as them two eloping?"

"I never expected that," he could say truthfully.

"Nor me either. Of course, it comes hard on you, I know that, happening suddent like the way it has. I didn't even know she knowed Mr. Nash."

He noticed the scrupulous deference in her use of the "Mr."

"Did she know him long?" she asked.

"I don't know. She skated with him on the factory pond during the cold snap."

"I want to know! Well, that explains it! I seen the' was something that had gone wrong betwixt her and you, but I didn't know adzactly what. I jes' set it down to some little tiff or other, like lovers is al'ays havin'. I 'lowed it would come all right with time. I was that sorry! I did so want that her and you should get married. I thought it was as good as settled."

She paused, and wagged her grey, unkempt head mournfully. Then she strained a few last drops of coffee from the pot into her cup, drank it, and said, philosophically: "Well, what's done's done."

"I'm sorry for you and Mr. Grow, ma'am," Carter said, feeling that he should say something.

"Well, it's hard on all of us. Course, the Nashs are a fine fambly, there's that about it. They're the best they is. And rich! Laws a'mighty! It'll be a fine thing for Gertie, and I believe, from all I've heerd tell, that Mr. Nash is a good, steady, clean-livin' young man. I don't know why he wanted to elope onless it was because he hated the fuss of a weddin'; or mebbe it 'as because he thought that Grow couldn't afford the expense of a grand weddin'; I've thought of that, too. We're poor folks, I know, but we're just as good as anybody. Grow's fambly back East where he come from was the best they was, and my fambly, well, we never give in to nobody. I hope Colonel Nash will forgive him. Do you think he will? He seems such a kind man like; he was awful per-lite to Grow the other night, I must say, when they held their debate, though for my part I wish Grow wouldn't meddle in that question; I don't see as it's likely to do us any good. You think he'll forgive him, don't you?"

"Why, I reckon so; I certainly hope so, ma'am."

"I 'spect they'll want to set up housekeeping in a home of their own when they get back from Cincinnati, don't you?"

"I reckon," said Carter. He had finished his breakfast, and longed to get away. But Mrs. Grow held him. She looked at him closely, appealingly, an instant, as though there were on her heart a question she feared to put.

"Carter," she said, and she glanced about over her shoulder, fearfully, as if even there she might be overheard. "Carter— you think he'll marry her, don't you? as soon as they get to Cincinnati?"

He looked her in the eyes and saw how deep the trouble was that lay there; he felt an immense pity for her, and he said:

"Of course. Why shouldn't he?"

But the word "Cincinnati" brought up a vision—the dark streets near the river, and the girl with the dark eyes; and her "Howdy Honey!" He thought of Gertie, and shuddered. He rose from the table.

"I wouldn't worry about it now, Mrs. Grow, if I were you. It'll all come right. Let's hope for the best."

She burst into tears, and Carter went round the table, laid his hand on her shoulder, and said:

"Don't cry, Mrs. Grow, don't. It'll turn out all right."

She dried her eyes, and said:

"Oh Carter, you don't know what it means to have someone to talk to! You don't know! It's hard to talk to Grow. He's the best man in the world, but you know how he is. He won't talk about it. He won't let it be mentioned. Trouble affects some people dif-ferent. He feels as bad as me, but he shuts it up inside him and won't let it out. He's proud—he's proud! When I said to him this morning that we're just as good as the Nashs, he flew out at me and said that my saying that only showed I had my doubts. But you—you understand a body."

She pressed her apron to her swollen eyes to dry her tears. Then she said:

"Carter, don't leave us yet awhile like you said you would the other night? You won't, will you? It'd only add to the talk—there's bound to be talk now anyway it turns out—and then—it'd be so lonely now without you!"

XXI

The silent and austere Grow was almost as depressing a companion as his voluble and tearful wife. All that day he never said a word. He sat at his desk as usual, with his paper in his hand, but he did not read; he merely sat and stared over his spectacles at nothing. The store was filled with a silence that fairly throbbed with anxiety and concern. Carter stood in the front doorway, gazing out into the blank and sprawling square, as silent almost as the store itself. But the silence of the Square was more endurable than the silence of the store, for it was an empty silence, untroubled, on that spring morning, by human preoccupation with the larger issues of life. A few people drifted aimlessly in and out of the shops that occupied the lower storeys of its squat wooden buildings, or sauntered in provincial indolence along the walks, but their movements had no more interest or significance than the yoke of oxen that, with slow and deliberate steps, their great heads swaying low and rhythmically under their heavy yoke, trundled a cart across the Square.

No one came into the store. Indeed, ever since the night of the debate, customers had been growing fewer and fewer, and Grow was already beginning to pay the penalty of espousing, publicly and sincerely, an unpopular cause. And when it became known that his daughter had eloped, he would doubtless suffer still more in public disfavour. Looking out into that dull, flat Square, a symbol of life in general in Macochee, Carter longed to get away, to go somewhere else. But he must get away from the store, at any rate, for a few moments at least; he couldn't stand it if he didn't.

"I'll just step over to the post-office a minute," he said to Grow, who merely gave a grunt which Carter chose to construe as permission.

He went to the post-office and then walked towards the Court House, and on the way, just as he had expected, he met Fowler Brunton, and as they walked to Joe Tappan's they talked of the sensational news that already was flying from mouth to mouth all over town. Brunton, Carter observed, was trying to pump him; Nash, Brunton said, had not been seen in public lately, and someone had said it was because he had a black eye; Brunton wondered where Nash had got it. But Carter was wary, and would tell Brunton little that he did not already know. It was embarrassing to discuss the subject at all, even with Brunton, and yet it was a subject not just then to be avoided.

"I don't even know how or where they went," said Carter in response to one of Brunton's leading questions.

"They say," said Brunton, "that Tom took one of his father's horses and a buggy, and drove to Springfield. Is the old man going to pursue them?"

"I don't think so."

"I guess if any irate parent pursues them it will be old Nash," Brunton laughed, rather cynically, and the innuendo had its sting, even for Carter, who knew how the Grows were suffering.

"They might be married before he could overtake them," said Carter.

"Married!" exclaimed Brunton. "What in hell would he want to marry her for? There's no necessity for doing that. In fact, everybody wonders why he even took the trouble to go away with her at all. Of course, Tom Nash is all kinds of a damn fool, and a sort of sap-head, but I don't believe he'd be fool enough to marry a girl like that—unless she had a baby and swore it on him under the bastardy act. And even then, he could buy her off."

Carter was troubled and humiliated. He could feel Brunton's eyes upon him in suspicious enquiry, and he tried for, and flattered himself that he had achieved, an air of indifference that would admit no personal relation to the case or any interest in it.

"The ones I feel sorry for," he said, "are Mr. and Mrs. Grow. They're all broken up, Mrs. Grow crying all the time and he frozen up tight as ice, and suffering, no doubt, the worse of the two."

"Poor old Grow!" said Brunton. "I feel sorry for him, too. I felt sorry for him the other night, and I felt sorry when everybody turned on him. And now this thing happens. Let's have another drink."

They were standing at Tappan's bar, and when Brunton made this convivial proposal, he was answered by a voice behind him.

136

"A most excellent thing to do, provided you don't allow it to become a fixed habit."

And there was Giles Paten.

"What'll you have?" asked Brunton.

Old Giles, with an air of originality, said that he would take a little of the hair of the dog that had bitten him; Carter, in a swaggering loyalty to Kentucky, said: "Bourbon," while Brunton called for rye. And whilst Tappan set out the bottles and glasses, Brunton leant over towards Carter and, in a confidential tone, said:

"For my part, I hope Gertie lands him, if that's what she took him away for. It would lower the Nash pride, for you know, Blair, 'way down deep in my heart I'm ag'in the rich. And so, here's to Gertie all the same!"

Old Giles filled his small tumbler to the brim and, holding it up, said in his solemn, whiskified voice:

" 'Tis but a drop,' the father said, and gave it to his son."

They clinked their glasses and drank. Inevitably they talked of little else than the flight of Gertie and Nash, and Paten and Brunton speculated on the causes that might have led Nash to take a course that seemed to them so unnecessary. Carter listened whilst they talked. He was troubled and humiliated to learn that Gertie's reputation had been of a sort to make such an unflattering question possible; if she was that kind of girl, then he had been a fool. But he had this consolation: Nash had been a greater fool. Looking back he could see now that Gertie had been flattered by Nash's attentions, and perhaps, as she had intimated, she had been able to deceive him and lure him into marriage as the only way of possessing her. These questions, and the now still more important question whether Nash would marry her or not, kept running through Carter's mind as they stood there at that bar and drank.

He was, of course, no such accustomed toper as old Paten, who went to bed drunk every night, nor was he able, as yet, to carry his liquor as well as Brunton, so that before long he realized that he was getting somewhat fuddled. But some canny inner sense warned him not to show it, and above all to hold his tongue, especially when Gertie's name came up in the noisy conversation.

As he stood at the bar, drinking and listening to the loud talk, he was aware of a double consciousness, or personality, within him; one consciousness, sly and canny, looked on with a satirical wisdom at the other, saying, from time to time: "Look out! You're getting drunk! Be careful! Remember you've got a quick temper and don't make a fool of yourself!."

But he felt that he was carrying himself very well; no one would dream that the whisky affected him any more than it did old Paten. Giles was a good old soul, genial and kind.

"By God," old Giles was saying, "I don't blame Tom for running off with her! I wish she'd run off with me! I told you once, my boy, that you didn't appreciate your good fortune in knowing such a damn fine gal."

The sly little being in Carter's mind, peeping out through one of his eyes, detected Brunton in the act of scowling, of signalling a warning to old Giles; the sly little being chuckled and said to his drunken companion: "Look out, now! Just pretend not to notice it!"

And so Carter only smiled, enigmatically, so that old Giles wouldn't know what he was thinking.

It was noon, and time to go home to dinner. No use to go back to the store now! But he didn't care. The store might go hang. Let old Grow run his old store. He wasn't going to stay in the store any longer and be a poor clerk. No, sir, not by a damn sight. He was going to be admitted to the bar in a few weeks more and be a lawyer—Attorney and Counsellor-at-Law and Solicitor in Chancery—just like good old Giles and good old Fowler. Fowler was his friend; he loved Fowler, his friend for life, come what would! He was free now; he suddenly realized that stupendous fact; free of the store, and best of all, free of Gertie! For there was no good denying it, when a fellow got mixed up with a girl in that way, or in any way, he was a slave; couldn't call his soul his own; couldn't even go out o' nights; couldn't see another fellow even look at her without getting mad. What a fool a woman made of a man to be sure!

When he got home Mrs. Grow came running to meet him and asked anxiously:

"Any news?"

But he evaded her and went up to his room. He must lie down a minute before dinner ... When he awoke it was nearly dark. He lay a moment, trying to collect his scattered senses ... Oh yes; he remembered. He had got a little drunk at Tappan's; had come home and lain down; he had fallen asleep and slept all afternoon. Then he heard voices somewhere in the house, men's voices, in a low bass rumble of conversation. For a moment he couldn't decide where the voices came from; it was always hard to tell where sounds came from; he decided, however, that they came from the little parlour downstairs. One of the voices sounded like Grow's; yes, it was Grow; he had a caller. But who? After a while the parlour door opened; Grow was showing his caller out.

"Good-night, Colonel. I thank you for your visit."

"Good-night, Mr. Grow. My respects, if you please, to your lady."

Carter leapt from his bed and went to his window, and looked down into the street. Yes, it was Colonel Nash. The purpose of his visit, however, or what passed between him and Grow in the intimacy of that closed parlour, were secrets that, so far as Carter knew, never transpired. Mrs. Grow was immensely flattered by the visit, but if she knew why the Colonel had come, she never let on to Carter. As for Grow, he never mentioned the visit so far as Carter knew, though Carter felt, by some subtle apprehension, that the visit had, in a way, comforted him and salved his wounded pride.

As the days passed and no word came from Gertie, Mrs. Grow spoke less and less of her daughter to Carter; the extravagant hopes she had built on Gertie's escapade gradually began to fail, and finally she must have given them up altogether, for she, like Grow, ceased to speak of Gertie, and became almost as moody and silent as her husband. She traipsed about at her household work in an untidy state that became more and more dishevelled, her hair falling from its fastenings, her skirt sagging and gaping behind, showing a strip of white chemise between the band and the bodice; in short, a forlorn and depressing slattern. Then, the meals were not what they once had been; she took no interest in her cooking, and Carter who had pitied her at first now began to resent her neglect, and soon to dislike, almost to hate her.

It was not much more cheerful at the store. Trade which had fallen off ever since Grow's unfortunate debate with Colonel Nash, showed an even more lamentable decline since the scandalous elopement of Grow's daughter with the scion of the nobler house. There was much sympathy for Colonel and Mrs. Nash, but scarcely a word of pity for Mr. and Mrs. Grow. In short, the fortunes of the house of Grow seemed to be at a low ebb, and Carter was almost superstitiously eager to dissociate himself from them. He was determined to do so as soon as he was admitted to the bar; he had practically finished his course of reading, and was only waiting for the Supreme Court, as it made the circuit of the counties, to come to Macochee, when he would be presented by Judge Diller as a worthy candidate for examination. In the meantime, he spent his evenings with Fowler Brunton and Giles Paten, generally in the convivial atmosphere of Joe Tappan's grocery, glad of his new freedom, and congratulating himself that he was henceforth to have nothing whatever to do with females.

XXII

One morning late in the month of June, Carter was standing in the doorway of the store whence, across the Square and a little ways up the main street, he had a glimpse of the white pediment and Doric columns of the Court House. He gazed at them this morning in a less absent-minded way than usual, for now that he had been admitted to the bar, he felt a personal, almost a proprietary interest in the classic structure which was to be the scene of his forensic triumphs. But as he gazed, his attention was suddenly attracted by a sight that always had a superior interest for him—a thoroughbred horse came cantering down the street. The horse was a dark chestnut, and it was superbly ridden by a woman. She crossed the Square and drew rein before the store. Carter rushed to the kerb and, making his best bow and offering her his hand, said:

"Allow me to assist you to alight, ma'am."

She gave him, perhaps with a touch of hauteur, her gauntleted hand, leapt with a light spring to the ground, and with a formal manner, said:

"Thank you, sir."

Something in her voice thrilled him. It was low and well modulated, and its cultivated tone was familiar, arousing in him strange, almost nostalgic memories; in short, he recognized it instantly as of Virginia—far other than the throaty voices he had hardly grown accustomed to in Ohio, or the high-pitched nasal voices of the Yankees who had settled there.

"May I hitch your horse for you, ma'am?"

"If you please, sir," she said in that soft Virginia voice.

He threw the bridle-rein over the horse's head and tied it to the long hitching-rack at the kerb. She was gathering up the vast and cumbrous folds of her black riding-skirt and, with a sinuous twist of her slender, little waist, she turned and looked down to see if her skirts were quite clear of the ground, but not raised above the ankles of her riding-boots. They were, he thought, the

140

tiniest boots he had ever seen, and as he looked at her he thought that she was the tiniest girl he had ever seen, a veritable little fairy queen, in fact. Her waist, in its tight-fitting black habit of innumerable gores, was so slender that he could have spanned it with his two hands, and her little head with the stiff riding-hat perched on top of its thick coils of dark hair, hardly came to his shoulder. As she gathered her voluminous riding-skirt in her left hand and, evidently satisfied with her self-inspection, looked up at him, he had, almost for the first time, a good look at her face. She couldn't have been twenty, and yet that slender, oval little face with its white skin, its blue eyes, had the commanding dignity, the pride, the aloofness, of a woman twice as old and used to the world. In fact, this slender, delicate little horsewoman bore herself with the grand manner of a great lady.

As they entered the store, Carter asked:

"May I be of any service to you, ma'am?"

She looked about the store, and then raising her blue eyes to Carter, she said:

"I believe not, thank you, sir. Is the elder Mr. Grow here—that is the name, is it not?"

"That is the name of the proprietor, ma'am," Carter said; and, not caring to be taken for Grow's son, hastened to add: "My name is Blair—Carter Blair."

"Ah?" she said, as though this interesting distinction were not of prime importance. "I prefer to be waited on by Mr. Grow."

The rather pale little face, Carter noted, suddenly blushed, but without softening her dismissal of him, she proceeded at once to the back of the store whence Grow emerged, thrusting his glasses up on his forehead. The young lady approached with the confidence one might feel in a sober and ageing man, and made her wants known in a voice so low that Carter could not hear what she said. Grow, in his uncertainty about the disposal of his own stock, scowled a little, scratched his head reflectively, and then, scanning the labels on the shelves, began to pull down the boxes containing ladies' stockings. And Carter, feeling that it would be more delicate on his part to withdraw, went back to his station in the doorway.

But he had no vision now for the Doric columns of the Court House, or any interest in the languid life of the Square, unless, indeed, it were for the young lady's horse, impatiently pawing the cobbled gutter. He thought that he knew every horse in Macochee worth knowing, and this bald-faced chestnut gelding looked familiar. He concluded presently that he had seen it mounted by Mr. Congreve, a gentleman who lived on a large stockfarm about a mile north of town. But the identity of the horse was not important, except as it might serve to establish the identity of its fair rider, and Carter placed himself in the doorway in such a way that he might keep a fascinated eye on the young lady herself. She had drawn off her gauntlets and laid them beside her riding-whip on the counter, and her tiny hands were rummaging among the long white stockings with a swift and reckless unconcern for order that was beginning to get on Grow's nerves. Carter could not hear what the young lady said, though the pleasant tones of her voice floated to him now and then in a most agreeable, though tantalizing manner. She made Grow turn the store inside out. He hauled down box after box, and, before he could do so himself, she pulled out their contents and then, with a positive shake of her small head, flung them unfeelingly aside. It was plain that she had not found what she wanted, and finally Grow, with that undisguised contempt he had for women who did not know their own minds, said curtly:

"Well, madam, that's the best I can do for you."

He said this as though having already done all that was in human power and not finding his efforts appreciated, he would make no further attempt. But she addressed a few words to him, and he took his pencil from behind his ear and, whilst she leant over the counter to see if he got it right, and pointing with a rather imperative finger, she made him write something down on a scrap of paper. Then, drawing herself up, her tiny figure straight and trim, she drew on her gauntlets, gathered up the skirts of her riding-habit, picked up her whip, and, with an inclination of her head in Grow's direction, turned to leave the store. As she drew near, Carter's heart began to flutter with a delicious but fearful excitement. She came on, carrying her small head proudly, a certain magnificence in her manner, and when she reached the door the adoration in Carter's eyes must have touched her, for inclining her head towards him, she graciously bestowed upon him ever so slight a smile.

"May I have the honour?" he began, and since he was not instantly blasted for his presumption, he accompanied her across the pavement. He untied the horse, led him round the rack to the kerb and, passing the reins over the horse's head, placed them in her hand. She prepared to mount; and Carter, bending his knee, held his hand as a step and, when she placed her little foot in it, gave a graceful little spring, and he raised her as by a gesture to the saddle, light as a feather. Happy and exultant, he held the stirrup for her, and an instant later she had settled herself in the saddle.

"Thank you kindly, sir," she said, as she gathered up the reins. And just then the chestnut began to rear and plunge.

"Prince!" she said, speaking sharply to her mount. "Prince, behave yourself!"

Carter seized the horse by the bits, but, gathering the reins tightly in her gauntleted hand, compressed now into a diminutive fist, she said:

"You may give him his head if you please."

Carter stood aside.

"I'll bid you good-morning, sir," she said. A bright little smile flitted across the oval face, then instantly her lips were tightly compressed and, drawing her rawhide whip, she furiously lashed her mount in the flank, wheeled him about and, sitting her horse as straight as an Indian, galloped off helter-skelter across the Square. Carter stood and watched her, the galloping chestnut, the ballooning black riding-skirt, the tiny waist, the erect, flat back in the tight-fitting black bodice; he watched her in admiration until she disappeared beyond the Court House, and so from his view beyond the Methodist church.

"By God!" he exclaimed as he turned back into the store, "By God, that gal can ride!"

For some extraordinary reason Grow had come to the door to watch his client mount and ride away. He assented to Carter's opinion.

"Who is she?" asked Carter.

"I don't know," said Grow; "didn't give her name. Stranger, I guess."

"Yes—from Virginia," added Carter, impressively. "What did she want?"

"Stockings."

"Couldn't find the right kind?"

Grow shook his head.

"None small enough. She takes a 7—girl's size foot—but I don't know as a girl's leg would fit her. She's terribly particular. Wants I should write to Cincinnati and get 'em to send up some by the stage. You might send a letter down by Steve next stage, now. And you'll have a day's work cleaning up the mess she made of those stockings."

"And she didn't mention her name or tell where she's stopping?"

"No. Acted as if it was none of my business. Said she'd call again."

Carter went to the tangled pile of stockings and began to assort them. And, as he turned them over, smoothed them out, matched and assorted them, now and then he would look at the large foot intended for these pioneer women of Ohio, and then think of the tiny foot that had rested for that brief instant in his hand before she sprang, light as a bird, into the sidesaddle. No. 7! That very afternoon he wrote the letter to Messrs. Clayton & Webb at Cincinnati, and gave it into Steve Ruggle's own hands, charging him solemnly to see that it was delivered as soon as the stage reached Cincinnati. And far into the night he was engaged in composing a poem entitled: *Lines addressed to a Young Lady, for whom the Author, unknown to her, had had the honour to order a Pair of Stockings.*

XXIII

Not that he had any intention of presenting the poem to his divinity; not at all. In the first place he did not even know her name, and had he known it he should not have dared. But she had so deeply affected him by her charm, she so completely filled his waking and, indeed, his sleeping hours, that he must find some relief in expression. In short, he was in love, as it is called. Hence the poem, and that anxious scanning of the Square every day to see her ride by on the spirited chestnut.

"Who's the gal visiting the Congreves?" he asked with a sly effect of casualness of Fowler Brunton the next time he saw him.

"Damned if I know," said Brunton. "Didn't know there was one. Why?"

"Nothing. I just wondered, and thought you would know if anybody did."

Brunton glanced at Carter with a sudden suspicion, as if in Carter's words there were some hidden sting. His dark face flushed to the roots of his long black locks, which the young ladies of Macochee considered romantic; they were all sentimentally devoted to him, or ready to be. But he wouldn't so much as look at one of them. He, too, was in love—notoriously, hopelessly, in love with Sallie Congreve. And she, by all accounts, was as desperately in love with him. But the trouble was—and this is where tragedy came in—Brunton drank, and the Congreves would never consent to their daughter's marrying a man who drank.

Brunton had hardly ever mentioned Sallie Congreve to Carter; he was sensitively reticent, and often protected himself with sarcasm.

"I thought you had no longer any interest in the sex," he said.

Carter winced just a little and felt his cheeks grow hot; this sudden recalling of Gertie was distasteful; he could not bear to think of her now, or to mention her in the same breath with the unnamed divinity of whom he was so unworthy. Writing a poem, indeed, to this pure, bewitching angel on the very table on which Gertie, so short a time before, had sat and dangled her legs! It was hardly decent. He told Brunton of the young lady riding up to the store on Congreve's thoroughbred chestnut gelding.

"She's from Virginia; could tell by her voice; that's all I know—that, and that I never saw a woman with such a seat on a horse."

"God! you Kentuckians! You think more of your horses than you do of your women! To say nothing of Bourbon whisky. Let's go and get a drink. And as for this young female, I'll find out about her. Mrs. Congreve's got some Virginia relatives; maybe she's one of them."

Carter's deduction proved to be as sound as he thought it clever. Brunton dropped into the store two or three days later to report that the young lady was, indeed, a cousin of Mrs. Congreve, a kind of forty-second cousin, to be sure, but nevertheless, in Virginia, a cousin—and her name was Lucretia Harris.[25] She lived in Loudon county. And Sallie Congreve said to come out any time they felt like it; the latch-string was always out.

On Sunday afternoon, then, the two young men set out to ride to Congreve's, Carter mounted on Dolly D. and Brunton on a hack hired at a livery-stable. Carter's heart was in his mouth; he had been frightened ever since Brunton had told him that they were to go. But he had a new beaver hat, a Bolivar, the first he had ever owned (bought on tick at Green, the hatter's), and this gave him confidence—this and Dolly D., for he was certain of one thing at least, and that was that however far short he himself might fall, and even though the Bolivar itself were to fail, Dolly D. was sure to make a favourable impression.

The Congreve stock-farm lay a mile or so north of Macochee on a soft dirt road that ran as straight as surveying instruments could lay it out through a country that had hardly been reclaimed as yet from its original wildness; patches of dense forest still remained, though marked for wanton and pitiless destruction by gaunt, girdled trees and blackened stumps in fields bounded by zigzag rail fences. The Indian corn was already high in some of them, and in some the yellow wheat was almost ready for the cradlers. They rode along at a hard canter; the dust raised by the horses' hooves quivered in the hot air and powdered the riders' garments, and Carter was relieved when they came to the edge of a green pasture in which mares with their long-legged colts were grazing, and Brunton, pointing, said that that was Congreve's. They turned in at a whitewashed gate and rode through an apple orchard up to a wide low house, part of which, the original structure, had been built of hewn logs, though to this a more pretentious frame structure had been added. There was a long, low verandah, and through a wide front door they caught a glimpse of the dim, cool interior of the hall. The rambling house had a comfortable hospitable look, but no one was in sight. They dismounted, tied their horses to the horse-rail, and went up to the door. Brunton sounded the knocker, and then sat down in one of the rocking-chairs on the verandah, took off his hat, and mopped his face with his handkerchief.

"Might as well sit down and take it easy," he advised Carter. "Ladies always make you wait when you call; it's a strict social rule. They are supposed to be lying down, and have to get up and dress from their stays out."

They waited.

"Haven't they got a nigger?" asked Carter.

"Yes, three. But they're lying down, too."

After a while there was a step in the hall, and Sallie Congreve appeared.

"Oh!" she exclaimed, as in surprise. "It's you, is it, Mr. Brunton?"

"Yes, it's me; and this is my friend, the Honourable Carter Blair."

They laughed, and Carter made his bow to the tall, fair girl who extended her hand. There was a merry expression in her eyes, which were blue as cornflowers. He looked in vain for the sad and tragic expression he had expected to find in one with such a romance in her life. Doubtless she was doing her best to hide it heroically.

"Mamma and Cousin Lucretia will be down presently. They were not quite ready." And then she turned to Carter and said: "I believe you are a recent comer to Macochee, Mr. Blair. How do you like Ohio?"

"Very well, thank you."

Carter, as usual in social emergencies, felt a little embarrassed and tongue-tied. When people talked like that it always sounded

146

trivial, affected and insincere. If they had anything important, or new and startling, or funny to say, let them say it; if they hadn't, then they'd better keep still. But "How do you like Ohio?"— what sense was there in that? Miss Sallie might be considered good-looking by some; but she was too big, too much on the order of a heavy dragoon. Her ankle, just showing in its white stocking amidst the flounces of her skirts, was too large; no No. 7 there! He was sure that she didn't like him; she didn't think he was anybody. The way she said "a recent comer to Macochee" had shown him that. How long, he should like to know, must one live in Macochee before becoming somebody? Wasn't he from Kentucky—and from Bourbon county? What more could anyone ask? It was the next best thing to coming from Virginia . . . A strange change had come over Brunton; he wasn't the same fellow at all. The moment this girl had come on the verandah he had become another person entirely. He was showing off, that was it. And neither Miss Sallie nor Brunton was interested in him; they were interested in each other; they were carrying on a kind of conversation without words; the words that they spoke in this general, this silly, giggling, three-cornered conversation meant nothing at all. And so, gradually, Carter dropped out of the three-cornered conversation and sat there in silence, feeling out of it all. And the rocking-chairs in which Miss Sallie and Brunton sat began to drift, as they rocked, nearer and nearer to each other . . .

Dolly D. was restless, switching her long tail viciously and stamping irritably at the flies; the sharp, impatient noise of her hooves as they struck the ground sounded loud on the Sabbath stillness of the hot afternoon. Then she laid back her ears, thrust out her lips and began nipping at the neck of the livery hack and worrying him. And, glad of an excuse, Carter got up and leading Dolly to the far end of the rack, tied her there. Then, looking her over, he saw an enormous horse-fly on her rump, and crushed it with a sudden, loud smack of his palm.

As he walked back to the verandah he saw Miss Lucretia Harris; there she was, at last, standing in the doorway. She was all in white. Her flounced batiste skirt spreading from her small waist filled the entire doorway from side to side. A cambric handkerchief was crossed on her breast, and her hair, parted in the middle, was dressed over her ears and a curl hung on each side of her forehead.

"Oh, Cousin Lucretia," exclaimed Miss Sallie, in that artificial company voice, "oh, Cousin Lucretia; there you are! Come on out and let me present these gentlemen."

And Cousin Lucretia stepped out on the verandah and stood there whilst[26] Miss Sallie presented, first Brunton, then Carter; and as each made his best bow she acknowledged it by catching her wide skirts on each side in her fingers, making a slight inclination and a graceful step backward, but not enough to be called a curtsey, and said each time:

"I'm right pleased to make your acquaintance, sir."

The conversation at first was slightly constrained.

"Isn't Mamma coming down, Cousin Lucretia?"

"Cousin Amelia wasn't quite ready, Cousin Sallie. She hadn't finished craping."[27]

And then there was the heat, oppressive at that hour of the afternoon. As Carter gazed at Miss Lucretia sitting there in her white muslin as cool as a cucumber, he wondered how she managed it. Miss Sallie, in fact, was just by way of remarking:

"You certainly look cool, Cousin Lucretia!"

"Ladies don't feel the heat," observed Brunton, and Carter wondered how he dared.

"They do not show it, sir," Miss Lucretia replied.

She spoke in the somewhat formal and rather severe style that Carter had observed that day at the store, and it made him a little afraid of her.

"You mustn't pay any attention to what Mr. Brunton says, Cousin Lucretia," said Miss Sallie in a proprietary way. "He's a great quiz—always trying to plague us females, and is quite impertinent, though he can be right agreeable when he likes." And she smiled archly at Brunton.

They bantered one another for a moment, and then the two young ladies entered upon a reminiscent conversation from which the gentlemen were subtly excluded, a conversation that had many dark and mysterious allusions to persons and things that Brunton and Carter knew nothing about; it was carried on with a good deal of giggling, and apparently had some relation to a visit Miss Sallie had made in Virginia, and to two beaux who had come to pay their addresses and to drink tea with them at one time. One of them, it seemed, was "very agreeable, though not handsome"; the other was "homely, but a mighty worthy man—didn't you think so, Cousin Lucretia?"

"Oh, very polite and genteel; and tolerably clever."

"Clever! I never saw such a laughable creature. The minuet he danced! I was highly diverted. No wonder Cousin Betty gave him his discard. And he was her slave!"

"Cousin Betty looked so pretty and genteel in her blue lutestring."

"We played grind the bottle and hide the thimble—do you remember?"

And they laughed again.

"You see, Blair," said Brunton solemnly, "what is in store for us. Our characters will be so thoroughly canvassed and nothing left of them!"

But Carter was minding his p's and q's, and somewhat basely glad of the cover afforded by a conversation of which he could not make head or tail, for he rather dreaded being left alone with Miss Harris, as he inevitably should be in a few moments, when Miss Congreve and Brunton forgot everybody else for themselves. It would be fearful to be left alone with Miss Lucretia, but it would be delicious. He had hardly caught his breath yet, so great had been the emotion her appearance had caused him. And now Miss Sallie's and Brunton's voices having sunk to a low tone, he was practically left alone with her, and he didn't know what to say. Miss Lucretia had not given the slightest sign of ever having seen him before, and of course it was not his place to recall the incident at the store. To do so would hardly be delicate in view of the object of her visit there. Doubtless she refrained for the same reason, unless she thought that it might be embarrassing to remind him of his humble occupation. Confound it, why hadn't they told her that he was a lawyer! He wondered how he might casually bring out this important fact without seeming too boastful. He had intended to compliment her on her skill as a horsewoman, but with this assumption that they had never met before that was now impossible. And yet, though the conversation might have been said to drag at first, the thought of all this could not have been very far from her mind, for as she sat there her eyes had wandered across the gravelled drives to the horses tied to the whitewashed rail. Presently she said:

"That's a mighty fine horse there. The bay, I mean." She pointed to Dolly D. "Is it yours?"

"Yes."

"Tuckahoe, isn't it?"

"Yes."

"I didn't know they bred Tuckahoes in Ohio."

"They don't. I brought this one from Kentucky with me."

"You are from Kentucky then?"

"Yes."

"I reckoned as much—from the way you spoke. You don't speak like the people here in Ohio."

He might, he thought, have returned that compliment; it was a joy to hear her speak, no matter what she said; her voice was music—to his ear, at any rate. Compared to Miss Sallie's for instance, it was as the mocking-bird's song to the blue-jay's.

However, it was perhaps simpler to talk about horses. Miss Lucretia asked if they had races in the fall at Macochee; she admitted that she always felt a strong inclination to go to races, even stronger than her inclination to go to balls.

"I always go—when I a'n't too lazy!" She laughed a little. And so there were no races in Macochee? It was a pity.

"Yes," Carter agreed. "But if you could see our races in Kentucky!"

Oh, yes, she had heard of them. She and Cousin Sallie only the other night had had a serious conversation and decided that it was better to occupy oneself with something more serious and improving than balls, races and novel-reading.

"I have too strong a liking for novels," she confessed. "But when you have read something more serious and improving you soon grow to prefer it. That has been my experience. Do you approve of reading novels?"

"I don't disapprove of it. In fact, I like to read them. I'm very fond of Sir Walter Scott. Aren't you?"

"Oh, I admire him vastly! Have you read Miss Sedgwick's novels—*Clarence*, for instance?"[28]

Carter had never heard of Miss Sedgwick, or read any of her novels, but he said he thought he had.

"I have just finished *Hope Leslie*," Miss Harris went on. "I was much affected. Her style is most beautiful. I reckon you have read it?"

Carter had to own that he hadn't, but he intended to do so at once. The allusion to reading, however, gave him just the opening he wanted.

"I haven't had time for reading anything of late," he explained, "except law books. You see, I—well, I've been studying for the bar. But now that I am admitted, I expect to have more time for reading other things." He thought that he had brought it in rather neatly. Then he hurried on: "I'm fond of poetry. Are you?"

"Of *some* poetry," she said, significantly. "Much of it, I have been told, is hardly suitable for females."

It would be better, then, not to drag in Byron! But there were always horses.

"Are you fond of riding?"

"Oh, very! Cousin Congreve lets me have a mount, and I go for a ride out every morning when the weather is fine, and occasionally I ride out for a little airing in the evening. The horse I usu-

150

ally ride is the most hard-going horse I ever saw; it makes me very tired sometimes. I reckon your horse has a good mouth?"

"Oh, yes!" He was debating in his mind whether he might offer Dolly D. to her as a mount—he would gladly have given her outright—and whether it would be proper to ask her if he might ride with her, when Brunton spoilt everything by saying:

"Miss Lucretia, I heard a fine compliment for you. Blair said you were the finest horsewoman he had ever seen—not excepting those in Bourbon county, Kentucky."

He felt distressingly awkward, and didn't know what to say. But Miss Lucretia said promptly:

"Well, now, I am sure that was mighty civil of him, sir!"

She turned and looked at Carter with a sudden, bright little smile; he wondered if it were intended to recall the morning when he had assisted her to mount, but he could only gaze at her in hopeless adoration. And just then Mrs. Congreve having at last finished her craping and dressing, came out on the verandah. She was a large, amiable matron, with auburn hair and a pink complexion, her round arms and plump shoulders showing ruddy under the white film of her bodice. Carter had hardly been introduced to her than Congreve himself appeared, a tall, raw-boned man with sandy hair and moustache. He was in shirt-sleeves and linen pantaloons, and took his place at once at the edge of the porch, whence he could more conveniently spit the tobacco he incessantly chewed. His eye, too, soon roved to Dolly D.

"Fancy bit of horse-flesh you've got there, Mr. Blair," he said. "How old?"

"Four, sir."

"Let's have a look at her."

And he stepped off the porch and crossed the driveway. Carter felt that he ought to follow. Congreve looked her over with the critical eye of the horse-trader.

"Want to sell her?" he said finally.

"Oh, I couldn't sell her, sir!"

"Not for two hundred and fifty dollars?"

Two hundred and fifty dollars! The sum was staggering. He could live two years on $250—until he had a law practice. He could buy land—do anything. He looked at Dolly D., swallowed, and said, hastily:

"Oh no, sir! Not for anything!"

Congreve gave his good-natured laugh.

"Well, don't know as I can blame you. But if you ever do want to, why, let me know."

Then his wife called imperatively from the porch:

"Mr. Congreve! Remember the Sabbath day! And come in and put on your coat and get ready for refreshments."

Congreve laughed, took his quid in his fist and chucked it away. When they went back to the porch a negress was handing round sillabub[29] and cake and tea.

XXIV

When Carter took his leave that afternoon the young ladies both asked him to call again—Miss Harris with her small head inclined to one side, her small hand in his, and her blue eyes looking up at him with a serious expression that was part of her grave, wistful little smile. He was not sure just how long he ought to wait before calling again; he felt that he could not live a whole week without seeing her again, and so, a day or two later, business being very slack in the store, he asked Grow if he might take the morning off.

"Might as well, I guess," said Grow. "You don't seem to be good for much lately, anyhow. Seem to have something on your mind."

Carter did not mind what Grow said now; there was a kind of exultation in his breast that made him feel superior to all the minor annoyances of life, and for that matter, all its major difficulties as well. He lived for but one single object, and that was to be with Lucretia Harris; nothing else mattered now. If Grow had refused his consent, Carter would have thrown up his place then and there; he was only waiting for some good excuse to leave the Grows anyhow. He would acquire a better standing in Miss Harris's eyes, he was sure, if he were to hang out his shingle, and cease to be a mere dry-goods clerk. And he would acquire a better standing in his own if he were to have lodging in another house than that one in which he had had, well, an affair which, however difficult it was for him to regret, he should not like to have known in certain quarters. But it was hard to leave the Grows without hurting their feelings; the only thing he could think of was to pay a visit to his kin in Kentucky whom he hadn't seen for a year; he would stop on the way to show himself to Tom Corwin, and when he came back, board with Mrs. Brewster, where Brunton lived. But he couldn't leave so long as Miss Harris was visiting the Congreves.

And so this morning Grow having let him off, he went home, saddled Dolly D., and by a roundabout way, circled the town to the eastward and came out on the main road not far from Congreves. Then he allowed Dolly D. to choose her own gait. And it was not long before he was rewarded; there was Miss Harris, riding to town on the chestnut gelding. Miss Harris was vastly surprised, and Carter pretended to be even more surprised than she. After they had exchanged civilities Carter asked if he might accompany her, and she replied:

"I shall be right pleased to have you attend me, Mr. Blair—as far as the town, where I intend to make a few purchases."

They rode on then, side by side, but as it turned out she made no purchases. She could just as well, she explained, make them the next day, and so they rode together all that morning. After that they rode together frequently. The following Sunday Carter and Brunton called again, and after that Carter would ride out to the Congreves' and make an evening call, which was the more conventional way to go a-courting. And so, before long he was definitely established, in public opinion at least, as the suitor of Miss Harris.

But in just what relation he was established in the opinion of Miss Harris, he was not at all sure. She was kind, gracious, and a little condescending, and for such a mite of a girl, she had a grand manner that was almost terrifying. She would never go riding with him deliberately and of express purpose; if she went at all it must be contrived as an accident, a happy accident, to be sure, but still, an accident. Once he ventured to ask her to go, but she was forced to decline, though with regret, because there was "no groom at Cousin Congreve's to attend them."

It filled him with despair when he thought of it. What right had he, a poor young man, a budding lawyer, a briefless barrister, what right had he to aspire to the hand of a young lady who was used to living in such grandeur in tidewater Virginia? To ask her to come out here to the wilderness of the West, to a small town and live in a cottage and do the housework herself! With those white little hands! It was absurd and presumptuous. To ask her to wait? Even though he were certain to become as great as Tom Corwin, he couldn't expect that of her!

Nevertheless, he couldn't stay away. Somehow or other he found himself at the Congreves' every evening, sitting with the family on the porch—as if the impenetrable reserve with which Miss Harris surrounded herself were not sufficient protection! They would sit there on the porch in the cool of the summer eve-

153

ning, the girls white blurs in the soft darkness. Mrs. Congreve would sit with them, and sometimes Congreve himself; he would talk horses for a while, and then get up and say he guessed he had better go to bed, and stalk into the house and up the creaking stairs, to undress in the dark.

One evening Carter and Brunton had gone to call. It was always livelier when Brunton was there, for he stood in no such awe of the young ladies as did Carter. Congreve, faithful to his principle of early to bed and early to rise, had soon withdrawn, and the negress had handed round cakes and tea. As they were eating their cake the young ladies got to giggling over something, and Miss Sallie said:

"Too bad it isn't dumb cake!"[30]

And at that her mother had said:

"Girls, don't be silly!"

Just at this moment Congreve's voice came peremptorily booming down the staircase demanding to know of his wife what she had done with his nightshirt, and Mrs. Congreve, considerably flustered, had sprung up and rustled into the house.

The two young ladies for a second or two tried to control themselves; Miss Sallie was rocking violently to and fro, her handkerchief to her mouth, trying to suppress her laughter, and though Miss Lucretia did not rock, she too was obliged to press her handkerchief to her mouth, and then they gave way and went off into gales of laughter. Miss Sallie became almost hysterical; she laughed, then stopped laughing, then laughed again worse than before. It was almost alarming. Miss Lucretia advised a sip of tea. At last Miss Sallie regained her self-control and wiped away her tears, sighed and exclaimed: "Oh dear! Oh dear!" And then they were silent for a moment, there in the darkness.

"What were we talking about?" asked Miss Sallie.

"Dumb cake—whatever that is," said Brunton.

"Oh Lucretia!" she said; "he doesn't know what dumb cake is! Think of it!"

"I'm sure you couldn't make it!" Brunton retorted.

"Don't make me laugh again!" Miss Sallie pleaded. And again addressing Miss Lucretia she went on: "I reckon he never heard of salt and egg, either."

"No, but I've heard of tying a girdle round the bedpost."[31]

"Oh, you think you're smart!"

Carter spoke to Miss Lucretia in a low voice.

"What are they talking about?" he asked.

"Things that gentlemen are not supposed to know about," she said.

In the darkness he could barely see her faint smile, but he could see her shining eyes. They were quiet for a moment, gazing at each other. The dim forms of Miss Sallie and Brunton at the other end of the porch had merged into a single blur, and their voices had sunk to a tone so low that their words were but an indistinguishable murmur, a part of the mysterious sounds that intensify the silence of the countryside at night—the shrilling of katydids and crickets, the croaking of frogs, the baying of a coon-dog at some distant farmhouse, the mournful cry of a whip-poor-will in the wood. The effect of the silence was to make the hour seem very late. The air had grown cooler, and it bore now the fragrance of the honeysuckle vine that climbed over the porch, the odour of the peonies, ghostly white in the darkness, and the aromatic scent of the spice-bushes over whose dark masses the fireflies flashed the blue lights of their fairy lamps. Miss Lucretia's oval little face was palely visible, and Carter sat and gazed at her with the fervour of the sentimentalism in which the night had steeped him. And suddenly, when the whip-poor-will called again, he thought he saw a slight shudder in the frail figure in white.

"You are feeling chilly!" he whispered in solicitous alarm. "The dew is falling!"

"No," she protested. "I'm quite all right." He could see the smile with which she said this, a wan, almost pathetic little smile. "Do you know, sometimes the night here almost frightens me. It is so still. I can imagine Indians and wolves and bears and wild cats and all kinds of terrible beasts skulking in those woods over there. I reckon you'll think it right silly of me. Of course it's only a fancy."

"It's because you come from an old State. But really it has been a long time since there has been anything like that in Ohio—a whole generation!"

"Yes, I know. I'm not really afraid. I said it was a silly fancy."

"Not silly!" he protested, "poetic. Nothing you could say or do or think would be silly." He paused, and then "Tell me," he said, "should you like to live in Ohio?"

"I don't know," she replied. "I never thought of it."

Carter felt like weeping; he didn't know why. He said nothing, but leant over, took her small hand in his and reverently kissed it. She allowed him to hold it a minute, and then slowly, gently withdrew it. They sat there a moment in that throbbing silence.

And then, all of a sudden, they were startled by a voice, the voice of Mrs. Congreve calling from her room upstairs:

"Sal-lie! Girls!"

"Whoo!" replied Miss Sallie, in a thin, high voice, with an over-sweetened rising inflection.

"Getting late!"

XXV

By a highly curious coincidence at which they could only marvel, Miss Harris and Carter happened to fall in with each other the very next morning, as they were riding along the North road just outside of Macochee. They slowed down their horses to a walk, and rode along side by side in the crisp air that tingled in the northern breeze. The horses were not quite satisfied to walk. Dolly D. was in especially high spirits that morning; she tossed her head, jingled her bits, blew through her delicate nostrils and soft lips, and sent tiny showers of fine spray flying back in the riders' faces. After they had marvelled sufficiently at their accidental meeting, and praised the fine weather of Ohio, there was a moment or two of silence and constraint. Carter thought at first that Miss Harris was slightly embarrassed, and he had never seen that proud little manner of hers compromised by such a thing as embarrassment. She seemed above such a possibility.

"I was that mortified," she confessed presently, "by what occurred last evening! You divine what I mean, do you not? I should never have thought Cousin Amelia capable of such a thing! Cousin Congreve, perhaps, yes—for he is such a quiz. But Cousin Amelia! It was not quite genteel!"

"But it was all our fault, Brunton's and mine! We ought not to have—"

"Oh, I pray you!" she interrupted him hastily. "Let us not refer to it again! It is too distressing!" And she raised her gloved hand for an instant to her eyes as if to shut out the painful memory. The influences of that evening, however, were still upon them, even in the bright sunlight of this summer morning. She raised her eyes to him with that smile which lit up her face now and then with an expression so bright, so frank, so almost childishly appealing that Carter felt he might as well take up their conversation at the very point at which it had been broken off by Cousin Amelia's inelegant intervention the night before, and propose then and there. But there was always that ticklish question of the proprieties; one false step, one slip, and he should get his discard, like the homely and laughable creature whose minuet had so highly diverted her in Virginia. Still, he had better risk it all on a single throw, than to endure this uncertainty any longer. He leant forward now, whilst that bright little smile was still lighting up her face, and began:

"I was going to ask you something last night, Miss Lucretia; I know I'm not worthy, but, now, may I pay you my humble addresses — ?"

He did not get to finish his formal little speech. The bright smile on her delicate face became more brilliant, her eyes sparkled, and saying "You'll have to catch me first, Mr. Blair!" she gave her horse a cut with her riding-whip and galloped off helter-skelter down the road.

He heard her laugh, and she was half a furlong away before he could realize what had happened. Then he spoke to his mare, and put off down the road after them. Dolly D. could run and she was soon going at her best lick; he felt exultant at the thought that he should soon overtake her. And then! He laughed. "Come on, old gal, come on!" he said to Dolly D. But the chestnut gelding could run too; and before they had covered a quarter of a mile, Carter knew, and Dolly D. knew, that they were in for a race. "Get along, honey, get along!" he urged the mare. Her hooves were drumming merrily on the dirt road, and he could hear the clods flying behind him.

And there, ahead, was the tiny figure of Miss Lucretia, with her riding-skirt billowing enormously like a balloon; she glanced back over her shoulder, and waved her riding-whip. Once he thought that she was going to put the chestnut at a rail fence, leap it, and gallop across some pasture-land—as she had spoken several times of doing—and his heart was in his mouth; the fence was too high. The chestnut galloped on, scattering clods of the soft earth in showers behind him as he went.

Dolly D. was easily good for a mile and a half at this gait, and Carter felt that she was gaining on the chestnut. No need to push her, however, just yet. It was very pleasant, very exhilarating, and capital sport, this race—and with what a prize! He would save the mare for a gallant spurt at the finish—just before they got to Congreves'. What a mare she was, this Dolly D. of his! What bottom, and a heart of steel!

And just then something happened; something had gone wrong. Miss Lucretia was trying to pull her horse up; she was swaying slightly in the saddle. Yes, she was trying to pull her horse up; he heard her cry, "Whoa Prince! Whoa!" But the hard-mouthed chestnut would not stop; he went galloping on, harder than ever. And then Miss Lucretia swayed again in the saddle.

Carter spoke to Dolly D., pressed with his knees, and she leapt forward; she thundered on and was at the chestnut's heels; the sound of her hooves, of course, made the chestnut strain forward all the harder, but now he was only a length ahead; now only half a length; and Carter saw what was the matter—the saddle-girth. He saw with relief that the chestnut had his head up in the air, sure sign that the pace was telling on him and that he was in distress, while Dolly D. had her head down; he urged her on and, riding close on the chestnut's near side, Carter caught Miss Lucretia just as the saddle slipped and turned, and raised her slight figure in his arm. She fainted. He spoke to Dolly D., and she stopped, and still holding Miss Lucretia, Carter managed to dismount. The chestnut bolted on down the road towards the Congreves'.

Carter knelt beside the road, the girl's head resting on his knee. He fanned her with his hat—he called her name—and presently her eyes opened and looked up at him wonderingly an instant, and then with understanding.

"Oh, Miss Lucretia—" he began.

But the horsewoman in her spoke first.

"It wasn't my fault, Mr. Blair; the saddle-girth broke."

XXVI

When Carter, still anxious about Miss Lucretia, rode out to Congreves' that evening, he was delighted to find her on the porch all alone, and none the worse for her adventure of the morning.

"It was nothing," she protested, and laughed at his lingering anxiety.

"But it might have been! It was a close run thing!"

They spoke in the lowest tones, there in the dusk, fearing at any moment the members of the family might hear them and come out.

"The saddle slipped, that was all. It's over now. There is no use to discuss it further."

"But you haven't answered my question."

"Your question?"

158

"The one I asked you just before you dashed away. You told me to catch you—and I caught you!"

"Well?"

She was smiling up at him again, and he took her in his arms. She hid her face for an instant against his shoulder, and then whispered:

"You may ask my father, Mr. Blair."

Then she looked about prudently over her shoulder, as if to make certain that no one was in sight, raised her face to his and said:

"Just one!"

He kissed her, and then Miss Sallie appeared, to be followed soon by the others of the family, so that the chance of being alone was over for that evening. The talk, of course, was all of the narrow escape of the morning, and it came out that the girths had not broken in the race, but had merely been insufficiently tightened. Miss Lucretia had not been prevented from having her afternoon ride; in fact, as soon as the sun had got low in the west and the afternoon breeze had begun to cool the air, Miss Lucretia had ordered the chestnut to be saddled again and gone for a gallop.

"Damn plucky, eh Blair?" said Congreve.

"A perfect Trojan!" exclaimed Carter fervently.

"It will never do to let a horse think he has gotten the best of you," explained Miss Lucretia.

"Damn good horse sense, that," observed Congreve.

"Mr. Congreve," said Mrs. Congreve, "it isn't genteel to swear in the presence of ladies. I wish you wouldn't do it."

Miss Lucretia had given Carter permission to speak to her father, and it was agreed that, as soon as she returned to her home in the course of the summer, Carter should set out on Dolly D., claim his bride, and when they had been married, mount his wife on a pillion behind him, cross the mountains into Kentucky, visit the Blairs in Bourbon county, and then come on to Ohio in the fall. The pillion was the approved way for men to bring their wives from the East into the Ohio country, though Miss Lucretia thought it was going out of fashion. However, she was not averse to the plan; the pillion was cheaper than the stage, and they must economize.

"And your mare has already shown that she can carry double," said Miss Lucretia.

Carter had felt rather guilty about the way he had been neglecting his duties in the store of late. He felt rather sorry, too, for old Grow, first because Grow was about to lose him, and then because Grow had been losing business more and more. In the capricious and whimsical way in which the fates deal with mortals, having no more regard for justice than the devil himself, his own fortunes had been soaring whilst poor old Grow's had been declining. And every bit of bad luck that Grow had, seemed to mean just so much more good luck for him. Well, he couldn't help it; he himself, of course, was intrinsically more deserving than Grow. And bad luck didn't matter so much to Grow anyhow, for Grow was getting to be an old man. Carter, therefore, was not very much surprised when a few days after his engagement to Miss Lucretia, Grow, instead of reproaching him for neglecting his duties, told him that he was going to sell out to a Yankee—a man named Spooner from Connecticut; he was compelled to; during the panic of 1837 business had gone completely to the dogs. Carter tried to appear sympathetic, but secretly he was delighted, since this relieved him of the painful necessity of announcing their separation himself.

As if the hard times weren't enough, some malignant and remorseless fate seemed to pursue Grow.

"Things have been going against me," he said, with a shake of his head, more melancholy than ever, "things have been going against me ever since that debate I had with Colonel Nash. Ever since Gertie—" Grow's voice broke on the name that he never uttered any more, and having uttered it now, he was unable to go on; his lip trembled, and he turned away. Carter felt a great pity for him, but inwardly he resented this intrusion of a painful subject, this reminder of an incident he was anxious to forget. He could tolerate now no slightest cloud on his perfect happiness.

"If I can drive any kind of advantageous bargain with Spooner," Grow went on, "I ought to clear enough to buy that small ten-acre piece a little ways west of town on the Blue Jacket road.[32] It has got a little house on it, and we can raise enough garden-truck to live on; I shall have time to devote myself to my work. I'm going to get out a paper—a paper devoted to the cause of Abolition. After all, that's my work; that's my mission, and I must be about it. It is time; yes sir, it is high time!"

He looked narrowly at Carter, and Carter felt vaguely troubled; he had no faith in this wild, impracticable scheme of Grow's, and he knew that Grow's searching eye had sought out and found the scepticism and worldly disapproval in his own heart.

"You think I'm crazy, Blair!"

"Oh, Mr. Grow, don't say that!"

160

"Oh yes, you do! I know it; I can see it!" Grow's eyes had begun to burn with a light that would enable him to see all the hidden things in men's hearts. "A man's foes are they of his own household! You believe in slavery because you were born and reared in the midst of it. Well, you are young—I make allowances. My women-folks, if they didn't exactly believe in it, were not opposed to it. They go the way of the world! Everybody in this town, everybody that counts for anything, is of the same mind. You won't find as many righteous as were found in Sodom and Gomorrha."

"I was only thinking, sir, of the difficulty of making a living on ten acres and by publishing a paper which you say yourself will be unpopular. I was thinking, too, that it would be hard on Mrs. Grow."

"Oh, I know, I know! That's what everybody will say! We are sent forth as sheep in the midst of wolves! It's always been that way! But we are told to fear not them which kill the body, but are not able to kill the soul. And so, Blair, I must go forth—even though I have neither gold nor silver nor brass in my purse, nor scrip for my journey."

The strange light was blazing in Grow's eyes. He had drawn his thin body to its full height; he seemed to have grown suddenly tall; he trembled in his fanatical exaltation; his beard wagged as he poured forth his impassioned speech, with its mixture of scriptural phrases; he pointed his long, bony forefinger at Carter, and Carter was not sure whether he had to do with a prophet or an insane man. He did not know what to say or what to do; it was embarrassing to be thus harangued, there, almost one might say, in public. Carter longed to get away, but he stood patiently listening to what Grow was saying, and wishing that someone would come in so that Grow would have to stop. But it was not often that anyone came into the store any more.

Finally, however, Grow stopped, and after a pause he said, in another and more human tone:

"Carter,"—he had never addressed him by his Christian name before—"Carter, you've been a good boy since you worked for me. You've been somewhat like a son to me. I had hoped—but no matter now; that's gone. If you want to stay on with this man Spooner when he takes over the business, you can. I've given you a good name to him. But I guess you'll want to practise law now."

"Yes, sir."

"Well, I can't blame you. I wish you success, and I think you'll

161

go far. But there's one thing I want to say to you. You oughtn't to drink. You oughtn't to associate with that fellow Brunton, and those other companions of yours. Next after slavery whisky is the great curse of our land. It ought to be prohibited. For some reason lawyers seem to think they ought to drink more than other people. They think it's smart to get drunk and a proof that they are brilliant."

Carter thought that he was in for a temperance lecture, for Grow was almost as fanatical on that subject as he was on slavery. But Grow suddenly growing sententious again merely said:

"I suppose they *do* feel more brilliant when they're drunk."

And then he dropped the matter and said no more.

Three or four days later, coming into the store one morning at nine o'clock, Carter found Spooner, the Yankee who was to buy the store, there with Grow. They had been going over the terms of the sale, discussing the value of the stock and of the lease and the goodwill. Spooner who, of course, had made inquiries, was contending that the goodwill was worth nothing, and Carter could see that Grow was in a bad temper; his hair and beard were bristling angrily, and he was talking in a loud voice. Spooner was as tall and thin as Grow, but several years younger; he had dark reddish hair and a wisp of red beard on his chin, his upper lip being smooth-shaven. Carter, who in any event would have contemned him as a Yankee, liked him no better for his looks, and when Grow, in his surly fashion had introduced them, and Spooner looked up in his brisk businesslike way, and in his Yankee nasal twang, began: "Well, young man!" Carter fairly hated him.

"Well, young man," twanged Spooner, "ain't you getting down to business rather late? When I take over this store, it's going to be run strictly on modern lines, and if you expect to work for me, you'll have to keep better hours."

Carter's temper flared up at once.

"Run your store on any lines you damn please!" he retorted. "Who in hell wants to work for you? I'm sure I don't!"

"Wal, I want to know!" exclaimed Spooner.

XXVII

Grow and the Yankee struck a bargain, though they were nearly a week in doing so, and even then, the negotiations had to be suspended for the last two days to enable Grow to attend an Anti-Slavery Convention at

Granville, a village about twenty miles from Macochee, a hotbed of Abolition and a station on the Underground Railroad. Grow was deeply interested in this convention, and had been looking forward to it eagerly; he expected to meet there and confer with some of the leading lights in the movement, men from Oberlin and other towns in New Connecticut where, because that part of the State had been settled by people from New England, the Anti-Slavery sentiment was strongest and most aggressively militant. To Grow the occasion had a deep, almost a religious significance; in his mind it celebrated his release from uncongenial labours, and his consecration to the cause to which henceforward he was to devote his life. He would allow nothing to stand in the way of his going; Spooner would simply have to wait until he could get back before finally closing up the contract. He would be gone, he guessed, two days, and he asked Carter to look after the store in his absence. But this was not all. Grow asked him, as a last favour, to lend him Dolly D. to carry him to Granville and back. Grow was somewhat embarrassed in making this request. He was a proud man, as Carter knew, and not given to asking favours of anybody.

"The fact is," Grow explained, with something almost like shame, "I'm not any too flush of ready cash right now."

"Why, certainly, Mr. Grow, if it will be of the slightest service."

Carter hastened to consent in order to spare Grow and himself pain. But he had his misgivings; no one had ever ridden Dolly D. but himself; she was the most highly-prized of his possessions, in fact, his one valuable possession, and his proprietorial feeling was something more than the pride of ownership, it was a jealous affection. Besides, Grow was no horseman, and then—an abolition meeting! He didn't like the idea; there was something demeaning in it. Miss Lucretia, he was sure, would not consider it genteel; he should be ashamed to tell her. However, there was nothing to be done. He had given his consent and if he had it all to do over, why, he would give it again.

And so the next afternoon, after reiterating his minute instructions about feed and water and gaits, he helped Grow to mount, adjusted the stirrup-straps, and, with a sinking of the heart, watched him ride away, the most ungainly and ridiculous figure, surely, ever seen on horseback.

That evening he walked out to Congreves'.

"But your mare, Mr. Blair?" asked Miss Lucretia in surprise and alarm. "I trust nothing—"

"Oh no!" he hastened to reassure her, "I lent her to Mr. Grow to ride over to Granville. He has got to attend a meeting of some sort or other over there."

The following evening after a long, hot, tedious day in the store (with Spooner constantly hanging about, prying and poking into everything and pestering him with questions in that twanging Yankee voice) Carter closed up somewhat earlier than usual and went home with half a hope that Grow might have got there before him. But no Grow and no word of him. Mrs. Grow had prepared the supper and was keeping it hot for him on the back of the stove, and every few minutes she would rush out to the front porch and down to the front gate to see if there was any sign of her husband. She was in a nervous and irritable state. The day had been one of those hot, sultry days in Ohio that wear the nerves to a frazzle. The lifeless air, saturated with moisture, clung to the skin like a sweat-soaked garment of sticky wool; there was not a breath of air, and the heat became more oppressive as the day declined. A thunderstorm was brewing and, while its rain would be welcome, people were filled with dread by the electric menace of its sinister clouds.

"Feels like we was going to have another tornado like the one we had seven years ago," said Mrs. Grow. "You wouldn't remember it, not bein' here, but I do. It raised three children high in the air and killed 'em, knocked off the steeple of the Methodist church, and jus' blew the feathers offen our chickens.[33] Dear me! I wisht Ethan would come! He'd ought to be here by now. What do you s'pose is keeping him?"

"I don't know," said Carter, who was anxious and troubled himself.

"I wonder if your horse could have run away and throwed him!"

"She wouldn't throw anyone who treated her right, and knew how to ride," Carter replied rather testily. The heat and this waiting had affected his nerves too, and he wouldn't have her blaming Dolly D.

Mrs. Grow went out to the front gate again, and presently dragged back, looking more anxious and troubled than ever.

"Nary a sign of hide or hair of him," she said, shaking her frowsy head mournfully.

Then Carter, unable to endure the suspense any longer, went out to the gate himself and hung over it, looking down the road. And after a long while he saw a figure on horseback turning in from Main Street. He rushed back to the front door and shouted into the house: "He's coming, Mrs. Grow!" and then went back to his post of observation at the gate. And as he did so, he heard a noise, the noise of a hostile and ribald crowd, and looking down the road he saw a great crowd of men and boys, following the figure on horseback. The crowd trooped along in the dust of the road, jeering, hooting, and howling; the noise attracted the residents of the quiet street, and they came running out from their supper-tables, as Mrs. Grow came running out to join Carter. The horseman and the mob that pursued him drew nearer; they could hear the howls of cruel, derisive, inhuman laughter, and presently they could hear a shout of:

"Bobolitionist! Bobolitionist!"

They were drawing near now, near enough for Carter to see... Grow, sitting his mount in that ungainly fashion, his long legs hanging almost limp at his horse's sides, his body bent forward, his back bowed, his head hanging in weariness and silent endurance... And Dolly D.? Could that be Dolly D., that slow, shambling nag, with head hanging low, and ears drooping in defeat? Both horse and rider were covered with dust and stained with yellow splotches. And so Grow, home from the Anti-Slavery Convention, rode up to his own door. Mrs. Grow covered her face with her hands and began to cry. And the mob, as Grow drew rein, shouted again:

"Bobolitionist! Bobolitionist!"

Carter gazed; he saw Grow, smeared with eggs from head to foot, turn half way round in the saddle to face his tormentors; Grow began to say something to them, but the words were drowned by the shouts of the mob. He saw Grow's lips moving, his thin beard wagging. But he had no eyes for Grow now. He was looking at Dolly D., standing there, her head down, her sides heaving, her coat smeared and matted with eggs and thick with dust. Grow's wife had gone out to him and he had dismounted, his distracted and hysterical wife wringing her hands and trying to aid him. And now that Grow had dismounted Carter could see Dolly D. She was trembling violently: he looked and saw that her mane was gone, hacked off in great ugly patches, and, in place of her flowing, splendid tail, there was now but a short, fleshy stump, grey like a rat's tail, and with no more hair on it, and it was bleeding where the mob had crudely shaved it that day. He gazed at it a moment in dumb horror. Dolly D., his beautiful Tuckahoe mare, thus horribly mutilated and ruined! He could not realize it, could not accept it as a fact. He could only gaze in stupefaction.

The crowd for the moment was fallen silent. They stood, looking at Carter. And as Carter took his eyes at last from his ruined horse, he glanced about him, at Grow, at the faces of neighbours who had come up in curiosity, and when they saw what had happened had gathered round in sympathy; then looked at the crowd that had followed Grow home, and his eyes rested on the sallow face of [   ], the leader of the rowdies from the Bottoms; the bully looked at him with an inane leer of triumph. And suddenly, beside himself with rage, Carter struck [   ] a blow on the jaw and stretched him out cold and stunned in the road. He heard Grow shout at him:

"It wasn't they that did it! It was the mob at Granville!"

But what difference did that make? Carter sprang into the midst of the other rowdies.

"It wasn't us! It wasn't us!" they cried. But he knocked two more of them down. And then, having a belly full, the crowd, or the ruffians from the Bottoms at least, withdrew.

And Carter returned to Dolly D. and she nuzzled her nose into his hand. Grow came up to him and said:

"Too bad it had to happen, Blair. But it's a sacrifice in a good cause."

He would not trust himself to speak to Grow just then. He led Dolly D. round to the stable, and when she stood once more in her stall he put his arms about her neck and wept.

XXVIII

When Carter had groomed Dolly D. and done what he could to dress the cuts on her fleshy tail, he went into the house to find Grow, rid of his egg-stained garments, bathed and combed and dressed in fresh linen, sitting at the supper-table. His wife was adjuring him to "eat something," for he "must keep up his strength"—as indeed he must if his new life were to consist in such adventures as that through which he had passed that day. She urged Carter to eat too, but he was too sickened by what had happened, too much distressed by the sorry state in which Dolly D. had been brought back, to be able to eat. And Grow had no more appetite than he, though his want of it came from no depression of spirits, but rather from a peculiar excitement. As he talked of his adventure, Carter noted a certain exaltation in him, a kind of pride, and he realized that Grow was already enjoying the meed of martyrdom. His account of the day's events was brief, and it could not have been too brief for Carter, who had learnt all that he need know by one glance at his ruined mare. It was no such consolation to him as it was to

Grow to know that, in spite of the fact that no one in Granville would let the Anti-Slavery Society a hall in which to meet, in spite of the fact that the town authorities would give them no protection, and in spite of the fact that the mob had forbidden them to hold any meetings at all, and had threatened to tar and feather the speakers and ride them out of town on a rail, the society had succeeded in meeting in a barn. The mob had shied stones at them, and they had driven off the mob with staves made from hoop-poles they had taken from a cooper-shop. Judge Birney had made his speech and Grow had made his, and what was more, Judge Birney had complimented him on it. And when it was over and the resolutions had been adopted, and Grow had gone to the livery-stable to get Dolly D. he had found that she had been "bobbed." He had mounted her and ridden away, pursued by the mob pelting him with eggs.

"But your horse wasn't the only one that was bobbed," said Grow, casually. "There were three or four others."

And with this consoling information Grow began to tell what was said in the speeches, and so far as Carter ever knew, never gave another thought to Dolly D.

Carter, however, could think of little else. He almost sat up with her that night. She was excessively nervous. The thunderstorm that had been brewing all day broke in the evening, and Dolly D. had always been afraid of thunder. At each crash she would start with terror. And then, the next morning though the storm was over it had not cooled the air in the least; it had only made it hotter, more suffocating than ever. The hot moisture in the air fairly scalded the skin. The flies were ferocious, and Dolly D. was driven half mad now that she had no longer any tail to switch them with; she could only flap her poor unavailing stump frantically, stamp her feet and bite her own flanks with her long teeth.

Carter consulted Congreve, in whose household he found the sympathy that a family of horse-lovers was bound to feel for him in such a misfortune. Miss Lucretia, when he told her of the outrage, had turned pale with anger, stamped her little foot, and exclaimed:

"Oh, the wicked brutes! The wicked, wicked brutes! Hanging would be too good for them!"

And then her large eyes filled with pity, she clasped her hands under her chin, and, looking up at Carter, said:

"Oh, Mr. Blair! That lovely, lovely creature! To think that she should be so wantonly mutilated! She was the prettiest animal I ever saw!"

Her sympathy and her sorrow wrung Carter's heart, and his pain increased as more and more he realized the extent of his loss. There was the sense of shame, the indignity of it all, which Dolly D. herself seemed to share. There could be no riding her back in triumph to Kentucky now, to be jeered and hooted all the way as a Bobolitionist! No going over the Blue Ridge to Virginia to bring back his bride on a pillion.

Congreve himself in his indignation cursed and swore with a vehemence that was consoling. He damned the mob, damned the Anti-Slavery Society, and not only damned Grow, but urged Carter to sue him for damages.

"Her tail will grow out again in time, at least enough to be properly bobbed, and her mane could be decently hogged, but she'll never be the good-looking horse she was once. And Grow is responsible," he said.

But Carter shook his head. He could not pursue Grow. Angry as he was with Grow, and exasperated by his apparent indifference, there was something in Grow that caused Carter, deep down in his heart, to respect him, almost to like him.

"The way he stands up to odds, the way he faces the music, and stumps fate to do its worst—no," said Carter, "I can't help admiring him for it."

"He's a God damn stubborn fool, that's what he is," said Congreve, with a definitive gesture. "He's crazy, like all them damned Abolitionists. They've got an itch for notoriety. If they can't get it one way they will another—even if it's only riding through the streets on a bob-tailed nag."

Something, however, had to be done. Dolly D. was in a bad way and growing worse. Worn out with nervousness and tormented by the flies, she refused to eat: her coat was losing its lustre and she was beginning to look gaunt and haggard. Carter consulted Congreve.

"Well, she might do better out here at the farm. You fetch her out here, and we'll turn her out to grass. She's high-strung, but she'll come round with a little rest and good air and care. By and by she'll do in the stud, and by the time you're married you may have a good colt out of her."

And so the next morning Carter led Dolly D., covered by a linen horsecloth, out to Congreve's. It was almost the last act of his old life at Grow's and the beginning of a new phase of his existence. Grow had closed his bargain with Spooner, who had taken possession and called his place "The Yankee Store," to show how modern and efficient and up-to-date it was. Grow had

168

bought his ten acres on the Blue Jacket road, and was busy with the first number of his new weekly, *The Torchlight*.[34]

Carter had taken lodgings at Mrs. Brewster's boarding-house where Fowler Brunton lived, and though Brunton had suggested more than once that they form a partnership for the practice of the law, some instinct in Carter had held him back and now he had accepted a connection with Judge Diller, and the new shingle for the firm of Diller and Blair was being painted in bright gilt letters on a sanded black background, and Carter was hoping that it would be swinging from its iron bracket before the small one-storey law office in Court Street in time for Miss Lucretia to see it before she left with Mrs. Congreve and Miss Sallie in the stage for Cincinnati on her way home. And Carter was looking forward to the day when he himself should go to Virginia and be married.

BOOK II

I

Before Carter Blair left home to go to his law office on that September morning in the year 1840, he carefully brushed his black broadcloth coat, adjusted his beaver hat at the exact angle of conventional respectability, and, in the mirror that hung in the hall, studied the solemn expression of countenance proper to a candidate for the Legislature on the Whig ticket. He was proud of the honour; it was no small thing, he felt, to find himself, after less than three years practice at the bar, on a ticket headed by General Harrison as candidate for President and Tom Corwin for Governor. In that short space of time he had become a man of family, a man of property, and a prominent citizen. Such was the liberality of opportunity offered to a young man of [promise] in the Ohio of those days. He bore these gratifying facts in mind as he walked up Main Street and around the Square, his broad shoulders thrown back, surely a fine figure of a man, for among the changes that had come with the passing of those few years, he had grown stouter.

As he was passing along North Main Street he heard the crack of rifle shots. It was a sound that always made his heart beat a little faster because it recalled those boyhood days when he used to shoot squirrels in Kentucky, and he hurried on to the vacant lot where a crowd of men were holding a turkey-shoot. It had been advertised as a more important contest than the ordinary turkey-shoot. The prizes were described as "elegant and valuable"; the first of them, for instance, a full set of china dishes! Blair went in and stood a moment or two watching the contestants shoot. Those free and equal sovereigns, of course, could not be expected to betray any interest in a leading citizen, or show themselves in the least impressed, even if he did wear broadcloth and a beaver hat and had been nominated for the Legislature. But they did cast surreptitious glances at him now and then, and presently Turner, one of the promoters and managers of the contest said genially:

"Try your hand, Mr. Blair!"

Blair had not fired a rifle in a long while, not indeed since the visit he had paid to his kin back in Bourbon county that fall two years before when he was on his way to Virginia to marry Luc-

170

retia; at that time he had gone squirrel-shooting with his brother Joe. But his finger itched for the trigger, and besides, in this year of 1840 with its log cabin and hard cider campaign for Tippecanoe and Tyler Too, a Whig candidate with any of the more picturesque accomplishments of the pioneers ought to show them off. For Ohio was just emerging from the pioneer epoch; a new generation had grown up, a generation that had not known the cruel and savage reality of that epoch, and was ready to romanticize it and to find a sentimental interest in its rude sports and games, and in all that pertained to its life. Blair, to be sure, hadn't known the pioneer life either, except in its very last phases, and as one of the new generation he could be as romantic about it as any of them, but Simon Kenton and old Daniel Boone couldn't have handled their long, trusty rifles with greater skill than he could handle his. And so he said:

"Well, I used to be able to hit a barn-door, but it's been a long time since I drew a bead on anything. However, I'll just try my luck."

He drew off his coat, laid aside his hat, and said:

"Let's heft those pea-rifles once."

He balanced them, one after another, in his hand, tested their weight and the feel of them, selected one and took his stand. At the far end of the vacant lot a live turkey was stalking about picking up the kernels of corn strewn there for the victims of this sacrifice. It seemed hardly fair; but then, the pioneers were not noted for their loyalty to the spirit of fair-play; they could be as unfair and as cruel as the Shawanees or the Delawares. However, if he hadn't lost his old skill he would make it easy for the turkey. He fired and shot the turkey through the head.

After that he was sure of himself. He won the first prize, and then, in a spirit of reckless bravado, he told them to fetch a candle; he was going to give them an exhibition of fancy shooting—show them how it was done in Kentucky. The candle was set up at forty paces and lighted. Blair snuffed it with his rifle. Then he shot again and put the candle out. And then, amidst the hurrahs of the crowd, he handed the man back his rifle, drew on his coat, put on his hat, told them to deliver the set of china dishes at his residence, and, bidding them all good-morning, he went on to his law office.

When he went home to dinner at mid-day he asked Lucretia, the first thing, if a china service had been delivered at the house that morning.

"Yes," she said, "some men came an hour or two ago with a

service of china and told me that you had won it at a shooting-contest of some sort or other."

"Well, and where is it?"

"I told them to take it back."

"Take it back! But why did you do that?"

"Because, Mr. Blair, as I told the gentlemen who brought the dishes, I will have nothing in my house that has been won in a game of chance."

He looked at her in amazement.

"Chance!" he exclaimed when he could get his breath. "Chance! Why, there was no chance about it! It was all pure skill. If you could have seen me snuffing a candle after I had won first prize, and then with the next ball putting it out, as well as I ever did it as a boy in Kentucky, you wouldn't have thought there was any chance about it."

But she was unmoved, quite unpersuaded. She had that serious air she generally wore.

"I have no doubt, Mr. Blair," she said, "that if we were reduced to the necessity of living like the pioneers—of whom we are hearing so much just now—you would be able to supply the larder with your rifle. But fortunately that isn't required. And whether chance or skill, I don't approve of these round[35] pioneer contests."

"But you are not opposed to horse-racing."

"Not among gentlemen, and under proper conditions. But that is quite another matter."

Blair set his lips. He was slightly irritated. She was making him ridiculous in the eyes of those merry boys who had applauded him that morning as a crack shot. But there was nothing to be done about it now. He had not been long after their marriage in discovering that his wife had a set of principles that were apt now and then to interfere with his liberty. She had a will of her own, and could be a little adamantine rock when the occasion required. It had amused him at first; he had rather liked it, and was too much her willing slave to make any objection; it was merely one more of her charming little ways which he was glad to indulge in her in a pleased, patronizing and manly superiority.

However, he said nothing, and by the time they sat down to dinner he could laugh at the joke of it and at her, though she saw no joke in it at all.

They sat there facing each other across the small table in their dining-room. Her lips were slightly compressed with a firmness that asserted her principles so long as there was any lingering question of their validity. Her lips were thin; in fact, she had grown somewhat thinner since the birth of her baby; she had had a hard time, small as she was, and the baby a bouncing ten-pound boy. Blair was for an instant rather surprised to observe that she was looking a little pale and peaked. But that was largely the effect of the Ohio summer which pulled everybody down, more or less, and having to nurse Jamie. She would be all right again with the coming of fall and cool weather. But she must keep up her strength.

"You ought to eat more, my dear," he said. "You just peck at your food."

"I never was a hearty eater, Mr. Blair."

She looked up from her plate with that appealing shadow of a smile that was so characteristic of her. She was, of course, right—she was always right—and he was reassured and the slight momentary anxiety about her health vanished. She never had eaten much, hardly enough to keep a bird alive. It was part of her delicate, fairy-like charm. He was mighty proud of her, proud of the place she had at once assumed in Macochee, beside Mrs. Nash and Mrs. Chatterton and Mrs. Congreve, and all the other best people. She had quietly assumed that position as of right.

"Oh yes," he had once overheard Mrs. Nash say, "she is, you know, an F.F.V."

He was mighty proud of the way she managed the house, she did it with extraordinary skill, and so quietly that you would hardly know she was doing it at all. The cooking, for instance; it was all Southern; she had brought the recipes from Virginia; such ham (hickory-cured), and fried chicken with Maryland gravy, and spoon-bread and beaten biscuits. The house resounded every morning with the noise as Jem in the kitchen pounded the dough to make them. It had been a lucky day for him—that on which she had ridden up to Grow's old store on Congreve's chestnut gelding, and he had said to himself: "There's the gal for me!" Yes, he was mighty proud of her, proud even of the way she managed him.

He was proud of his house, too. It was of brick, two storeys high—or practically two storeys; anyhow, a storey and a half. To be sure, the bedrooms upstairs were rather dark, like an attic, for the windows in the gable-ends were small; but that didn't matter so much at present since they were never occupied. By the time the family grew sufficiently to require them he should be able to build the extension he and Lucretia were planning. He would do that just as soon as he paid off the mortgage. The house, one of the few in Macochee that were built of brick, was old; having been built in 1815. It stood in Miami street at the corner of Walnut street, and Blair had bought the vacant lot next to it, so that he owned nearly an acre of ground. The place had endless possibilities. There was room for stables at the back, room for a flower garden and a kitchen garden. He had set out a few apple-trees and peach-trees, and built a grape-arbour from the back-porch all the way to the barnyard. Already in front of the house a rose-vine was growing from a slip that Lucretia had brought with her from Virginia, and Blair had planted elms along the kerb of Miami street, spindly young saplings tied to stakes and protected now by perforated boxes, but destined in Blair's prevision to spread a lordly shade before his wide house and to shelter a large family of Blairs.

As he sat looking about the dining-room, somewhat dim because the green blinds at the windows were lowered to that point which gave the illusion of coolness and produced a yellow half-light that the flies did not like, Blair was considering its possibilities. It was an ordinary dining-room, with a fire-place, (stuffed just now with feathery branches of asparagus), a mantelpiece with a clock, and a walnut sideboard on the other wall. But beyond, through open folding doors, there was a sitting-room with the little low rocking-chair by the front window in which Lucretia sat to rock her baby, or to sew. But Blair always saw things not as they were but as they ought to be, and as they were to become, and just now he saw this sitting-room thrown into the dining-room and made part of it. Then they could draw out the table and seat twice as many; a large family—all those Blairs of the future. And they would give grand dinners on the generous scale of Kentucky and Virginia hospitality, with the latchstring always out. The present parlour would become a sitting-room, and the parlour—or parlours—would be in the new part of the house; they would get a new set of rosewood furniture. At present the parlour was filled with furniture that Lucretia had brought from Virginia, having had it shipped down the Ohio. The furniture was all shrouded in grey linen covers now—from where he sat he had a glimpse of it through the open door. It was very gratifying and reassuring, and he had reason for feeling proud. For a young man who had come to Ohio only four years before with nothing in the world except the horse he rode and what he had in his saddle-bags, it was no inconsiderable achievement.

Perhaps it would have been impossible anywhere else than in Ohio. He was beginning to take a pride in Ohio too, now that he had a stake in the country. He was beginning to think of himself not so much as a Kentuckian as an Ohioan; not a Corn Cracker but a Buckeye, as Ohioans had begun to call themselves since they had been singing [Otway Curry's] spirited song in this present campaign. That he had accomplished all this in so short a time proved how wise he had been to come to Ohio. It was indeed the promised land, the land flowing with milk and honey. When he had decided to study law, he had quailed at the thought of the long time it would take him to establish himself in a practice. And yet, after all, looking back upon it now, how easy it had been! To be sure, he had had luck: Judge Diller had taken him into partnership, but nevertheless he had had to work like a nigger. Nobody had ever got anything out of old Judge Diller for nothing, Connecticut Yankee that he was! For instance, there was the Hoag case; he had done all the work in that himself—drawn the pleadings, prepared the case, appeared in court, examined the witnesses, addressed the jury, obtained the verdict, in fact done everything—even collected the fee, the most important and often the most difficult thing of all. It was the largest fee they had ever received—a thousand dollars! And what was more, that success had opened up a pocket of business in Goshen township, so that everyone in that part of the county who needed the services of a good lawyer always consulted Diller & Blair, with a leaning towards Blair.

With such a fee as that in the Hoag case they could go on for a good while. And even though money was scarce and fees often slow in coming in, credit was easy and they could live well, even extravagantly, as Judge Diller would occasionally point out to him when he gave him advice, as he liked to do. But Blair was indifferent to money and careless about it. When he was flush with it he was apt to lend it to Fowler Brunton, or to Giles Paten, who came now and then to "borrow" from him. Blair was interested in other things; money was a kind of disagreeable and contemptible necessity, and only good to spend. And so he spent it freely when he had it, and when he hadn't, went in debt.

Just now, of course, his thoughts were all on his campaign for the Legislature. If he could be elected it would be the beginning of a political career. General Harrison and Tom Corwin who were stumping the State together, were coming to Macochee, and the Whigs were arranging for a monster rally and barbecue. And as he sat there at dinner that day, an idea, a real inspiration, came to him—he would write an original song in Tom Corwin's honour, to be sung when the candidate for Governor came to Macochee. And after dinner, when Lucretia went to look after the baby, Blair went into the sitting-room and to the press where he kept his books (until he could build the extension and have a proper library) and got down his copy of Byron.

II

If Blair's song were to be sung at the Whig rally there was no time to lose. Here they were already in September and the great day only a fortnight away. General Harrison was to speak at Dayton on the 10th, the anniversary of Perry's victory on Lake Erie, and on the theory that all great patriotic victories were due to the Whigs, they proposed to celebrate it by an immense mass-meeting. The General was to come from Dayton to Macochee where the rally would be held on the 15th. And besides the song, there was the speech he was expected to deliver—from the same platform as Tom Corwin. The thought of it elated him, or would have elated him if it had not filled him with fear and apprehension; what if he should fail? Why hadn't he begun to prepare long before? Why did he yield to this lazy habit of procrastination? He never began to get ready for these events until the last minute, and then it was always a scramble to be ready at all. But besides these things, there were the frequent meetings of committees, the arrangements of details, the preparations for entertaining the distinguished guests, and for feeding and lodging the vast crowds that would come to town on that day. In fact, everyone in Macochee was in a fever of excited preparation.

Everyone, that is, except Lucretia. She maintained her poise and serenity as though nothing extraordinary were happening. She had done her part, of course; she had promised and prepared her contribution of food for the dinner. The ladies of the churches—united in this purpose if in no other—were to serve to visitors; she had offered to put up Mr. Corwin and to give a dinner for him—which Blair was eager to do; but it had been decided that General Harrison and Tom Corwin were to be the guests of Colonel Nash, whose house was the grandest residence in town. She was somewhat disappointed by this decision.

"I should have admired to meet a gentleman of whom I have heard you speak so often," she said.

"But you can meet him at the speaking," Blair replied.

But she shook her head.

"Ladies do not attend political gatherings, Mr. Blair, I should not like to be exposed to the jostling of a promiscuous crowd."

"But shouldn't you like to see and hear old Harrison? Perhaps we can arrange—"

"No," she hastened to say. "I can hardly approve of an old gentleman who is a candidate for the Presidency galloping and gallivanting about all over the country, soliciting the votes of the masses. It is unseemly. A candidate for the Presidency should remain dignifiedly at home, on his estates. However, politics are not my province. I leave all that to you. I am sorry, though, on your account, that we could not have had the honour of entertaining Mr. Corwin."

The silvery autumnal haze that lay upon the fields that morning of the 15th, announced one of those burning September days that seem to radiate the accumulated heat of a whole summer. Ever since dawn people had been pouring into town; farmers with their wives and sleepy children, having got up two hours before dawn, and driven long miles in jolting waggons over rough roads to catch a glimpse of the hero of Tippecanoe and to hear Tom Corwin speak; companies of militia; delegations of men on horseback from neighbouring counties; and people in carriages and coaches from one knew not where. Ever since daylight preparations had been going on in Colonel Nash's hickory grove for the great barbecue where all these people were to be fed; a Dallas steer was being roasted whole over the coals of wood-fires burning since midnight in holes dug in the ground; twelve tables, each 300 feet long, had been laid on trestles, and barrels of hard cider had been rolled up, ready to be broached.

In the town, the Macochee Blues were early under arms, drawn up in the Court House grounds, now standing at ease, now coming smartly to order arms, as Captain Ames issued a command in a strident voice that, at any minute, might split his throat. The allegorical floats that were to appear in the great procession that afternoon were being hauled into Main Street, and Joel Gersham, Grand Marshal of the Day, in his red, white and blue scarf worn baldric-wise, and attended by his staff, was already dashing about, suddenly reining his horse to its haunches to shout an important order, then spurring it on again, galloping from one point to another at a rate that must wind half a dozen mounts by night.

The sun got up and, dissipating the silvery mist, hung like a brazen ball in the cloud of yellow dust that was stirred up by all this movement and the constant shuffling of excited throngs through the streets. Brass bands were marching at the head of delegations, filling the air with the blare of martial music.

Blair mounted on his skittish bay filly, Kittie (a daughter of Dolly D.) rode as one of the delegation that was to meet General Harrison, who had spent the night at the house of Major Kirkpatrick, on the Springfield and Dayton road, and escort him to town. They rode six miles along the road before a cloud of dust told them that the great man was approaching. And presently, there he was, mounted on a white horse, surrounded by a civilian staff and escorted by a troop of mounted riflemen. Ex-Governor Metcalfe of Kentucky rode with him, dressed in a buckskin hunting-shirt.[36] Blair glanced about eagerly for Tom Corwin, but he was not in the cavalcade; he was coming on, someone said, by coach. After that Blair had eyes for no one but Harrison. Like everyone else, he was under the impression of the legend that had caught the fancy of the people, and served better than any declaration of principles or any political programme as a party platform, the legend of the rough old frontiersman and Indian fighter who lived in a log-cabin in the back country and drank hard cider. But now he was presented to a spare, long-faced, kindly old gentleman, wearing simple grey homespun and an uncomfortable high stock, sitting his white horse with the ease and grace of a man who had spent a lifetime in the saddle, but worn out and weary, bored to death and perhaps a little bewildered by all the fuss that was being made over him.

No doubt the Van Buren men were right when they said that he would have asked nothing better than to be let alone to drink his hard cider in his log-cabin at North Bend, and perhaps if they had not said it with a sneer he might have been. As a matter of fact, it was a great deal more than a log-cabin, even if a part of it had originally been built of hewn logs, but, in the inverted snobbery of a democracy, nothing could have made a stronger appeal to people who for the most part had been born in log-cabins if they were not living in them still, than this reproach of humble origins, and the Whigs were making the most of it. They had routed the poor old man out of his retirement and were dragging him about all over the country as the principal exhibit of a travelling circus.

Colonel Nash had not only lent his vast grove for the barbecue, but he had invited a dozen prominent men to dine with General Harrison at his house. Blair, as the party candidate for the Legislature, was, of course, invited, and it was there that he expected to see Tom Corwin once more. He had not seen his hero since that day long ago at Lebanon when he had seen him for the first time; (he had stopped at Lebanon on his way to Kentucky the year following, but Tom Corwin was not at home.). He was eager to present himself to Tom Corwin, to let Tom Corwin see how he had profited by his advice. Would Tom Corwin remember him?

Great crowds of noisy men in buckeye hats or coonskin caps were trooping into the Grove, shouting and singing, in the spirit of frontier rowdyism. They had already filled the twelve long tables, and were swigging the watered cider from gourds that were handed round, and cramming their mouths with the "salt-rising" bread and the scorched meat. The air, hazy from the dust, was filled with the rank odour of trampled ragweed, the smell of the burning flesh of barbecued beeves and sheep, and the exhalations of the sweaty, unwashed human crowd. At the sight and at the smell, Blair had a feeling that a candidate would never dare avow, an undemocratic sensation of relief that he was not to dine in that company, but was to sit at table with the quality at the big house. He felt more at home in the white pillared portico of Colonel Nash's Georgian house with the Colonel's old negro servant, Cassius, togged out today in a blue swallow-tail coat with brass buttons and a buff waistcoat, to open the door for him.

Within the door of the high-ceiled drawing-room that opened off the wide hall, Colonel Nash welcomed him with that courtly manner which caused so many in Macochee to refer to him as a gentleman of the old school, and a moment later he was bending over the white, plump hand of Mrs. Nash, who, the only woman present, was there to do the honours of her house. Mrs. Nash was a stately matron, with a magnificent bust and a certain over-ripe full-blown beauty, like that of a gorgeous double peony. She smiled on Blair, asked after his "sweet little wife," dabbed her slightly perspiring face with the lace handkerchief that hung from a gold chain, fluttered her fan an instant at each pink cheek, gathered her full, sweeping skirt, and turned to receive Judge Diller.

Blair glanced about the long drawing-room, looking for Tom Corwin, and—yes, there he was, with a knot of men about him, all craning their necks and straining their ears to hear every word he said. Blair could just see him—the broad shoulders in the broadcloth coat, a bit of the velvet waistcoat, the immaculate shirt, the fat chin tucked into the white collar and black tie, and the large, fleshy, smooth-shaven swarthy face, the incessant play of its features as the various emotions quickly succeeded one

179

another. He was strangely moved. There he was, Tom Corwin, his exemplar, hero and idol; Corwin had stopped speaking, having come, no doubt, to the end of his story. He paused, was silent, pursed his humorous mouth, and rolled his great, dark eyes drolly about the circle of his auditors. And they burst into one great peal of delighted laughter. Blair eagerly started forward, and then suddenly, he was arrested in his progress by the sight of another face, the face of Tom Nash.

He had not seen Tom Nash since that night so long before when they had fought in the street in front of Grow's house. He had not seen him, or known what had become of him; and he had not thought of him when he could help it, for the whole episode of his life at Grow's was one he did not like to recall; he wished to forget it, to erase it from his memory and from his life, as though it had never been; he had a superstitious dread of some influence or result of that life stealing down into this new life and affecting it. He did not like to be reminded of it, as the face of Tom Nash, with its curiously sly and significant expression was reminding him of it now. He had had no idea that Tom Nash had come home. It had been years since Nash had gone away, and months since Blair had heard anyone mention his name. At first people used to wonder and speculate about his fate; somone had heard that he and Gertie had been married and were living at Cincinnati; someone said they had a baby, but no one knew for sure. And then it had got to be a kind of joke, and if anyone expressed any curiosity about them or wondered what had become of them, someone was certain to say with the laugh the standard jest required:

"Oh, I expect they've gone down into Symmes' hole."[37]

Neither Colonel Nash nor Grow ever mentioned them, and bore themselves with a dignified and distant reserve that would have brooked no inquiry.

But now, whatever might have become of Gertie, here, at any rate was Tom Nash, looking at him through narrowed eyes, rather quizzically, as though wondering how they should meet after this long time. Blair determined not to dodge the embarrassing rencounter, and with recognition patent in his face he was just taking a step towards Nash when Mrs. Nash, sweeping by and pointing with her fan, said:

"Mr. Blair, do you know my boy, Tom?"

"Very well, ma'am," Blair replied, and, holding out his hand, he said:

"How're you, Nash?"

180

"How're you, Blair?"

Blair looked Nash full in the eyes; their gaze met; there was, for an instant, a conflict of wills. Then, slowly, Nash's gaze wavered and in another instant, fell. Blair felt, somehow, a sense of relief, a sudden restoration of power. But there was still an inevitable moment of embarrassment which Blair, taking the lead and assuming command of the situation, met by saying:

"I didn't know you were at home."

"I only came last night."

"I trust you are well?"

"Oh, yes. And you?"

"Oh, I'm always well."

And then he got away. "I must pay my respects to the Governor," he explained in excusing himself—they were already speaking of their candidate as the Governor—and in another instant the moment he had been dreaming of, longing for, and looking forward to for years, had come at last—the moment in which he stood before Tom Corwin.

But, of course, according to the inexorable and remorseless law of contrariety, the moment could not be what he had imagined or expected. He held Tom Corwin's hand for a second, and he looked into Tom Corwin's face. But he never uttered one of the phrases he had prepared so long ago for this occasion; now that he was in Tom Corwin's presence, they all at once seemed silly—and there were all those men standing about. And plainly Tom Corwin did not remember him; why should he? And Blair shrank delicately from subjecting him to one of those harrowing tests of memory to which public men were daily subjected in a democracy, and did not mention the fact of their having met before. And so the moment which meant so much to Blair and so little to Tom Corwin, who met thousands every day—the moment passed. And, worst of all, the moment was poisoned for him by that sudden apparition of Tom Nash. Tom Corwin was smiling at him, to be sure, with that humorous and charming smile on his dark features, but before that face there swam the sarcastic countenance of Tom Nash, and the ruddy face with the high cheek-bones and the black eyebrows meeting across the nose, of Gertie Grow. It was just as well, perhaps, that General Harrison should have appeared in the doorway of the drawing-room just then; he stood there a moment, a grey wraith of the Indian wars, glancing about with the confused and startled gaze of an old gentleman who, having been on the go since dawn, had just awakened from his nap to find that he was hungry and ready for his dinner.

III

But the General did not have much time to devote to his dinner that day, or to linger over Colonel Nash's madeira, which was so much better than the hard cider he was supposed to prefer, for at one o'clock an anvil was fired off—the signal for the procession to start.[38] Soon after, mounted on his white horse, he was escorted in noisy triumph to the Square where a tall mast had been set up, and from its truck an enormous flag with twenty-five stars and thirteen stripes lolled upon the lazy air, and a long blue pennant undulated, upon which one might read in gilt letters "Harrison & Tyler." A great stand built of unbarked cedar logs and decked out with cedar boughs, and gay with flags and red, white and blue bunting, had been erected at the foot of the mast, and from it the General was to review the procession. With him were Tom Corwin and ex-Governor Metcalfe of Kentucky, still in the buckskin hunting-shirt which he must have found more appropriate to the occasion than to the weather. And seated at the rail, their hands crossed on their sticks, their trembling chins resting on their hands, their faded eyes gazing out over the crowd, were three old, ancient men, who had, or thought they had, fought under Washington in the War of Independence. Behind them and around them in a sticky huddle were numerous Vice-Presidents, the clergyman who was to make the prayer, and the Tippecanoe Glee Club which was to sing the campaign song. The whole Vast Square was packed with people—a black mass that filled it to every corner, and overflowed into the four streets that centred there. Stationed on the outskirts of the crowd, or wriggling through it, were fakirs vending pain-killers and ague-cures, water-melons and lemonade, and Yankee pedlars with gewgaws to tempt the farmers' wives. The fronts of all the stores and houses fluttered with flags and bunting, and at their windows were knots of people, and people swarmed upon the roofs. The air was full of noise; the cries of hawkers, the shrill neigh of stallions, the wails of tired and nervous infants. From the vast, restless crowd, incessantly in movement like the sea, rose an endless hum of excited interest; strange, mysterious waves of feeling swept over it; a great laugh would go up for no reason at all; then a great clamour and wild cheers; sometimes it would fall suddenly silent, and for an instant swirl about some point of tragic interest, where some farmer's wife, worn out by fatigue and excitement and the heat, had fainted, and for a moment was thought to have dropped dead.

It was only by a miracle—for which Grand Marshal Gersham took to himself the credit—that a way was ever made through that crowd for the procession, and even Gersham's miracle could not have accomplished it had not the crowd been so good-natured and in such gala spirits that it did all it could to help him. And at last from somewhere far away came the shrilling of fifes and the roll and throb of drums. They were coming at last. A thrill of realized expectation ran through the crowd, a wave of emotion and excitement, and then as the blaring brasses of the Dayton Military Band suddenly burst into a vast crescendo as the head of the column debouched into the Square, and General Harrison advanced to the rail to review the procession, a mighty roar went up from the crowd, and spontaneously all those excited people began to sing to the jolly tune of *Little Pigs*.

For Tippecanoe and Tyler too!

Blair felt goose-flesh creep over him, and little tremors ran up his back and into the roots of his hair. He looked at General Harrison standing there in his suit of grey homespun, thin and erect, and he saw that the General was deeply moved. His lip trembled slightly, and to Blair he seemed at sixty-seven, very old. Tom Corwin was on his right and ex-Governor Metcalfe on his left; and Blair had succeeded, without a display of too much eagerness, in getting a position beside Tom Corwin.

Grand Marshal Gersham, riding with his staff at the head of the procession, rode up to the stand and saluted General Harrison, then turned out and flourished about on his horse in an effort to keep the way clear for the picturesque column. The band passed and the Dayton Greys, and then a delegation of men in dress of pioneers—something like that affected by ex-Governor Metcalfe of Kentucky—rode by on their farm horses. Then on the platforms of farm-waggons, were trappers' lodges, half-faced camps built of saplings and cedar boughs; and there were canoes—intended to suggest Tippecanoe—one of them made out of the hollowed log of a sycamore tree, with long-haired trappers sitting in it, seriously wielding their paddles with an air of conviction.

The Macochee Blues marched by, Captain Ames flashing his sword in salute, and with his plumed head turned rigidly towards the stand, fixed the General with a stern, martial expression, and the General raised his hand wearily to his head in acknowledgement of the salute. The Blues passed; the fifes screamed and the drums rolled and rattled; the dusty air danced in the September sun; the crowd cheered and now and then broke into a rhythmic chant of:

Van Van is a used-up man!

A great Conestoga wain with a red body and blue wheels and a hood of canvas, rumbled along, as in the early days when the first settlers came over the mountains. The settler, his rifle over his shoulder, walked beside his horses, and out of the flap of the wagon-cover his wife, in linsey-woolsey and a sunbonnet, looked gravely on the crowd, her children clustered about her staring in wonder.

The procession wound its slow way through the crowd, like a current through the sea, with flags and banners and emblems and mottoes. One man carried a hickory pole, on the top of which, attached by a chain, perched a raccoon, its sharp, ill-tempered little face screwed up in an expression of snarling and unavailing anger. One delegation bore a banner inscribed:

The People is Oll Korrect.

And as they marched they sang:

"Old Tip, he wears a homespun suit,
He has no ruffled shirt-wirt-wirt;
But Mat he has the golden plate,
And he's a little squirt-wirt-wirt."

They bawled their song, and another delegation sang:

"Farewell, dear Van,
You're not our man;
To guard the ship
We'll try old Tip."

But nothing in this log-cabin and hard-cider procession made quite so big a hit as the log-cabin itself. When its bulk was trundled into the Square a great shout went up to greet it. Six horses drew the waggon on which it was borne, a genuine log-cabin, built of buckeye logs, and roofed with clapboards; it had doors and windows (with greased paper for glass) and a chimney made of sticks and clay with smoke coming out of it. On its wall was stretched a coon-skin, fastened by the four sprawling feet. A well-sweep stood near the cabin, and beside the door was a barrel of hard cider, from which the wife of the pioneer ladled out a noggin of hard cider to the men and boys, already tipsy, who shuffled along beside the waggon. A boy in linsey-woolsey was niggering corn, and a bevy of girls flung out corn-dodgers to the crowd. And in the doorway—where the latch-string always hung out—sat the hardy pioneer himself, his rifle across his knees, resting from his labours.

The heavy float lumbered on, the log-cabin joggling with the movement, and when it was abreast of the stand, it stopped. And then the Tippecanoe Glee Club rose, and to the tune of *Highland Laddie* sang:

> Oh where, tell me where, was your Buckeye Cabin made?
> Oh where, tell me where, was your Buckeye Cabin made?
> 'Twas built among the merry boys who wield the plow and spade;
> Where the Log-Cabins stand in the bonnie Buckeye shade.

The review was finished, it was time for the speeches, and, at the thought of addressing that immense crowd in the presence of Tom Corwin and that distinguished company, Blair's heart came into his mouth, and his throat was parched and dry.

Colonel Nash was to preside, and as the procession trailed away with all its noise and tomfoolery, he arose and in his impressive way stood beside the table. He stood and waited a moment for the excitement to subside. A large white pitcher filled with water for the orators stood on the table with a tumbler beside it, and as Colonel Nash drew the pitcher towards him, a wit in the crowd shouted:

"Is that hard cider, Colonel?"

A great guffaw rose from the crowd. Then another wit shouted:

"Don't drink it all up! Leave some for old Tippecanoe!"

And again the crowd burst into a coarse and boisterous laugh. Colonel Nash, Blair could see, was annoyed, but he stood there in the cuirass of his impenetrable dignity, waiting for the crowd to settle down into silence and seriousness.

Tom Corwin had been looking on at all this horse-play and tomfoolery with an inscrutable air of solemnity. He looked on at it now through half-closed eyes, studying the crowd, that vast sweep of upturned, vapid faces before him, and Blair thought that he shook his head ever so slightly, and not so much disapprovingly as in sadness and despair. And presently he said, almost as much to himself, it seemed, as to Blair:

"Though it make the unskillful laugh, it cannot but make the judicious grieve."

Colonel Nash, however, had at last got under way; his somewhat inadequate voice ringing out with unwonted distinctness in the silence which now, after so much noise and clamour, filled at

last the Square. He was speaking indignantly of the panic of
1837, for which he was holding President Van Buren personally
responsible, and presently he was introducing ex-Governor Metcalfe of Kentucky, and presently the ex-Governor, perspiring in
his buckskin hunting-shirt, was dealing the Red Fox of Kinderhook those mighty blows that seemed to justify his sobriquet
of the Stone Hammer, quite as much as the fact that he had begun life as a stone-mason.

Strange, thought Blair, that all great Americans must have these
picturesque nicknames testifying to a lowly origin! Henry Clay
was the Mill Boy of the Slashes; General Harrison was Old Tip;
Van Buren was the Red Fox of Kinderhook; and Tom Corwin was
the Waggon Boy. But he had an intuitive feeling that Mr. Corwin
did not especially relish this frontier familiarity even though he
endured it, as a man in politics must endure so much of the sort.
He determined, at any rate, that in his speech he would not refer
to Mr. Corwin in any such way... He wondered whether he
should ever earn some such nickname, and what it would
be... He was trying to keep his speech in his head; and as the
time for him to deliver it was drawing near—he was to follow
the Stone Hammer—he was wondering what parts of it he might
leave out, besides the bit about the Waggon Boy—for this crowd
was not waiting to hear him—they were waiting to hear Tom
Corwin.

"I'm going to cut mine short," he said to Tom Corwin, as he
rose to speak.

"Take your time, my boy; take your time—and take it easy."

He was standing at the rail, looking out over that great welter
of faces, turned up to him. The faces were all unknown to him;
they were strange and, he imagined, hostile. But presently the
vast congeries began to dissolve into its individual, human elements; familiar countenances emerged from the mass, faces that
he knew. Somewhere he saw the red face of Giles Paten, and beside it that of Fowler Brunton, and he was encouraged. Then he
saw another face that disconcerted him—the sharp, cynical face
of Tom Nash, turned up to him with an expression of sneering
malevolence. He looked away and there, all at once, on the outskirts of the crowd where it must have been standing for some
time without his having noticed it, he saw an open carriage driven by a negro coachman in a blue coat and a white beaver hat.
Yes, it was Colonel Nash's turn-out; that was old Cassius, and beside Mrs. Nash, sat Lucretia. She smiled out of the depths of her
flowered bonnet, and fluttered a handkerchief at him.

Well, it was over, anyhow, and not so bad after all. The bit about Mr. Corwin as a boy having carried supplies to the brave General Harrison and his gallant army when, fastened in the trackless swamps and brushwoods of the St. Mary's country they had been exposed to the dangers of the northwestern frontier, that bit had been well received. Lucretia had waved to him again when he had finished, and when he sat down Tom Corwin laid his hand on his knee and smiled and said:

"That was a first-rate speech, my boy."

There was no time just then to say more, but that much sufficed to produce in Blair a glow of satisfaction, of gratitude and affection; he had a sense of exquisite relief that the ordeal was over; now, in the delicious sensation of having won the approval of Tom Corwin, he could lean back at his ease and enjoy the other speeches. The Glee Club had advanced to the front of the stand; the leader had struck the key with his tuning-fork and the different parts were clearing their throats and humming preliminary sol-fa's. Then they burst into song:

> "Oh, what has caused this great commotion,
> motion, motion,
> All the country through?
> It is the ball a-rolling on
> For Tippecanoe and Tyler too.
> And with 'em we'll beat little Van!
> Van, Van is a used-up man;
> And with 'em we'll beat little Van![39]

The Glee Club hadn't finished the first verse before the crowd had caught up the well-known tune and joined in the chorus, and when the song was sung and Colonel Nash had risen to introduce General Harrison, the crowd, a boiling maelstrom of enthusiasm now, would not listen to him and he could only smile and wave his white hand as General Harrison slowly advanced to the rail, and stood there, a little pale, bowing and raising his hand now and then for silence. He tried several times to speak, his lips moved, but he could not be heard. But at last, with a suddenness that was startling and far more impressive in its emotional quality than the wild cheers a moment before, silence fell and the General, in the thin voice that did not carry very far, began his speech.

He stood there, a grey eidolon of a swiftly vanished epoch which, for a little while, the crude pageant that had swept by had reconstructed in the imaginations of all those people. He had known this land, the very spot on which he then stood, as a [vast] wilderness; in 1794, as a young aide-de-camp on the staff of Mad

187

Anthony Wayne, he had marched through it with two thousand regular troops and fifteen hundred mounted riflemen from Kentucky, to defeat the Indians at the foot of the rapids of the Maumee in the Battle of Fallen Timbers. In 1811 he had defeated Tecumseh and his brother "The Prophet" on the banks of the Tippecanoe, and two years later, when he defeated General Proctor and Tecumseh in the Battle of the Thames he won a decisive victory in the war of 1812. And it was all this, this war to wrest the land from savages, and this pioneer epoch that in the lifetime of one man had vanished to make way for the civilisation in which they were living now, that those people were thinking of as they looked at the weary old General, far more than the patriotic words he was trying to shout across the Square. This was what it meant to young Carter Blair, at any rate, and all that was slightly pathetic in the spectacle, and even all that was slightly ridiculous to the young whose lives lay all before them, was swallowed up and lost in the larger significance of these mysterious implications. Let him shout on, poor old man, for another hour, if he wanted to; he had the right in this Ohio he had done so much to create, to shout and wave his arms as long as he pleased!

The vast crowd stayed, hung on to the end, for they had come, most of them, to hear Tom Corwin, and those who ever heard Tom Corwin had something to remember, to think about and talk about and even brag about, all the rest of their lives.

IV

It had come at last—the charmed moment for which that crowd had patiently waited all that afternoon, and they began to shout: "Corwin! Corwin!" But no; before Tom Corwin could speak, it appeared that the Glee Club must sing again, and whilst they were getting ready, Colonel Nash, in a light, facetious vein, intended to keep the crowd in a good humour, said that he had an important announcement to make; they were about to have the pleasure of listening to a new song, composed especially for this occasion, and about to be rendered for the first time in public. The song had been written by a talented young citizen of Macochee who united in himself the genius of the poet, the erudition of the lawyer, and the wisdom of the statesman, and the Colonel's only regret was that the extreme modesty of the author forbade the divulgation of his name.

"But I have no alternative," continued the Colonel with a pleasant smile at Blair, "and must respect his desire for anonymity."

The members of the Glee Club looked at Blair at the same time, and smiled significantly, and then they sang his song.

During the singing of the song many knowing glances were turned on Blair, and many heads nodded approval in his direction, and, when it was done and the crowd were applauding, Tom Corwin looked at Blair and rolled his eyes and drew his mouth down with such a droll expression of reproof that everybody burst into laughter.

Colonel Nash, observing that the next speaker needed no introduction, eulogized him at length; and finally Tom Corwin stood at the rail to be greeted with a great roar of applause. He stood there with a grave and serious expression; a hush fell suddenly; he looked about over his immense audience—five thousand, it was estimated—and the crowd settled itself for the greatest treat that Ohio could offer.

The sun, with the waning afternoon, had by this time got so low in the sky that its level rays, shining through the gap in the wall of buildings made by Miami Street, shone full in the speaker's stand, and almost into Tom Corwin's eyes. Someone opened an umbrella and held it near him to shield him from the sun's rays. But Tom Corwin passed his hand over his swarthy face and said:

"I don't think there's any danger of the sun's spoiling my complexion."

The crowd, at this, burst into such a roar of laughter that he had to wait for them to quiet down again before he could proceed. But at last there was silence and the rich, mellow voice was sending its accents to every corner of the Square.

As Blair sat there, bound by the spell in which Corwin held the enraptured crowd, he noticed that Giles Paten was slowly working a way up to the front and presently he stood immediately before the platform and under Tom Corwin's eye. Paten, of course, was a Democrat, and, as Blair knew, would be a little drunk by that hour of the day and be spoiling for an argument, especially as Van Buren had been heavily pummelled by all the Whig orators for the last three hours. Tom Corwin who, by his irony, his wit, his sarcasm, his extraordinary pantomime, and by his sober eloquence, his command of pathos, and in fact of all the

189

emotions, had his hearers laughing one moment and crying the next. He would quote from Burns, from Shakespeare, from Byron, but he would quote most of all from the Bible which he seemed to know by heart, and had at his fingers' ends; and as the Bible was the book his hearers knew better than any other, they understood his allusions to it better than to any other literature. In picturing the hard times and the evils of the land under the administration of Van Buren, he had drawn an analogy between those times and the state of the world before the flood. He had done it in a solemn and impressive strain of lofty rhetoric. He had drawn an impressive picture of Noah, the only preacher of righteousness in the midst of the universal antediluvian corruption. He described the building of the Ark, and the coming of the Deluge. The crowd listened in tense and breathless silence to the picture of the awful catastrophe. And then, all at once, Tom Corwin's eye caught the eye of Giles Paten, looking up at him with an expression of cynical scepticism, and he paused. Blair saw that old Giles was about to speak; Tom Corwin looked at him, his mobile mouth working humorously, and before Giles could say a word, Tom Corwin said:

"But I think I hear you say, my unbelieving Democrat, that the old commodore did once get tight."

The spell was broken, and the solemnity that had held the crowd a moment before was dissipated by the great chorus of laughter. The laughter was perhaps loudest on the stand where Macocheeans wondered by what unerring and prescient precision Tom Corwin had selected, out of all that multitude, Giles Paten to impersonate his opponents. But Tom Corwin was not done.

"Yes, my fellow citizens, I fear me you had forgotten that the righteous old patriarch was a man. He was a farmer as most of you are—the only occupation for a gentleman. He cultivated the vine, as all of you should; his vintage, no doubt, was the best ever tasted in this world. Once, we are told, he took an excusable glass too much, and fell asleep and lay uncovered in his tent. A sad plight, you will say, for an old man just entering upon his seventh century. He was observed in that naked, pitiful condition by his younger son, Ham—they say a gentleman of my colour— the father of the Canaanites, a satirical rascal, who, instead of behaving with becoming reverence toward his old father, ridiculed and made sport of him, and went to tell his two brethren without that they too might enjoy the spectacle."

And then he turned to Giles Paten, and, leaning over the rail, in face, voice and manner imitating to the life a Methodist cir-

190

cuit-rider at a revival, he raised his hands imploringly and, in unctuous tones, apostrophized old Giles:

"Oh, my unsanctified brother! I will not repeat to you the curse that was pronounced when 'Noah awoke from his wine and knew what his younger son had done to him.' But, I pray you, be warned by it. Turn from your evil ways. Quit your ridicule and abuse of your good pioneer father protector, General Harrison. Help to avert the flood of evils about to overwhelm the nation. Go along with us; we will do you good. And may God have mercy on your soul!"

Whilst the crowd roared and rocked with merriment, Blair watched the play of expression in old Giles's blotched and purple face; it twitched a moment, then broke up into ripples of amusement, a smile spread over it, and at last the broad mouth opened, showing the brown and rotting snags of teeth, and emitted a burst of laughter as wild as anyone's. Tom Corwin stood there enjoying his mastery of the emotions of the crowd. He drew out an enormous handkerchief and mopped the perspiration on his glistening face; he jerked up his coat sleeves to allow the air to cool his wrists, and then, serious and solemn as a judge, he began one of those long periods of spread-eagle oratory that ended in a burst of eloquence.

Blair, enchanted by the performance, found an especial interest in studying the faces of the crowd, as he had studied the face of Giles Paten. There was one especially that interested him, the face of a farmer, prematurely aged by the bitter toil of a frontier farm. The man had stood there, tall and gaunt, all the afternoon, with his wife and children, a touching family group, the wife lean and sallow, with two aguish children hanging to her skirts, dragging her down, whimpering and complaining with the weariness and the heat, and another in her arms, clinging to her scrawny, wrinkled neck. She would shift it now and then from one angular hip to the other. Earlier in the afternoon when the log-cabin went by, she had given it a few sips of cider from a gourd, and since, whenever it cried with colic, she would jounce it up and down in her arms to distract it. At her side stood her eldest son, a tall, thin, gawky boy whose great eyes, glowing like stars, were fixed in the awe and wonder of imaginative youth on Tom Corwin, as in a trance. Now and then, whenever he thought of it, the farmer relieved his wife of the restless baby for a while, but he didn't think of it often; he was wholly absorbed in Tom Corwin. His tall, gaunt frame was clad in worn and threadbare garments that had long since taken on the neutral colour of the earth in which his life was passed. His coarse, unkempt hair

191

hung lank from the hat of woven leatherwood that he wore; the skin on his lean face was tanned like leather, and from his lantern-jaws, moving incessantly as he chewed his quid of tobacco, hung a scraggy sunburnt beard. But in his blue eyes and in that tanned face, there was reflected, as in a mirror, every emotion that Tom Corwin by his art evoked. At times his face would twitch with pain, his lip would tremble, tears would gather in his pale, blue eyes, and stream down his leathern face. And then a moment afterwards he would laugh and wag his head from side to side and say: "Ay, golly!" in the impossibility of expressing the satisfaction he felt. And when Tom Corwin soared away on one of his loftier flights of oratory, the farmer would stand with gaping mouth and strained expression on his face, rapt in naive amazement. And Blair understood how these poor folk could stand there all through the long hours of that afternoon, for this was the only pleasure, the only distraction, the only entertainment, the only break that ever relieved the bleak monotony and killing toil of their squalid lives; they would remember and treasure up and talk about this day for years to come.

Tom Corwin finished his speech. His collar lay in wet, wrinkled folds about his neck; a great splotch showed in the middle of his back where he had sweated through his coat. He would not stop for congratulations, and was driven away in a carriage with General Harrison to Colonel Nash's, amidst the cheers of the disintegrating crowd. And all that evening great clouds of dust rolled along the streets of Macochee as farm-waggons rattled away on their long journeys home, their occupants, many of them, full of whisky, whooping it up for Tippecanoe and Tyler too.

V

Blair was sitting alone in his law-office one morning, three or four days after the Whig rally, when, somewhat to his surprise, Ethan Grow came in. He had not seen much of Grow since his marriage. Grow was either working on his small "farm," or was absorbed in his anti-slavery agitation and in editing the newspaper which, by some miracle, he managed to keep alive. As for consulting him professionally, Blair was certain that Grow would never dream of doing such a thing; not that Grow was in the least unfriendly to him, not at all;

but merely on the principle that a lawyer whom one has known as a youth before he was called to the bar cannot, of course, have sufficient learning and judgment to give his opinions weight. Blair had deduced this disheartening principle early in his practice from the fact that no elder person of his acquaintance ever consulted him professionally. His only clients were found among those who had never known him but had merely heard of him, and so had faith in his mysterious powers. Nevertheless, he could feel that he was friends with Grow, even though their ways lay wide apart. Grow, because he published a newspaper and was the acknowledged leader of the Abolitionists in those parts, was a man of importance, and with the influx of more people from Connecticut and New Connecticut, abolition sentiment was increasing, and Grow was becoming a political power whom the Whigs were courting. Grow had given Harrison and Tyler and Tom Corwin only mild support, not considering them quite orthodox on the slavery question—that is, they were too willing to compromise. But, so far as he himself was concerned, Blair had no complaint to make, for Grow had given him several flattering, if somewhat patronizing, puffs in *The Torchlight*.

He supposed, therefore, that Grow had come on some political mission—perhaps, he for a moment feared, to urge him to come out whole-heartedly and unconditionally for immediate abolition. And indeed they did, for a moment, discuss politics; that is, they talked about the great rally, as everybody continued to do and would do for years to come. For Macochee had not recovered from the boisterous frontier frolic. The litter had not been swept from the Square, and the speakers' stand still stood there, the cedar-boughs drooping and yellowing in the sun, but still somehow recalling the great figures who had trod its boards and made the welkin ring with their eloquence. Colonel Nash, perhaps, was the only one who might have complained of the great event, though he did not do so, patriotically waiving aside all commiseration for his losses, and saying that he was more than repaid by the honour of having the future President of the United States and the future Governor of Ohio under his roof and of having them break bread with him. Colonel Nash's grove had suffered more from the barbecue than it had from the tornado of 1837;[40] for this time a human whirlwind—the most destructive of all— had swept over it, breaking off the boughs of its trees, trampling its grass, strewing the ground with débris, and rooting it up like swine. And, as if this were not enough, the crowd had not left a bushel of feed or a sheaf of grain or a bundle of hay in his barn, whilst trace-chains, hames, and hame-strings, horse-collars, bridles, and whole sets of harness had disappeared from his stables. And yet, the Colonel would only smile in his bland, rosy way, and quote old Cassius, his black man-servant, who had said in reporting these losses:

"No, suh, it was n' de Whigs dat done took 'em, no suh. 'T was dem an'inted Dimocrats, de o'n'rycuss villyans!"

But when Blair mentioned this fact to Grow and quoted old Cassius, the incident did not call forth the laugh that it could confidently be relied upon in most instances to produce; it did not even produce a smile; smiles to be sure, rarely brightened the stern features of Ethan Grow, and this morning at mention of the name of Nash they set in a frown, hard as a rock.

"H'm, yes," he said, drawing his hand slowly across his wide, firm mouth and down over his long, scraggy beard. "Might have expected as much from all that tomfoolery! Running an old man for President without a platform, without a principle—nothing but a reputation for fighting Indians—when there's this burning, live, throbbing issue about which you're all afraid to say a word! Do you think that songs about coonskins and log-cabins and hard cider, or the jokes of Tom Corwin, can long drown the cries going up from millions of human beings in chains in the South?"

Blair hardened a little at the slighting way in which Grow spoke of Tom Corwin, and he felt the sudden rush of resentment that came whenever he heard the South criticized; he sat up in his chair as though to take up the challenge. Perhaps Grow saw the movement, for he suddenly put forth his hand and said:

"But never mind that now; I came to talk of other things."

"Well?"

"Do you know what fetched Tom Nash home?"

"No, I haven't the least idea."

"You saw him?"

"Yes, at his father's house."

"Talk to him?"

"No; I saw him only for a moment the day I attended the dinner in honour of General Harrison and Mr. Corwin and Governor Metcalfe."

Blair noticed a slight change in Grow's features; an expression of somewhat amused contempt that was not, however, quite a sneer, swept over them.

"Well," he said, "I thought maybe, since you go with such grand people—" And then Grow checked himself, and whatever bitterness he might have felt was resolutely suppressed. Blair

194

then suddenly remembered that Grow had not been invited to the dinner, a rather significant omission, come to think of it, since Grow was editing a newspaper that, nominally at least supported the Whig candidates. And yet, on second thoughts, it could hardly be that which had caused the rancour Grow felt; Grow, in general, ranged at an altitude far above the petty envies and jealousies and resentments of ordinary life.

"You didn't happen to hear whether Tom had come home for good, or just on a visit like, did you?"

"No; I didn't exchange a dozen words with him, or hear him or his plans discussed in any way."

Grow was silent for a moment, and scratched his head in some uncertainty and bewilderment. Blair studied him; he looked much older than he had seemed in those old days in the store; his sad, careworn face, his gaunt, leathery jaws, and his rough, workworn hands were those of a farmer who grubbed a livelihood out of a small piece of land; but the nervous tension at which his whole being was strung, the light that glowed in his deep eyes, the eager, wiry spring of his thin body, all showed that spiritual rather than material forces played the stronger part in his life.

"I didn't mean to be offensive in what I said a moment ago, Blair," Grow said, "or wish to hurt your feelings, but I had heard something—well, I had better begin at the beginning. It concerns my daughter, Gertie, of course, as you must have imagined."

Blair's heart went faster, but he kept his countenance.

"You see, she and Nash never got on very well together after the first few months of their married life. They lived in Cincinnati and they had a baby—a boy—but Nash, well, he wasn't a practical man, he was a spoiled child to begin with, idle and luxurious and extravagant in his habits; he couldn't or wouldn't, work, hardly made a living, and the only money he had was what he could wheedle out of his mother; they wouldn't recognize his marriage or his son. Said he had married beneath him—whatever that means." Grow gave a harsh, sardonic laugh and added: "In Ohio, where we all boast—most of us with reason—of having been born and reared in log cabins! Well, they had a hard time getting along. I've sent Gertie what little money I could, but the Lord knows that ain't much! And then, at last, he left her and came home—that is, deserted his wife."

"Well, I'm not very much surprised," said Blair.

"No, nor me. But that isn't all, nor the worst. Do you know

195

what he says now?" Grow, his eyes gleaming, leaned eagerly forward and tapped Blair's knee significantly, so that Blair moved slightly away for he did not like men to lay hands on him. "He claims that they never were married, and that the boy is not his; he says if she insists, if she sues him for support or anything like that, why, he says he is able to establish the fact."

"Who told you all this?"

"No less a person than Colonel Nash."

"Colonel Nash!"

"Yes, sir; Colonel Nash. He came to see me, hummed and hawed, beat round the bush a while, talked turkey—Well, you know the man, polite, suave, oily, and all that. He said that they could establish the fact that the marriage was not valid, but that they were ready to fix it up with money. I told him my daughter's dishonour couldn't be bought and paid for. Then he offered to apply to the Legislature for a divorce; an expensive process, to be sure, but that if you were elected, and he was sure you would be, you would manage the bill and get it through for them."

"I'd see him in hell first!"

Grow leant back in his chair and stroked his beard with the satisfaction that a pious man, in some emergency of life, vicariously finds in the profane swearing of another who has a resource denied him.

"That's what my wife said," remarked Grow with a dry satisfaction. "It was she who insisted on my coming to see you and to tell you."

"Mr. Grow," said Blair, "do you think that Colonel Nash could ever hold up his head in this community again if he were to become a party to such blackguardly action on the part of his son? Do you think the community would tolerate it?"

"Blair, this community, or any community, will tolerate anything on the part of those who've got money enough to do what they please and pay for it."

They talked the whole business over in all its bearings—or nearly all its bearings, for there were certain elements in the affair, disturbing to Blair, which naturally he did not mention to the troubled Grow, and it was a relief to both of them when, in response to a question by Blair, Grow said that the couple had been married by a Baptist preacher at Springfield, and Blair announced;

"Well then, that settles it. The boy was born in wedlock, and Tom Nash is his father."

196

"What shall I tell Colonel Nash when he comes again?" asked Grow.

"Tell him to go to hell, and that I so advised you," said Blair.

Grow got up and smiled shrewdly as he said:

"I guess I won't tell him that until after election."

Blair went to the door with him.

"And what of Mrs. Tom Nash?"

"Gertie? Oh, I'm going to have her and the boy come to live with us until something is decided."

"Well, make my compliments to Mrs. Grow."

VI

Blair might put on a bold and swaggering front with Grow, but the visit of his old employer left him rather limp and flattened out. Grow had broken in upon a very pretty reverie; the immense success of the great rally indubitably meant success for the Whigs; Harrison had already carried several states; Corwin was sure to carry Ohio, and Blair himself was certain of election. And he had been sitting there in his law office, leaning back lazily in his chair, his long legs stretched out to the littered desk, the smoke of his segar going up to the ceiling, dreaming of his brilliant future. The first step, of course, was the Legislature, and now that was assured; after that, Congress—the Governorship—the Senate, and perhaps, afterwards—who knows? At any rate, his career was opening before him. And now, here at the very last minute, with the elections only a fortnight away—they were to be held early in October—the sinister shadow of a scandal was creeping towards him, and, once in its penumbra, why, goodbye to all these bright iridescent dreams. For a man involved in a "woman scrape" there would be no more hope politically than for the woman socially. It would provide a succulent morsel of gossip to be savoured by the women at every quilting-bee in the district; and men in groggeries and on street corners would roll it over and over in their mouths with their quids of tobacco, and laugh and joke and snigger in prurient and envious relish, but in public all these good people, men and women, would pull the long face of the hypocrite whose stern and unforgiving morality is not to be appeased.

And then his home, his nice little home; and Lucretia. She would hear... Damn it all, when a thing was once over and finished and done for, why wasn't it ended? Why must it come up again? Those few passionate nights in the little upper bed-room of that small house in Locust street—weren't they gone, lost in the dark abyss of the past?

The worst of it was that now he should have this fear on his mind all the time; and have to think of that instead of pleasant things. He should have to guard his every word, and watch his expression even, and be ever on the look out for this thing to rear its head and strike, without warning like a copperhead. But no, that was hardly fair; it had given warning. Well, say a rattlesnake then. The next thing was to scotch it... If it could only be held off until the election was over; it wouldn't matter quite so much then. And Grow, who never had suspected, poor old innocent dreamer, how much his revelation concerned *him!*—Grow had shrewdly said that he wouldn't give Colonel Nash an answer until after election. Well, he must say that was damned decent of old Grow.

There was a moment's relief in the reflection that the Nashs, with their position in the community, wouldn't want any scandal in their family... And yet, was that conclusion quite sound after all? Tom had already dragged their name in the dirt... Still, they really were married, and if people were married, why, there wasn't anything to be said against them...

However, there was really nothing that he could do; the least move on his part would precipitate matters; he must wait on events, the victim of their uncertainty and caprice. He went about, then, with this preoccupation continually on his mind, and somehow, no matter where he went, Tom Nash and his domestic infelicities were always coming up in the conversation. Even at home it was not to be escaped. They were sitting, one morning, Blair and Lucretia, in the little sitting-room that opened off the dining-room. The breakfast was long since over and cleared away, and the dining-room was shrouded in that dim penumbra which was disliked by the flies. Blair had loitered late at home that morning, for now, with election only a week away, and all the possibilities of its outcome so well adjusted in his favour, he had an almost superstitious apprehension of destroying their delicate and sensitive equilibrium by even appearing on the public scene. Lucretia sat in her low rocking-chair with Jamie on her knee, supporting his back with one hand and with the other rais-ing his embroidered white bib to wipe away the saliva that constantly dribbled from his rosy, cooing mouth. He had had his bath, his morning nap and his milk; and now, after an elaborate toilette he sat on his mother's knee, the great mass of long flannel and muslin petticoats he wore sweeping the floor. His soft, downy yellow hair, parted low on one side of his head, was brushed up on the other in a dashing crest, and the large blue eyes in his warm, glowing, healthy face—his "Daddy's eyes," said Lucretia—were smiling, and he kept making aimless, awkward and convulsive gestures with the tiny, chubby arms he had not yet learned to control.

"Daddy's eyes," said Lucretia again, and then began to talk baby-talk to him. Blair put out his forefinger, and Jamie grasped it in a strong grip and tried to raise it to his mouth. And Blair and Lucretia laughed; it was so inexpressibly charming.

"You precious little mannie!" said Lucretia, almost crushing him in a sudden embrace.

In the movement, her eye had chanced to glance out of the window, and she saw someone going by.

"Isn't that Mr. Tom Nash?" she asked.

Blair looked, and there was Nash, sauntering by on his aimless way uptown, the most striking figure, in a sartorial sense, in Macochee, with his bell-crowned hat cocked on his head, his high stock and tight-waisted, wide-skirted coat. To hear his name on Lucretia's lips had rather shocked Blair, and he turned suddenly cold inside.

"Mrs. Nash presented him the other day when I went to drink tea with her," Lucretia went on. "He was civil and genteel enough, but I thought him a coxcomb. There is something unpleasant about him, I don't know what—the way, perhaps, in which he looks at a lady. Not that he wasn't polite to me. He looks as though he had led a fast life."

"You have formed no unjust estimate of him, my dear," said Blair. "He is even worse than you have said; in fact, quite a blackguard."

"So bad as that! But Mrs. Nash thinks the sun rises and sets on him."

"Yes; she has spoiled him."

"She told me about his unfortunate matrimonial entanglement. It seems that he married beneath him, a quite improper female—ran away with her, in fact. She was, I believe, the daughter of Mr. Grow—the man you used to work for, is it not?"

"Yes."

"Then you must have known her."

"Yes, I knew her. I boarded at the Grows', you know, for a short time when I first came to Macochee. She was a kindly sort of girl and, between you and me, my dear, a lot too good for Tom Nash. I hear now that he has abandoned her and her baby. All Macochee, of course, will side with Nash; but I must admit that my sympathies are with the woman."

"Well," said Lucretia, after perpending the question for a moment with that solemn and judicial air which Blair found so charming in her when the question was one that did not affect his personal interests, "well, there's nothing for him to do about it now. They are married, and that settles it; they'll just have to make the best of it. And it would have been wiser on the part of the Nashs if they had taken them in in the first place; by this time everyone would have forgotten it. Don't you think your mammy knows what she's talking about, honey?"

Lucretia addressed this last remark to little Jamie, and Blair was glad enough to drop the other subject, and join his wife in celebrating the amazing perfections of their offspring.

VII

The great rally held in Macochee wound up the Hard Cider campaign so far as national and state issues were concerned—or, since there were no national or state issues, so far as national and state candidates were concerned, and left little doubt that the Whig ticket would be successful. But Blair could not, he discovered, be quite so easy in his mind as, say, General Harrison and Tom Corwin no doubt were, for he learned a few days later that Tom Nash, whom he so thoroughly contemned, was taking an interest in the political campaign that one might not have suspected from the nonchalant indifferent and impudent way in which he sauntered, in his foppish clothes, along the streets of Macochee.

Blair's opponent for the Legislature on the Democratic ticket was a man named Henderson, a lawyer like himself, who lived in an adjoining county of the district, and it was reported that Tom Nash and Henderson had suddenly become as thick as two thieves at a fair, and were going about quietly over the district together, as enemies sowing tares. The reports were brought to Blair by those friends who so eagerly run with bad news, at his law-office, which had become a kind of Whig headquarters in

Macochee, the Whig candidate for Congress living at Springfield. Judge Diller was growing old and was much less active in his profession than formerly. He seldom came to the office any more, and was allowing the practice to slip gradually into Blair's hands. Thus since Blair had become so active in politics, the outer room of the law office of Diller & Blair, which occupied the single-storey frame building in [Court] street, just across from the Court House, was filled all day long with local Whig politicians who gathered there in their wide leisure and smoked and chewed tobacco, and spat and talked politics all day long. Privacy, not easy to obtain in Macochee at any time, was hardly to be had there at all, and Blair, late one afternoon, tired of their endless palaver, had excused himself on the ground of having an important speech to prepare, and escaped to the small private room in the rear of the building, which Judge Diller usually occupied when he was at the office.

Once there and alone, Blair leant back in his chair, stretched his long legs and cocked his heels on the table, lighted his Conestoga segar, and began to read the Cincinnati *Gazette*. But he had not read long when one of the loafers in the outer room, super-serviceably assuming the rôle of usher, opened the door and, thrusting in his head, said:

"Lady to see you, sir."

And Blair glanced up to see Gertie Grow peering through the doorway. He was startled, and, for a second, mortified and confused. This sudden apparition was a surprise and a shock; he had no idea that she was in Macochee; Grow, to be sure, had said that she was coming home, but Blair had assumed that her return was for some indefinite time in the future. And now here she was, inopportunely arrived on the scene. His heels came down with a bang to the floor.

"May I come in?"

"Yes," he said, not very warmly.

As she pushed the door open, he saw that she carried a baby in her arms, a baby so large and bouncing that it was with difficulty that she could disengage a hand to extend by way of greeting. He drew up a chair for her, and she sat down with relief. The baby had been asleep, but the change of posture, or the sudden cessation of movement, awakened it and it began to whimper, and presently to cry outright. She changed its position again, and began to dandle it on her knee, swaying slightly from side to side as she did so, and looking at Blair.

"A good deal has happened since we saw each other last, hasn't there, Carter?" she said.

"Yes," he replied.

"Yes," she went on; "you've got married, and I've got married, and we've both got babies. You've got a boy, haven't you?"

"Yes."

"I heard so. So have I. Don't you think he's a fine, big handsome boy?" She suspended her dandling long enough to set her baby bolt upright on her knee, stiffening his back with one hand whilst with the other she wiped his mouth with a ball of a handkerchief, and then, moistening her fingers at her lips, arranged the thin hair on top of the large and really well-shaped head, parting it on the side, and giving the child a certain sober and masculine air as he sat there, his head bobbing unsteadily from time to time.

"Ain't he handsome? And don't you think he looks like his father?"

Blair bestowed a somewhat indifferent and too casual glance upon the prodigy that Gertie thus proudly held upon her knee, exhibited for his admiration. Blair glanced at it quickly and then turned his eyes away. He was, in fact, somewhat embarrassed by its presence. Babies in general did not interest him deeply. In the best and most unequivocal of circumstances he found it difficult to talk to them, and even more difficult to talk about them; he could not indefinitely expand in that fulsome and indiscriminating admiration which their natures seemed to crave and their mothers to exact. Even in the case of his own offspring, that rosy Jamie who was not much more than a year the junior of the specimen under notice, even in that case he was apt, unconsciously no doubt, to assume the detached and irresponsible attitude common to the male progenitor of all species. Babies, in fact, as such, rather bored him; he found them irresponsive and uninteresting and at times, indeed, pathetic. He recalled a story, legendary in the family and often told as illustrating the sombre character of his own Grandfather Blair, a taciturn old pioneer, sore let and hindered in the race that was set before him, who, in his cabin in Virginia, whenever a new grandchild appeared, would regard it sadly a moment, shake his head and for all comment say: "Poor little thing! Poor little thing!", as if prophetically he discerned all the tragic changes and chances of this mortal life that would beset it on its pilgrimage. But in the present instance, that of the baby sitting there rather insecurely on its mother's knee, there was an even wider range of tragic possibilities, for already small and inexperienced as it was, this child, it seemed, from all that its grandfather had hinted to Blair, had however in-

202

nocently and inadvertently divided one family and was menacing another. There was something almost sinister about it. Blair was afraid to look it in the eye.

"Don't you think he looks like his father?" Gertie was asking.

"Oh, the very spit and image of him," Blair hastened to say, though he did not think the child bore the slightest resemblance to anybody. His features were as yet strikingly undeveloped. Still, it was unquestionably desirable that it look like its father.

He was looking rather at Mrs. Nash. She was dressed with a certain coquetry in a flowered gown and large bonnet that, whilst somewhat worn and tarnished, proclaimed the fashion of the city, and she spoke with a certain affectation, as though the opportunities of a larger life in Cincinnati had made her more of a woman of this world. In a word, it was plain that she was trying to live up to the Nashs. The old pride of union with that family, Blair could see, was still strong in her, and now pathetic.

"It's a boy, isn't it?" he naively inquired.

Gertie looked up at him in swift reproach.

"Of course it is! Can't you see?" And moistening her fingers again, she retouched the part of his thin hair which already proclaimed his sex.

"I meant what is his name?"

"Thomas Worthington Nash, Jr." she said, and smiled proudly.

Blair had a feeling of distinct relief, and found it easier to meet the now less disconcerting gaze of the boy.

"He was only a seven months' child," Gertie went on, quite in her old inconsequential and artless way. It was an indelicate thing to say, especially as the child was present and might easily overhear this statement and consider it a reflection: one never knew how much children understood, and Thomas already could say a good many words, as Gertie proceeded to prove by putting him through his paces, in which he acquitted himself creditably, responding readily enough with the names of various objects, and by appropriate imitative sounds identifying all the domestic animals—a horse, a cow, a sheep, a dog, a cat, a rooster, etc.

But Blair, growing somewhat weary of this discussion, could not much longer feign an interest in the child, and he found it even more difficult to respond to the questions that Gertie, whether by way of politeness or out of curiosity, now began to put to him about his own family, about Jamie and about "Mrs. Blair."

"Laws!" she said, forgetting that she was a Nash, and relapsing suddenly into her old vocabulary and looking strangely like her mother, "Laws! It seems funny that there should be a Mrs. Blair, don't it?"

She looked at him and deeply sighed with an expression of peculiar and intimate meaning. He was annoyed. He did not like this veiled allusion to the past. And he did not like to have her discuss so freely and familiarly his wife and his little family. And why all this inferential reference to the past, this assumption of intimacy, and old associations? He was now in no mood of *laudator temporis acti.* Surely she hadn't come merely to talk about old times!

No more, indeed, had she. Thomas Worthington had grown sleepy and, with a sign, she drew his drowsy head to her breast and disposed his body so that he might fall comfortably asleep. Then she sighed again, and said:

"You have been luckier than me, Carter."

He wished she wouldn't call him thus intimately by his Christian name. He looked at her as she sat there, holding her child, a constant, heavy, inescapable burden; he marvelled at the change those few short years had brought in her, and wondered how she could ever have inspired any interest or passion in him, even that evanescent passion which was all his feeling for her had ever been. Perhaps the change was in him. But no; any pretty face, any well turned ankle could too easily affect his senses for it to be that. No, the change was in her. There she was, once more in the same room with him, alone but for the presence of the sleeping child, and besides indifference, almost a physical distaste, the only feeling he had for her was one of pity. In spite of her effort to retain the rank she thought she had attained in marrying a Nash, in spite of her fashionable, or once fashionable dress, she could not escape a defeated and slightly bedraggled air; she looked weary; her complexion had lost its freshness; and her eyes, under their heavy black brows, no longer had that bright animation which once had sparkled in them, nor her lips that red, inviting pout which—well, no matter now how they used to affect him! And it was almost as if she divined his thought when she went on:

"Oh Carter, I've gone through a lot since I saw you last!"

And she began to tell him of her life with Tom Nash, unfolding, with that artless simplicity which was all of her youth that life seemed to have left her, the sordid tale of the precarious years spent in boarding-houses at Cincinnati.

"He was kind for the first year, at least until the baby came. He didn't like the baby much; sometimes when he was drunk he would throw it up to me that it was a seven months' child—as if that was my fault! I guess, though, it was pretty much because we didn't have enough money. We never could have enough of course for him! He couldn't earn any; he didn't know how, and really, being a Nash, I couldn't blame him. He was a spoiled child with a rich father, you know; but after we got married his father wouldn't let him have any more; his mother would send him some now and then, though she had to do it unbeknownst to her husband. I guess it was his mother that spoilt him."

"It usually is the mother that spoils children."

"Do you think so, Carter? I don't want to spoil my boy."

"Boys are what their mothers make them," said Blair with the judicial air he thought befitting a consultation that he wished to keep as professional as possible. "Fathers have nothing to do with rearing their children."

"Well, that's what Tom Nash seemed to think," Gertie said with all her former literalness. "He gambled his money away as soon as his mother sent him any. Gambled, and I guess he drank. Oh, Carter, Cincinnati is a wicked city! I did the best I could. I wanted to get work. But what can a women do? Nothing, except housework and a Nash couldn't do that. A Nash couldn't go and work out as a hired girl! Tom Nash wouldn't have let me, any-how. He didn't like to have me out of his sight. He was terribly jealous of me, terribly jealous!"

Gertie made this statement with a trace of almost happy pride, as if there were one thing in her experience of matrimony, at any rate, in which she could find satisfaction, and she leant forward over the body of her sleeping child as though this subject de-manded an even more confidential air, and said:

"Why, Carter, he was even jealous of things that happened be-fore our marriage—jealous of you, and—"

She seemed about to go on, but checked herself, to Blair's re-lief.

"Well, anyway, the time came when I just had to leave him and come home. There was nothing else for me to do. And that brings me to what I really came to see you about."

Blair looked up and fixed his eyes attentively upon her.

"You know how Father is; I believe he's been to see you al-ready, hasn't he?"

Blair nodded.

"Of course, he thinks the Nashs ought to do something for me—he thinks that Tom ought to be made to support his child, that I ought to have the law on him."

Blair nodded again.

"Well, now listen. I haven't said anything to Father about it, but I don't want anything of the kind. I don't know what the law can do to Tom—you know better than me—but I don't want anything done to him, Carter! I wouldn't hurt him for the world! Have a lawsuit and a scandal, and all the things that would come out and all the things people would say! Why Carter, I wouldn't have it for the world! I wouldn't want to bring disgrace on the family—the Nashs, I mean. And I want my boy, when he grows up, to respect his father. Don't you see? Tom—"

The long black eyelashes suddenly drooped and tears came. "Tom," she faltered, "well, I think he'll come back to me some day when he comes to his senses." She wept a moment, then dried her eyes, and leant a little farther forward and the expression in her face wrought a transformation and brought back the old, kind—the too kind—Gertie Grow.

"So if Father says anything more, you just tell him nothing can be done, will you Carter?"

"Yes, Miss Gertie, if you wish it. You may count on me."

"Law, it sounds funny to hear you calling me "Miss Gertie" again! You talk just like you used to: 'Cyount on me'!" She tried to pronounce the word as Blair did, and laughed. Then she got up.

"Father will be waiting for me," she said, "and I must be going."

Blair went with her into the outer office which was empty now, for the afternoon had grown late, and the politicians and loafers had all gone. Blair had shown her almost to the door when she suddenly stopped as though frightened by something she had seen, and shrank back into the obscurity of the office. And Blair, looking out at the door, saw across the street Tom Nash and Henderson. They had seen Gertie about to leave the office, and they had stopped and stood there watching in sudden interest. They stood for a moment, and then Henderson caught Nash by the sleeve of his coat, gave it a tug, and they went on.

VIII

The first tangible result of Gertie's return to Macochee was a notice which appeared, a few days after she had visited Blair's office, in that week's issue of Winship's newspaper *The Democrat*. The notice ran:

"I, Thomas Worthington Nash, hereby give notice that I
will not be responsible for any debts contracted by
my wife, Gertrude Grow Nash, either in her own name
or in mine."

When Blair read the notice it seemed to him like a formal declaration of war. Such an act, of course, could only create a great
sensation in a community like Macochee and provide welcome
confirmation for the gossip that was already rife, though Blair did
not fail to note that there was one bit of satisfaction in it which
must be consoling to the Grows, and that was Tom Nash's admission that Gertie was his wife. One thing, too, was certain, and
that was that Blair would have to be looking after his fences, and
he resolved to spend the last ten days of the campaign in making
a final round of his district, visiting places where he had not appeared before.

Meetings had been arranged at Blue Jacket, at Raymer's Ford,
New Prospect, and elsewhere, so that he would be absent from
home most of the time until election day. He did not like to go;
the prospect of separation from Lucretia filled him with nostalgia.
In the few brief years of their married life he had come to depend, more than he himself realized, on her counsel and advice,
her sympathy and support; he felt that her judgment was infalli-
ble, and, in short, he leant on his frail and delicate little wife
with a weight that must have crushed a body not inhabited by a
spirit as strong and as resilient as steel. The pain of separation,
short as it was, was all the more acute in the present instance,
because he felt a new tenderness in their relation, and a new appreciation of it, now that a sinister shadow, as he morbidly
feared, seemed to be stealing upon their happiness. His distress
was all the greater because he could not, in this instance, tell her
what was worrying him, as he invariably did; ordinarily, when
anything troubled him, he told her and then it troubled him no
longer. But he could not dispose of this worry in that easy way,
though his gloomy mien did not escape the sharp eyes of Lucretia.

"What is the matter?" she asked him that morning. "You seem
to be low-spirited."

He looked at her an instant, and then caught her in his arms.

"I can't bear to leave you," he said.

He strained her to him and held her close, as though to protect
her from unhappiness, and above all, in the strange egoism of
man's nature, from anything that might mar the ideal she had
formed of him. He kissed her, and she nestled in his arms a

207

moment, in a kind of purring contentment. After a moment she slipped out of his embrace as though it were weakness to remain there longer, and stood looking at him, her face flushed with pleasure. Then presently, resuming her habitual calmness and self-control, she said:

"We have our duty to do in this life, Mr. Blair. We can only go ahead and do it, that is all. In this case it isn't much. It will soon be over, and you will be at home again."

And so Lucretia packed his saddlebags and that afternoon he flung them across Kitty—saddlebags striking the right note for a campaign in which the candidates must recall the pioneers as much as possible—and rode away to Blue Jacket. He fancied that he could feel a change in the atmosphere of his meeting that night; the audience was not hostile and there were no interruptions by rowdies, as was usually the case at these remote political meetings. But his hearers were cold and unresponsive. He did his best to rouse them; he told funny stories and tried to be as much like Tom Corwin as he could, but to no use; those farmers sat there on the benches of the little log-schoolhouse, their faces set in the mask of bucolic stolidity, and never cracked a smile or moved a muscle except to keep their jaws going all the while as they chewed their tobacco and flooded the puncheon floor with its yellow juice.

He was to stay the night with a friend of Judge Diller named Pike, who lived in a log-cabin not far from the settlement, on a farm he had cleared with his own hands. Pike and his wife occupied a bed at one end of the single room, screened by a curtain of faded calico strung on a wire, and Blair was assigned to a bed similarly screened at the other end of the cabin—Pike's two sons, who usually occupied that bed, having clambered up to the loft to sleep there. It was already late according to the scheme by which Pike regulated his life when they got home from the meeting, and they said good-night at once, Blair taking his candle and retiring behind his curtain. When he opened his saddlebags he was surprised and touched to find, on top of the clean linen Lucretia had so neatly folded there, his old copy of Byron's Poems, and when he picked it up he was still more surprised to find a bit of red ribbon yarn marking a place. He turned it up at once, and by the dim light of his candle read a passage marked in pencil, evidently by Lucretia's hand:

"Man's love is of man's life a thing apart;
'Tis woman's whole existence."[41]

He read it, closed the book and sat down on the edge of his bed, wondering what this strange message from her meant. He had long since learnt that Lucretia's nature was one of great reticence, of proud and deep reserves. She, for instance, had never in all their life, addressed him by any other form than "Mr. Blair." To be sure, that was the fashion of the well-bred in Virginia, and Lucretia, he was vastly proud to think, was an F.F.V. There had always been something formal in their relation which his own reserve made it no less difficult to overcome. It was not that they would withhold anything from each other; it was rather a deep respect for each other's essential dignity. It was not that they had any secrets from each other—except on his side this little secret about poor Gertie, which in the beginning had seemed so trivial that he had practically forgotten it, until these past few days. Could it be that it was known to her too, and that this was a delicate way of telling him so, and of conveying a mild reproach?

He sat and pondered these things until, peeping out from behind his curtain, he saw that the Pikes' candle glowed no longer behind their curtain; the fire in the vast chimney had burnt low, and the firelight no longer flickered on the cabin wall, and old Pike was tuning up for a long night's snore. Blair hastily undressed and sank into the depths of his feather-bed, and lay there a long time, thinking, and vaguely wishing that in this life the law of causality were not so remorseless.

He rode off the next morning to Raymer's Ford where he was to address a meeting that afternoon. The meeting was not a large one, and he thought he could feel the same atmosphere of apathy that he had felt at Blue Jacket. But, on his ride of ten miles to New Prospect where he was to speak that evening, he succeeded in convincing himself that he was making mountains out of molehills, and that, after the immense mass-meeting at Macochee, any political rally organized in his interest could only be an anti-climax. Nevertheless, when he got to New Prospect, he went at once to see John Cartwright, who kept the grocery there and was the leading Whig of the neighbourhood.

Blair rode up in front of the grocery, where a small group of idle men and boys promptly gathered staring at him in curiosity.

"Well, Cartwright, how are you?" he said with the candidate's cordiality, as a burly man in shirt-sleeves, with red hair and an enormous, drooping red moustache came out to greet him.

"Howdy, Mr. Blair. Just 'light and come in, won't you?"

Blair dismounted and tied his horse to the rack, the group of

209

men forming a circle about him and—whatever they may have thought of him—admiring his horse.

"How do things look in Tecumseh Township?" asked Blair as he went up to the door. But Cartwright did not reply. After he had shaken hands he spat judiciously on the earth, wiped his moist moustache with the edge of his hand, and said:

"I reckon you'd best step inside."

Cartwright, as Blair at once divined, was not going to jeopardize his local prestige and cheapen himself by discussing the great affairs of state out of doors before a lot of idle loafers, and they went indoors, and to the sample-room that Cartwright kept at the back of his store. They sat down and Blair asked Cartwright to have a dram with him. They clinked glasses, tossed off their whisky, and sat down. Cartwright, Blair thought, was somewhat ominously solemn, but that may have been to give himself importance.

"Well, Cartwright," said Blair, "how are things looking? Shall we have a good meeting to-night?"

"I reckon we'll have a right good turn-out, Mr. Blair," Cartwright replied, and then, after this encouraging beginning he added, "but I'm not so sure about the election, your part of it, 't any rate. Old Gineral Harrison and Tom Corwin is popular, but well, Mr. Blair, an enemy of yours has been sowing tares."

"Ah, indeed?"

"Yes, sir. Henderson was out here a few days ago. You know most of our folks come from New Connecticut, and they're narrow-minded like. There's a good deal of abolition sentiment and you come from Kentucky. They say you're hardly sound on the slavery question."

"I'm a Henry Clay man, Cartwright, on that as on other questions."

"Yes, I know; so am I, though I hain't worrying my mind much about the niggers. From all accounts, too, Mr. Blair, you're like Henry Clay in being popular with the sex."

Cartwright's red face turned a deeper red with the smile that overspread it as he said this, and with a suggestive roll of his eyes, he laughed at his own joke. "No wonder, either, a good-lookin' young fellow like you."

"Well, I can't say anything as to that. I have never found that I was so very popular with the ladies. I've got the finest wife in the world, and all I want now is to get back to her as soon as possible. She's from Virginia, Cartwright. As for your abolitionists out this way, they ought to be satisfied with my views so long as Ethan Grow is, and he supports me in *The Torchlight*."

"Yes, I know. But I don't think it's really so much that. You know when them there damn Yankees get their teeth into a moral idea they can't let go of it; they've just got to chaw on it and chaw on it. And ever since the visit of Henderson a story's been going round. You see he didn't come alone; that 'ere young Nash, the son of the Colonel, was with him." Cartwright was suddenly overwhelmed by embarrassment. "I don't like to mention a lady's name, but a story's been going round about you and—you don't mind my saying—and well, Mrs. Tom Nash."

"Well, Cartwright, you have more delicacy than Nash seems to have had, and the fact does you infinite credit. He seems to have no objection to fouling his own nest."

Blair could feel his own face flush with anger, and for a second he had difficulty in controlling himself. He was, indeed, on the point of breaking out when Cartwright said in a mollifying tone:

"I don't know as it was him said so much as Henderson. I reckon it was more his doings. You've only got to drop a hint, you know, and such things spread like prairie fire. You know our folks are narrow-minded like, being mostly Yankee stock or from back East, and not like you and me who come from Kentucky."

"Well, Cartwright, I'm much obliged to you for being frank with me. Forewarned is forearmed. As far as Tom Nash is concerned, he is a God-damned liar and a blackguard. As for the tale that he, or Henderson, or whoever it may be, has spread, I can't dignify it, or insult the lady it involves, by discussing it."

"I think," said Cartwright, "that you needn't worry about the meeting to-night. I'll have a lot of bully boys there, and if anybody starts a row he'll soon have a bellyful. Then if you can stay over to-morrow, we'll go round and see a few men I know, and it'll turn out all right, I'm pretty sure."

Cartwright's faith in his bully boys was justified. The meeting passed off without an incident or an interruption. The following day Blair went with Cartwright to call on several influential Whigs in the neighborhood, and received sufficient reassurances to relieve his anxiety about the vote in Tecumseh Township, though his anxiety about the "story" remained with him; he almost regretted that Cartwright had told him that. He bore that anxiety with him on his way to Willow Springs, where he addressed another meeting the following evening, and it remained with him until he got home and held Lucretia once more in his arms.

211

There was a moment of slight embarrassment for them both,—or so Blair felt—because of the passage she had marked in the Byron. But it was easy, when her head was hidden against his breast, or easier than it would have been had he been looking into her eyes, to say:

"I read the passage you marked, and for once Byron was mistaken. You are my whole life, my whole existence—whatever anybody may say."

She caught him impulsively round the neck with her slender arms and gave him a strong, passionate hug, and kissed him.

IX

The last meeting of the campaign was to be a belated flag-pole raising and grand Whig rally at Salem, a few days before election, and posters had announced for a week past that Blair and Fowler Brunton were "to discuss the issues of the day." Salem was only eight miles from Macochee—an easy canter there and back—but Brunton had refused to ride.

"No horseback for me," he had insisted. "I'm no pioneer, and I've got no saddlebags, and as I'm not a candidate for office I don't have to pretend that I prefer the savage life to the little civilisation, such as it is, we've been able to develop. No, by God, we'll drive."

It was just as well for, as Blair observed, Brunton was a little drunk before they started, and Blair preferred to drive the buggy they had hired at McCullough's livery. They had not gone far before Brunton produced a flask of whisky, offered it to Blair, and then took a pull at it himself. He kept on taking pulls, and when Blair reminded him that they had speeches to make that evening, Brunton assured Blair that he knew to a drop just how much whisky it required to tune him up to the right oratorical pitch. Blair was not sure that there wasn't something in the theory when they got to the meeting, for he had never heard Brunton make a more rousing speech. Brunton, too, had his wits about him as they prepared to drive back, for he stooped and carefully inspected the hubs of the buggy-wheels to make sure that political opponents had not unscrewed and removed the nuts. But as they drove homeward through the dark woods of the Marmon Valley in the chill air of the autumn evening, the buggy squeaking comfortably along over the soft road behind the jogging nag, Brunton produced his flask again—he had it refilled at Salem— and it was not long before he grew confidential and sentimental, and, speaking with a decided burr, was telling Blair how much he rejoiced in Blair's success, his happy home, his charming wife, and the career that was so auspiciously opening before him. And Blair was touched, for he knew how entirely sincere Brunton was; there wasn't the slightest hint of envy or meanness in his nature.

"And I'm proud to think," Brunton went on, in that thick tongue, that buzzing accent, "it's a consolation to me to remember that I had the honour to introduce you to the future Mrs. Blair. You remember, don't you, Carter, that evening out at Congreves'?"

How could he forget? They recalled the summer evening, and then, a moment later, Brunton was speaking of Sallie Congreve—and, on the verge of tears, bemoaning his hapless fate.

"You know what Byron says," Brunton went on, and he recited the lines: [lines omitted].

Blair was moved, and sincerely sorry for his friend.

"But it isn't hopeless, Fowler,—not at all."

Brunton shook his head mournfully.

"But it isn't, I tell you," said Blair. "It all depends on you."

"It can't be, Carter; it can't be. It can't ever be. It wasn't ever meant to be."

"But I tell you it can be. Listen, if you'll just brace yourself up—"

"No, Carter, you listen; listen to me. I don't have to listen to you, for I know what you're going to say. But, Carter, I'm your friend. You know that; your friend, right or wrong. I'd go through hell and high water for you. And you're my friend; I know it; I feel it. But you and I, we're different; you can't help it; I can't help it. You're—you won't mind my telling you, Carter?"

"Of course not."

"We've got to be frank, as friends. Well, you're sagacious, prudent; you look ahead, and plan beforehand. You're my best friend, but when it came to practising our profession you wouldn't take me for a partner. I don't blame you. No doubt you were right. But I'm not that way; I'm more impulsive, more spontaneous; I wear my heart on my sleeve for daws to peck at. I'm—I'm—oh hell, I don't know what I am! I'm a Goddamn fool, that's what I am. And to think—to think of Sallie Congreve! Oh

213

Carter, tell me, did you ever see such a lovely girl, such an in—
inesh—"

He had the greatest difficulty in pronouncing the word, but finally, syllable by syllable, he managed it. "Such an in-esh-ti-
ma-ble woman!"

He was silent for a moment, and Blair laid his hand on Brunton's shoulder and gave him an affectionate pat. There was still
suite in Brunton's ideas, for, a moment later, he said:

"I didn't mean to talk about Sallie, Carter. I've got my own
disappointment, my own trouble; my own failure, if you want to
call it that, to bear. I meant to tell you something—to give you a
friendly little warning."

"Yes?"

"Look out for Tom Nash, Carter; look out for Tom Nash!"

"What of Tom Nash?"

"He's capable of ruining your happiness, Carter."

"You mean he's doing what he can to prevent my election? I
know that."

"Oh, hell, no! What political influence has he got? Anyhow,
you're elected now, man. Henderson can't come within forty
rows of apple-trees of beating you. No, I'm thinking of your nice
little home, of that jewel of a wife of yours; you mustn't let anything happen that will touch Lucretia."

Blair gasped.

"What do you mean, Fowler? Speak out, man!" he said, sharply.

"Wait a minute! Don't fret the cattle. You've got no idea of the
malignant hatred Nash has for you. But I have, for I've heard him
talk. Now, don't grow angry with me, Carter. I'm only fulfilling
the sometimes ungrateful rôle of the *amicus curiae,* and I must
tell you the truth. *Amico Plato, sed magis amica veritas,* or, if
you prefer, *in vino veritas.*"

Blair could usually find Brunton's whimsical fooling amusing,
but just now, with his curiosity and apprehension aroused, he
was impatient, and said:

"Oh, go on, Fowler; come to the point."

"I'm coming. Tom Nash, then, has been drunk for a week,
drunker than I am at this minute. But as you know, when he's
drunk, he's fighting drunk, like an Irishman; when I'm drunk I'm
even more genial and kindly, if possible, than when I'm sober.
He spends most of his time at Joe Tappan's, breathing out vengeance against you. He seems to have a hatred of you that is
positively mortal."

214

Blair was somewhat shocked at this, and, for an instant, somewhat hurt. He was still young, still the dazzled subject of his youthful illusions; he could not understand why anyone should actively dislike him or bear him positive ill will. With kindly feelings himself towards all the world, wishing everyone well, he had generally taken it for granted that everyone held the same favourable opinion of him that he held of himself. How could it be otherwise? Then this feeling suddenly vanished and he hardened into a mood of hateful resentment.

"It's nothing to me what Tom Nash thinks of me. For all I care let him go to hell. But he'd better keep out of my way!"

After this angry outburst, however, his curiosity got the better of him, and he asked:

"What does he say about me? What have I done to him?"

"My dear Carter, it's a delicate matter. I'm merely warning you; urging you, as your best friend, and in your own interest, to avoid him for a while."

"Avoid him? What for? Do you think I'm afraid of Tom Nash—or any other man?"

Brunton gave a groan of despair.

"Oh, my God!" he exclaimed. "I knew it would come to that! That's precisely the trouble, the very danger I'm trying to avoid!"

"Fowler, I wish to the devil you would explain yourself and tell me what it's all about!"

Brunton was silent a moment. He took a pull at his bottle, cleared his throat, and then began:

"May it please the Court. I said a while ago that you were a prudent man who kept an eye on the future. As a rule that is true, but there's an exception, as to all rules. You don't keep a guard on that fiery Southern temper of yours. You're from Kentucky, and, like all Southern gentlemen you've got an exaggerated notion of chivalry and honour, and the hot head that goes with those ideas. You're always on a hair trigger and ready to fight at the drop of a hat—pistols and coffee for two; a snake round your hat and a bowie knife in your boot; and all that nonsense. It's the chief defect of an otherwise pleasing and gracious character. But since you're like that, I want you to avoid Tom Nash, for if you were to meet now, with him in his ugly mood, there would be a fight—God knows what—maybe a tragedy. I want you to think of the effect on your life; on your career; and, Carter, on Lucretia. For God's sake, man, don't bring sorrow to that angel from the skies!"

"All you say, Fowler," said Blair, "is most interesting and moving. But you've failed thus far to tell me what Nash says about me, what he charges me with. In other words, whether I shall be obliged to send him a challenge and ask you to do me the honour to act as my second."

"Look here, Carter. We're not in Kentucky, we're in Ohio, the prosaic Buckeye State. We don't fight duels in Ohio; we just grapple and roll on the ground, and bite off each other's thumbs and gouge out each other's eyes. Don't be ridiculous! I'm drunk, I know, but I had no idea you were."

"I was never more sober in my life, Fowler. If Nash should even mention the name of my wife, I would shoot him down like a dog."

"My God, man, he hasn't said anything about your wife! It's his wife—he claims to be the injured party—and Carter, it is evident that his pride is grievously hurt."

"Yes, but what in God's name does he say?"

"He says, Carter, that the child isn't his."

"It was born in wedlock."

"Yes, but he claims that he is not its father. He seems only lately to have found out, or so he claims. You see, he never had any intention of marrying her; but she was too clever to consent without a wedding. Now he claims that she tricked him into a marriage, and that she was in the family way at the time. That's why the Nashs won't recognize the child or its mother."

They said no more for the moment, but drove along in silence. They were drawing near to Macochee when Brunton, laying his hand affectionately on Blair's arm, broke the silence by saying:

"Promise me; don't go to Tappan's for a few days—keep out of his way. Do this for me! Promise me, Carter!"

Blair did not reply for a moment. He was struggling with his pride. Then at last he said:

"Thank you, Fowler. You are a good friend to me. I appreciate it. But don't ask me to promise that. I never ran away from a man in my life and I am not going to begin now by running away from a blackguard like Tom Nash."

X

It was late when they drove into Macochee and the little town was wrapped in darkness and slumber. Brunton had long since emptied his flask and flung it into the bushes by the roadside. The drink was dying down in him; he felt the chill of the night, and sat huddled up miserably in the corner of the seat, shivering and depressed and no longer talkative. In fact, as they rode along the silent streets they spoke to each other no more.

Blair set Brunton down at Mrs. Brewster's where his friend still had his lodgings, bade him good-night, and then drove to McCullough's livery-stable to put up the horse. As he started to walk home, he found that his legs were stiff and he felt rather cold and numb from his night drive. His way home led him across the Square; it sprawled there, wide and dark and empty, the Whig flag-mast tall and naked under the gloomy night-sky, its flag and triumphant pennant, in accordance with Captain Ames's strict code of military etiquette, having been lowered at sunset. The withered boughs on the speaker's stand rustled dismally in the night air. In the buildings that presented their closed fronts blankly to the Square not a light showed anywhere; the very town itself seemed deserted and dead, abandoned to him and one other human being, a man, some late reveller no doubt on his lonely way home, his uncertain footfall echoing in the silence of the Square. But yes, one house was awake; there was a thin golden bar of light across the transom of Joe Tappan's grocery where the green blind just failed to touch the lintel of the door. And numb and cold as he was, Blair thought of dropping in there for one last drink before going on home. He thought, of course, in the same instant of Brunton's warning; but Brunton was drunk, and besides, it was ten to one that Nash would not be there at this hour. But he had no sooner thought of this excuse than he was disgusted with himself; prudent or not, and Tom Nash or not, if he didn't go into Tappan's now when he had a reason for going there, it would be because he was afraid, and he should despise himself all his life as a coward. Afraid of Tom Nash, a spoiled darling of rich parents, an insufferable little fop and coxcomb like Tom Nash! Great God!

He crossed the Square, pushed open the door of Tappan's and went in. The place was empty save for Tappan himself, who, with folded arms, was snoozing behind the screened bar at the far end of the room where the principal business of the "grocery" was transacted. Tappan roused at his entrance, blinked, and, in a tone just a shade less cordial than his customary greeting, said "Good evening," without mentioning the name.

"Some Oscar Pepper, please, Tappan," said Blair.

And as Tappan set out the glass and bottle, Blair heard the door-latch click, and turned to see Fowler Brunton who, evidently moved by a desire similar to his own, had not gone home,

217

but had come for another drink himself. Brunton approached the bar, and said to Blair:

"So you're here, heigh?"

"Yes," said Blair; "and so are you, just in time for a drink."

Brunton, Blair observed, had already cast a look of anxious inquiry at Tappan, and Tappan had answered by a nod of deep concern. When this pantomime had been enacted between them—Blair scorning to take any notice of it—Brunton asked in a low voice:

"Who are with him?"

"Henderson and Winship."

"Who is your mysterious and dangerous customer, Tappan?" asked Blair. "Some Simon Girty, some wild desperado and Bad Man from the West?"

"It's Mr. Tom Nash, sir," said Tappan. "He's on the spree and in a nasty temper—ready to kick up a row. And, you know, I can't afford to have a row in my place, sir."

"Well, Tappan, in that case if I were you I'd kick Nash out. And Fowler, here's your very good health."

They drank, and then Brunton said:

"Do be reasonable, Carter, and go home."

Blair laughed, and as he very well knew, ostentatiously lingered, twirling his small tumbler round in his fingers, and making little circles of moisture on the smooth surface of the bar. And then, a moment later, the door to the back-room opened, and against a background of tobacco smoke he saw Tom Nash. He was haggard and wild in appearance, his eyes were bloodshot, he was unshaven, his flowered satin waistcoat was opened and blotched and stained. His eyes glanced round the room, and at sight of Blair he stopped as though smitten with angry surprise. Blair took no notice of him, made as though he hadn't seen him, but in a swift glance he caught a vision of Winship and Henderson standing in the doorway behind Nash, craning their necks and peering, with astonished and frightened eyes, over his shoulder. There was a strange contrast between the faces of the two men; Henderson's face was dark and clouded with sudden concern; Winship's was red, redder than ever, and his large blotched nose glowing like a carbuncle, with his eyes blazing on either side. They hesitated an instant, drew back, then changed their minds and came into the room, recognizing Blair by sheepish, but somehow appealing nods.

"Good evening, gentlemen," said Blair, formally.

He had had the drink he had come for and was about to pay

his reckoning, when Nash approached the bar—a short counter at which not more than four or five men could conveniently stand. He approached and, leaning on the bar, demanded of Tappan:

"Didn't you hear me calling? Why can't you answer, Tappan? We want more drink."

"I think you've had enough, Mr. Nash," said Tappan in a low, conciliatory voice.

Nash made an impatient movement of anger and resentment.

"I'm the judge of that," he said, and in the movement lurched against Blair. Blair moved away to avoid him, but this movement irritated Nash and, obviously of set purpose, he rudely brushed against Blair a second time, as if to push him further away.

"Don't jostle me, sir!" said Blair.

"Then get out of my way," retorted Nash.

"I tell you not to jostle me, sir!" said Blair, peremptorily. He could feel Brunton tugging at his coat-sleeve on the other side of him.

Nash now turned an insolent glance on him and said:

"Oh, it's you, is it? Well, you're just the man I've been looking for. I've got an account to settle with you!"

"Very well," said Blair, in the calm, level voice he was, by a tremendous effort, imposing upon his anger. "Whenever you like. But this is hardly the place for such discussions." And then, turning towards Tappan he asked:

"How much did you say it was, Tappan?"

"Two bits, sir."

Blair was counting the coins in his palm, when Nash seized him by the arm, and said:

"See here, Blair, God damn your soul to hell, you're not going to get out of it like that. I've stood enough from you—"

The coins, knocked from Blair's hand, rattled on the bar and down on the floor. Blair wrenched away from Nash's grasp.

"Nash," he said, "you're drunk. But even so, don't go too far. I give you fair warning."

The room had suddenly grown very still, so still that, as Fowler Brunton said afterwards, he could hear Blair breathing; Winship and Henderson were standing with tense, drawn expressions at the end of the bar; Tappan was looking over it, horrified. But Blair did not take his eyes from Nash, standing there, glaring at him in hatred. Nash took a step towards him.

"You're afraid to discuss it, are you, you—"

"Be careful, Nash," Blair interrupted. "I've warned you once; don't lay a hand on me again, and keep a civil tongue in your head."

And then, suddenly, Nash burst forth into violent and incoherent abuse of Blair.

Blair gave a sneering laugh.

"Nash," he said, "you're not only drunk, but crazy."

And then, turning to Henderson and Winship, he said:

"Hadn't you better take your drunken friend home, gentlemen?"

But Nash stepped nearer, and went on with his tirade:

"I was fool enough to marry your cast-off whore, I know, but, by God, you mustn't expect me to support your dirty bastard brat! And so take that, you lying, cowardly, son-of-a- —"

Nash lunged at Blair, but Blair, the hair on his head fairly bristling with rage, fetched Nash a blow with his fist that dropped him in a huddle on the sawdust-strewn floor.

Nash was struggling to get to his feet, and suddenly Blair saw the glint of metal in his hand and knew that Nash had drawn his pistol. Then Blair, throwing back his great coat, drew his own pistol and stood waiting. And Tappan and Henderson and Winship, looking on an instant in horror, suddenly ducked behind the bar. Blair waited. He saw Nash, with incredible slowness, as it seemed to him, get to his knees, then scramble to his feet, and finally, standing up, his pistol raised, glare at him with a drawn, white, and perfectly sober face. He met his eye, and then before either could move Fowler Brunton had leapt between them and, springing upon Nash, seized him by the arms, forced him back to the bar, bent him backwards over it, and caught the hand that held the pistol.

"You mad, drunken, murderous damn fool you!" said Brunton.

He wrenched the pistol finally from Nash's grasp, and Nash stood there, trying to catch his breath.

And just at that instant the door-latch clicked, there was a slow and heavy step down the length of the room, and, a moment later, Colonel Nash appeared round the corner of the screen. There he stood in his large beaver hat, his greatcoat buttoned up to his chin, his gold-headed cane in his hand. He appeared not to notice, or even to be aware of the others in the room; his eyes were fixed in humiliation and pain on the wretched figure of his son, leaning with his back to the bar, his arms sprawled out along its edge as if to support himself.

"Thomas," said the Colonel, "Thomas, come home with me."

Tom Nash looked at his father an instant.

"Come, Thomas," said the Colonel again.

And Tom's chin fell on his breast, his limp legs gave way, and he would have fallen if Brunton had not held him up. They fetched his hat and greatcoat from the back room, and supported on one side by Brunton and on the other by Colonel Nash, he was led from the bar. As they were going round the screen, the Colonel turned and said:

"Gentlemen, this is a sad and distressing occasion for me. Pardon me if, for a moment—appearing as I did so abruptly—I forgot my manners. I bid you good-night."

Blair waited until Brunton had helped Tom Nash to enter the carriage with his father, and then they went away together.

XI

They parted in the Square, Brunton to return to his lodgings, Blair to go on home. They had not exchanged a word since they left Tappan's. The emotion of the scene through which they had just passed, the loneliness and the melancholy of the late hour, the mystery of the dark autumnal night, and the silent, sleeping, unconscious town, lay upon their spirits. They heard the hollow rumble of Colonel Nash's carriage as it crossed the bridge over Possum Run; the steeple-clock in the Court House struck two; then the vast, intolerable silence again, more oppressive than before.

"A close shave, my boy," said Brunton.

"Yes," said Blair. He took Brunton's hand, tried to say something, but all he could say was: "Thank you, my friend."

And Brunton was too full of feeling to say more than:

"Well, good-night."

"Good night."

Blair turned up the collar of his coat and strode on towards home. Now that it was all over and he gazed back into the awful pit of tragedy from which he had just escaped, he was filled with horror, and he felt faint and weak. The night, as he looked back over it, seemed immeasurably long; the meeting at Salem might have been the occurrence of months before; and since he had kissed Lucretia good-bye—how long ago that had been! And at the thought of Lucretia he was filled with a tumult of longing, of regret, of grief and shame. She, waiting at home for him whilst he, in his foolish, stubborn pride, his silly bravado, his desire to show off in Brunton's eyes and in his own as well, he had come within an ace of—my God! He looked down in that pit of darkness and shuddered, and shut his eyes, and drew back in horror. He daren't think of it.

The question now was: should he tell Lucretia? She must hear of it soon or late; it would be all over town in the morning. Yes, he might as well tell her—that is, tell her something of it. But how much? He could not plead his hot temper as an excuse in this emergency. He had never shown more coolness and self-possession in his life; he had shown even more than that; he had given the most convincing proof of that deliberation and foresight which Brunton had mentioned as they were driving back from Salem; with a lawyer's skill and knowledge he had so contrived events, that Nash had been the aggressor, and at every stage of the quarrel entirely in the wrong. That is, he had contrived a perfect defence for the homicide he was ready to commit. Tell Lucretia this? Tell her why? Tell her about Gertie—over whom he was brawling in a drinking-bar? Well, not to-night, at any rate.

He slipped into the house as quietly as he could, hoping that she was asleep and would not hear him. But nothing ever went on in that house without Lucretia knowing it. As he stole along the passage past the door of her room—they had occupied separate rooms since the birth of the baby—he heard her say in a loud whisper:

"Is that you, Mr. Blair?"

"Yes," he said, and paused at the door.

"You are late. I was beginning to grow anxious."

"Yes, I am late. I'm sorry. But I won't come near you—I smell too strongly of politics."

"You may come and kiss me good-night, but please don't wake the baby."

He stepped on tiptoe across the room and bent and kissed her.

The following morning as they sat at breakfast he told her of his escapade; that is, he told her something of it, though by no means all. He began his sketch in a somewhat casual and slightly amused tone, and as he went on he was somewhat surprised to find what an inevitable and creditable air the bare outline might assume, and what a picturesque, manly and even heroic rôle he had so dashingly played.

"We were cold after our drive in the night air, and I dropped into Tappan's to get a dram to warm me up. As bad luck would have it, Tom Nash was there—with Winship and Henderson, by the way—and he was roaring drunk. I tried to avoid him but I couldn't. He became abusive and insulting, and I bore it all until he called me a lot of foul names, and then I had to knock him down. You know what we say in Kentucky—the damned lie is the first lick. Then he drew his pistol, but Fowler Brunton leapt upon him and took it from him. I was glad of that; I didn't want to have to shoot him. And just at that moment, what do you think happened? Colonel Nash appeared—looking for his wayward son—and took him home. I felt sorry for the poor old fellow. It is humiliating to a man and a gentleman of his standing and pride to have a drunken worthless blackguard of a son."

Lucretia sat and listened in silence, her eyes lowered under their long lashes to her coffee cup. When he had finished she raised her cup, took a sip of the coffee, and he saw that she was trembling.

"The quarrel between you and Mr. Tom Nash is one of long standing, is it not, Mr. Blair?" she asked, presently, looking up at him gravely.

"Well, my dear," replied Blair; "I wasn't aware that there was a standing quarrel between us. It is true that long ago, in our youth, we did have a disagreement, a silly, trifling picayunish affair, —a quarrel if you like; but so far as I was concerned, it left no bad blood behind. I'm sure that I cherished no ill will and bore him no grudge. But he's got some crazy notion in his fuddled brain—he was drunk as a fiddler—that I had done him a wrong, and am somehow, God only knows how, responsible for the mess he has made of his life. I can't tell you all he said—"

"I don't wish to know, Mr. Blair," she said, raising her hand to stay him. "I don't care to hear any more about it. But, since your honour seems to have been satisfied, can't you avoid him in the future?"

"I'll try to, Lucretia. But of course I can't allow him to insult me openly and wantonly."

"No, I reckon not. In Virginia, and I presume in Kentucky, gentlemen settle questions of honour in duels. I don't know what the prevailing method is in Ohio. It is a barbarous practice and, Mr. Blair, I perfectly detest it!" She clenched her two little fists and her eyes flashed fire, and then, swallowing painfully and regaining that perfect control of herself which she so rarely lost, she said, "But, wicked as it is, it surely presents advantages over the bar-room brawl."

He hung his head, and said:

"You are perfectly right, Lucretia, perfectly right. I had no business to go in there last night; as a matter of fact, Brunton had warned me against Nash, but Brunton was a little drunk too, and I didn't consider it really serious. And besides, I couldn't admit that I was afraid—"

"Whoever would dream of saying *you* were afraid? But I am

223

afraid—I was afraid last night. I lay awake and waited—I knew that something was wrong, that you were in danger, that—"

Her eyes suddenly filled with tears, and he was touched.

"Lucretia, dear!" he began.

But she impatiently brushed her tears away and said:

"I'm all right—never mind. I'm silly to be so weak."

XII

To Blair's alert senses the town seemed unnaturally still on that morning of election day. The golden light of the October sun cast a glamour on that small world, and when after breakfast as he started on his way up town, he paused an instant and, in the vista of Miami Street, caught a glimpse of the low hills that were swimming in the haze of autumn, the loveliest season of the year in Ohio. The village was still so integrally a part of the country that, in the sparsely built quarter where Blair had his residence, it was pervaded by the atmosphere of the woods, the odour of ripening nuts — hickory, beech and walnuts—and its colours were repeated in the coppery-brown and crimson and gold of the maple-trees, and in the pale yellow of the long five-cusped leaves of the buckeye-tree which had done such yeoman service for the Whigs in the campaign. There were other odours, too, in the air that morning—the appetizing odour of the apple-butter and the pickles that [Elvira], under Lucretia's supervision, was making in the garden behind the house. Lucretia, her slight figure enveloped in an enormous gingham apron (with sleeves) had come to the gate with him.

"Ohio is lovely, isn't it?" he said. "Especially in the fall of the year."

Her glance swept the wide and sparsely built-up street, and went on to the glimmering little picture of the hills framed by its trees.

"Yes," she said; "but on days like this I sometimes feel—"

"Not homesick for Virginia?"

"Ah! Virginia!" she said, a little wistfully, and smiled and made no direct reply to his question. Instead she said:

"I believe, Mr. Blair, that you are fonder now of Ohio than you are of Kentucky."

"I'm not disloyal to Kentucky; but I'm a Buckeye now, and I love the Buckeye State."

But Lucretia had more important things to do than to stand there discussing State loyalties, and, in her formal way she bade him "Good morning," and returned to the great steaming kettle in the garden behind the house. Blair stood looking after the slight, energetic little figure until it had flitted round the corner of the house, and then started on his walk to his law-office.

As he went he sensitively felt, or perhaps imagined, a certain almost mystical quality in the atmosphere which made this day unlike other days—a sense of breathless expectancy in the air, an apprehension of those fates that were playing with the destinies of so many men—from President Van Buren and General Harrison, and Governor Shannon and Tom Corwin, down to Representative Henderson himself. He had a vision of all those millions of independent and truculent sovereigns walking solemnly to the polls, gravely folding up their little strips of white paper, and tucking them irrevocably into the ballot-box, deciding not so much perhaps the political issues of the rollicking campaign that had just closed—for no one could tell precisely what those issues were—as the personal fate of those who, like himself, had been struggling in the arena. He wondered whether even now, on this the fatidical day, he ought not still to step softly and be circumspect, lest here at the very last minute he do something to defeat himself. But no; there was nothing to be done now. His fate was already determined by those voters with their remorseless thumbs down, or their gracious thumbs up, and all he could do was to wait and see whether, in his case, it was thumbs up or down. There was a strange irrevocability, a mysterious fatality about this event of election!

However, first of all he must go and cast his own vote. The polling place was in the Market beside the town-hall, in a shed used by the Macochee Volunteer Fire Company to house its apparatus. In the wide doorway, with the fire-pump and the hook-and-ladder truck in the dim background, a deal table was set out, and on it the sacred ballot-box. Behind the table sat the clerks and judges of election, Whigs and Democrats, philosophically chewing their tobacco in the neutrality imposed by their positions, whilst in the dust of the Market outside, the challengers and watchers of the two parties waited for the voters with no such pretensions of impartiality.

Blair, as he turned into the Market, saw, beside the watchers, two or three other men; one of them was Tom Nash. And there flashed before his mind the oval face of Lucretia with its expression of sweet concern, and proud, high-born reticence, and he heard that last appeal wrung from her by her love of him, that he avoid Tom Nash in future. But he was powerless; he was being swept along on this day of days by fatidical forces that he could not control; he could not turn back now. He walked on, and, rather than show any hesitation, he quickened his pace and came swinging along with a confident and somewhat breezy air. As he passed the small knot of men and wished them good morning, they all returned his salutation with hearty promptness—all save Nash. In Nash's eyes, one of them still discoloured, Blair saw the glint of a remorseless and deadly hatred. Nash compressed his thin lips, and a kind of malignant pallor swept his thin, drawn, dissipated face.

Blair passed on, and, going up to Dines, one of the Whig watchers, asked him for a ticket. Blair took the long, narrow strip, ran his eye down over the long list of names—the Whig electors, Thomas Corwin, the candidates for the State Offices and for Congress, and his own name—and as he slowly folded it up he said:

"The vote is being got out pretty well, is it Dines?"

"Oh yes, sir! Full Whig vote. You'll win in an easy canter."
Dines spoke, thought Blair, with a strained, uneasy enthusiasm.

Blair had turned so that he might keep an eye on Nash who still stood there eyeing him with that steady and malevolent glare. He went up to the table and poised his folded ballot over the slot in the box.

"All right, Mr. Blair," said one of the judges; "I guess we know you."

He dropped his ballot into the box, and Giles Paten, who was one of the clerks of election, said, with his air of solemn mockery:

"*Alea jacta est.*"

Paten was very sober that morning, for, as it was election day, the drinking-places in town were all closed, and he was also very classical.

"*Latet anguis in herba,*" he said, looking at Blair with an expression of peculiar meaning, "if you remember your Virgil."

Blair, with a laugh as indifferent as he could make it, turned away, and was about to leave the polling-place when Nash, as though he had suddenly taken a desperate resolution, came walking swiftly towards him. The thin face was of a pallor even more malevolent than it had been a few moments before, the thin lips were set in a white line.

"Blair," Nash said when he came near; "Blair, you and I might as well have it out here and now. This town isn't big enough to hold us both; one of us —"

"Hold on, Nash," said Blair, interrupting him; "don't go too far. I've given you warning once, so look out!"

The sneer that he had seen on Nash's lips years before, the sneer that in those days had had the power to drive him into a blind rage, came to Nash's lips again; Blair saw it and recognized it, and remembered how Nash used to employ it to express his arrogant contempt for him because of his poverty and his home-spun clothes. Without compunction or regret he could have killed Nash where he stood, but for once he was strangely cool and terribly aware.

"Warning!" Nash was saying. "To hell with you and your warning!"

"Nevertheless, Nash," Blair went on, "I repeat it. I've given you fair warning. You are not drunk this morning; you are as sober as I am. But I reckon you are insane —"

Nash drew his pistol. And at this, Blair stepped back a pace, and drew his pistol. He kept on stepping backward until he was well out into the Market. He was conscious of its empty, dusty space strewn with straw and chaff from the farm-waggons that filled it on Saturdays. Nash, who had the sun in his eyes, was circling warily round as though seeking a point of better advantage. Blair, remembering Paten and Dines and the rest of them, manoeuvred for a position that would leave them out of the line of fire. Then, suddenly, he realized that they had all taken cover in the polling-place; there was not a soul to be seen in all the length and breadth of the Market; it sprawled there, yellow in the bland October sun, wide, deserted and unreal, as bare and empty as a desert.

He stopped, stood still and waited in an immense and appalling silence. Nash had stopped at a distance of forty paces, and now stood there before him, a slender figure in the wide emptiness of the Place, the skirts of his blue coat spreading wide from his narrow waist, his thin legs in their tight trousers tapering down to his high-heeled boots. He was deathly pale; and with each short, sharp breath he drew, one of the brass buttons on the breast of his coat would glint suddenly in the sunlight. Blair noted all these minute details with a vivid distinctness, and, seeing the brass button flash again, it suddenly leapt to his mind that when his Uncle John Blair had fought his duel with Theodore Proctor at Lexington, he had turned sideways in order to present a narrower target to his antagonist. Blair turned sideways, and over his right shoulder looked at Nash. He waited.

227

Slowly Nash raised his arm, his pistol pointing to the sky. Blair heard him cock it, the click of the hammer sounding with sharp distinctness in the oppressive silence of the Place. He raised his own pistol . . . .

He saw Nash's arm descend; he saw a flash of fire, and as the report rang in his ears, at the same instant something stung him in the leg. He felt his leg go suddenly numb, the strength run out of it; he felt sick and faint. But he held on; held on to consciousness, and held on, as it were, to that flashing brass-button on the breast of Nash's coat. He lowered his pistol and pressed the trigger . . . And then, there was Nash all crumpled up on the ground. The Market, miraculously, was suddenly full of men running from all directions. Some of them were crowding about Nash, and someone was shouting: "Stand back, damn it, give the man air!"

Blair felt a warm trickle down his leg into his boot. And then, there was Giles Paten standing beside him, supporting him. The fact rather annoyed him. His temper suddenly flared up.

"Let me alone!" he said. "I'm all right!"

"But, damn it all, man," protested Paten, "you're hit. The blood is running down your leg."

"But don't let Nash see it," he said. "I don't want him to have the satisfaction —"

And then suddenly the Market, the crowd, everything slipped away from him, retreated to an incredible distance, and disappeared, and he was, for an instant, before the world turned black, conscious of but one thing, and that was the comforting softness of Giles Paten's paunch and his velvet waistcoat on which his head was pillowed.

XIII

And then, the next thing he knew he was being borne home on a shutter, and Lucretia was standing on the doorstep in her gingham apron, her hands clasped under her chin, her face white with fear

"It's nothing, honey," he called out; "nothing but a scratch. I'm all right." And to prove it, he tried to sit up, but the effort made him faint and with a little apologetic laugh he sank back on his shutter. She ran down to the gate and laid her hand on his forehead, looking down at him, her eyes large and filled with anguish. He smiled up at her, and tried to reassure and comfort her.

"Don't worry, honey, it's nothing. You see, I couldn't help it. He—"

She nodded in comprehension, and laying her fingers on his lips softly, she said:

"I know. It is Mr. Nash's work. But you mustn't speak now. I understand perfectly." And then she drew her frail little figure up in authority, and took command.

"This way, gentlemen, if you please," she said to the men who were bearing him, and showed them the way to his bedroom. She brought whisky and gave him to drink of it, and asked if they had notified the doctor.

They lifted him from the shutter and laid him on the wide bed. When Lucretia, with the help of Dines, started to draw off his boots and to unfasten his garments, the others standing by with inefficient solicitude, he protested; he would be all right in a few minutes; he would lie there and rest a bit and then get up and undress himself. His mind felt almost brilliantly clear; he was filled with a stimulating excitement. The scene in the Market was vividly before his eyes, as though he were still enacting it. Nash, standing there before him with his hateful face, his scowl, the brass button on his blue coat glinting in the sunlight. And a great and all-important, all-absorbing question came to his mind, and assailed him with irresistible insistence. He must ask them; he must make them tell him. Dines was bending over him, trying with his clumsy fingers to unfasten his stock. He looked up into Dines's red face with the sandy moustache that drooped, moist and mournful, over his mouth. He caught Dines's eye.

"Did I get him?" he asked anxiously, almost eagerly.

But Dines had no chance to reply. Lucretia's deft fingers pushed Dines's fingers away.

"Let me do it, " she said to Dines; and to him: "I told you not to speak, Mr. Blair."

For some reason he dared not ask Lucretia. She had heard his question and a look of pain had swept over her face. He must not distress Lucretia. Her fingers were so soft, so tiny, so deft and efficient. He raised his hand and gave them a little caress; she blushed and smiled, fondly. And he felt a vast dependence upon Lucretia, a dependence like that of a child on its mother. Then he felt suddenly weary, his whole being invaded by an immense and enervating lassitude. His temples began to throb with pain; he turned his head wearily; he would not get up for a while. He yielded himself to the softness of the pillow, and to Lucretia. It was good to have Lucretia to depend upon. She was a comfort and a blessing.... He should have to be patient, and wait until

229

the others had gone, and then ask Lucretia.

They were talking in the room in low tones, so that he should not hear. Dines was whispering, but when Dines whispered, his voice, for some reason, sounded louder than when he spoke aloud.

"Your husband wasn't at all to blame, Ma'am," Dines was saying. "No siree, not the least bit. We were all there and seen it clear as day. Nash—"

"Your assurance is unnecessary, sir," she said. "Mr. Blair could not be to blame, in any event. When made the subject of a brutal and unprovoked assault he would naturally defend himself."

"Of course ma'am. Nash only got what he deserved."

Blair made an effort; strained his ears to hear the answer to the insistent question.

"In fact, ma'am," Dines was going on, "I don't think he got enough. They said he wasn't hurt very badly, ma'am."

Not hurt very badly! Then he hadn't got him after all. He had missed that gleaming button on Nash's coat! A bad shot! He felt a sudden, instinctive sense of disappointment. To be sure, he was out of practice, and then he had never been so good with a pistol as with a rifle. If he had only had his rifle! And yet—perhaps it was better so; better for Lucretia's sake—and Jamie's—at any rate. But what was she saying? He strained his ears again.

"I have no interest in the fate of Mr. Tom Nash, sir," she was saying. "I am only concerned about my husband."

And at this swift and passionate outburst of love and loyalty Blair's heart gave a bound of pride and exultation. God! What a woman!

"And just now I am anxious to have a doctor. Will one of you please to go for Dr. Pearce? And if you will have the goodness to retire, I shall try to make Mr. Blair more comfortable. I thank you all very kindly, gentlemen, for your services."

They accepted their dismissal and shuffled out, pausing in the doorway for a last solemn and sympathetic glimpse at Blair, who tried to smile and wave his hand, and said:

"Thanks, boys, thanks."

When Dr. Pearce arrived a few moments later, somewhat flurried by the tragic urgency of the summons, Blair treated his seriousness facetiously.

"It's nothing, Doc. We had a little argument at the polls this morning."

Dr. Pearce, who tried to conceal his youth by wearing a full beard and whiskers, nodded solemnly, and Blair could see that he was worried and anxious. Lucretia, standing rigidly at the foot of the bed with her hands folded, was watching the doctor anxiously.

"H'm!" said the doctor. "Let's have a look."

When he had examined the wound, he shook his head again and said:

"A very near shave, my friend, a very near shave. A little higher up, and—"

He left them to imagine the fatal complications that would have resulted had it been a little higher up. All that Blair knew was that the ball had entered his right thigh near the hip, and that, now that he was recovered from the shock, it was beginning to give him pain. Dr. Pearce dressed the wound, got out a cupping-glass and bled him, and left him stretched out in bed in a darkened room, under an injunction to try and get some sleep. The doctor said he would return in the afternoon. Then Blair could hear him and Lucretia holding a long, whispered conversation in the passage outside the door.

XIV

And then, after that, long days of weariness and impatience and pain, and longer nights of fever and delirium, when he was struggling impotently with persistent and insuperable obstacles, the nature of which he could not understand for, whilst at night, in his delirium, they seemed altogether real and plausible and normal, by day they became fantastic and absurd, so that there were no words, no symbols, by which he could communicate them to Lucretia. If he struck an antagonist with his fist, the blow fell, flabby, inert and powerless. If he shot at him, the ball would rebound, harmless, from its mark. If, in a cold sweat of terror, he tried to run, his legs were suddenly stricken with paralysis. Then, night after night, he was on his trial, there in the Court House, familiar in a strange unfamiliarity; on his trial for the murder of Tom Nash; Tom Corwin was by his side, defending him. They had entered upon the trial in jovial merriment, certain of sympathy and acquittal, but nothing that he could say by way of explanation could make the slightest impression on the minds of the judge or the jury. For every time he tried to explain, Tom Nash, who was sitting on the bench beside the Judge, would give a sneering, mocking laugh, and then the others—judge, jury, Gertie Grow, old Grow, Giles Paten, Fowler Brunton and Converse would all sneer and turn on him with pitiless expressions of a venomous and implacable hatred.

Then the dawn would come, pale through the windows of his room, and he would wonder what he had said in his delirium. He would ask Lucretia, but she would only smile—a little wanly now after a week spent in endless watching, day and night, at his bedside—she would only smile and brush back his moist locks from his brow, and smooth his pillow, and say:

"You were just a little flighty, and wandered somewhat in your mind, that is all."

Then, after a little respite in those early morning hours, when his fever would abate slightly, Dr. Pearce would come, examine and dress his wound, bleed him, give him some more febrifuge, and the long day would drag itself down to the long night and its horrors again.

But at last there came a morning when he himself knew, before the doctor came and took his pulse and looked at his tongue, that his fever was gone. The doctor came and did all those things, and then, for the first time, smiled, and then smiled at Lucretia, and said:

"Mrs. Blair, I want you should go to bed and get some sleep."

And Lucretia gasped, and a smile came to her wan face, and she came and stood beside him, laid her hand on his brow, and started to say something. But her eyes suddenly filled with tears, she bit her lip, and turned and left the room.

There were so many things he wished to know. One of the most distressing features of his delirium had been the incessant and exhausting toil of rolling a huge and heavy ball, a ball higher than his head. He was required to push it along and as he pushed it, to sing the campaign song:

As rolls this ball, etc.

But though he put all his strength into the effort, the immense ball would not budge, and if he did not roll the ball Tom Corwin would not be elected. Or perhaps Tippecanoe and Tyler Too would not be elected. The confusion in his mind increased his pain, and he would awaken exhausted by these Sisyphean labours. He would put his questions to Lucretia and to Dr. Pearce over and over again, and then forget their answers, or confuse them with what the people of his dreams told him. They could not answer all his questions, for it was days before the results of the election, even locally, could be known, and the result of the national election could not be ascertained for a fortnight. But now that his head was clear, he must get these things straightened out in his mind. First of all, Tom Corwin.

Elected, of course. [Over 16,000] majority.[42]

And old Harrison?

Yes, old Harrison—in fact, the entire Whig ticket, from top to bottom.

Including—me?

Of course.

But there was another question, a question that he hesitated somewhat to put. Then one morning, when the doctor was there, and Lucretia had gone for a moment from the room, he put it bluntly to the doctor. Tom Nash—how was he?

"But I have already told you—a dozen times."

"Well then, I've forgotten."

"He's all right. Why shouldn't he be? He escaped without a scratch."

"But I left him lying on the ground. I saw him fall."

"Yes, but he wasn't hurt. The bullet hit a button on his coat and glanced off. The blow, however, staggered him for a second, and he fell. It was a miracle—a hair's breadth either way, and—tschk!"

Blair made no comment, and was silent for a moment, reflecting on this strange chance. He wasn't such a bad shot after all—unless the bullet had hit some other button. He wouldn't ask the doctor which button had deflected the ball, or how they knew it had struck a button at all.

It was not many days before he could sit up in bed and see a friend or two, now and then, if they didn't sit too long—and Lucretia saw to it that they didn't—Fowler Brunton and Giles Paten, fresh from the barber's, shaven and shorn and smelling of bay rum, and his hair neatly plastered down, and his face as grave and solemn as if he had come to a funeral; and Judge Diller and old Grow, who seized the opportunity to urge Blair, now that he was elected, to come out flat-footed for abolition.

And then one day there came Scott Gardner, the Prosecuting Attorney of the county. Lucretia was present at the interview, which, in its official scope, did not last long. Gardner, after a few polite preliminaries, said:

"I came to ask, Carter, if you wanted to prosecute Tom Nash. If you will appear against him I shall lay the matter before the grand jury at the November term."

Blair leant instantly forward from the pillows piled behind him against the walnut head of the bedstead.

"Prosecute him! Of course I won't."

"I told you, sir," said Lucretia, with a complacent little smile. "I told you, sir, that that was what Mr. Blair would say."

Gardner smiled too, no doubt with a certain sense of relief, and said that he was not surprised; it was precisely what he had expected. "I do not wish to evade my duty," he said, and then as though a load had been removed from his mind, he added: "But I can't prosecute without witnesses, can I?"

"Of course you can't," said Blair. "And I assume all the responsibility. You see it was a private affair between gentlemen—just a little private row."

"That is hardly a nice word to employ, Mr. Blair," said Lucretia.

"What word?"

"The one you just used. Don't, pray, ask me to repeat it."

"You mean 'row'?"

"Yes. It is inelegant, if not vulgar."

"Well, my dear," he said, amused as always at her rather pedantic ways, "you see you've got a Kentucky backwoodsman for a husband, and I confess I didn't know that 'row' wasn't a proper word. Did you, Scott?"

Gardner, somewhat in awe of Lucretia, was forced to admit that he did not.

"And what would you call it, my dear?" asked Blair.

"I would call it a barbarous affray!" she said, her eyes flashing. "Without even the slightly civilizing formalities of the duel which, goodness knows, is barbarous enough as it is. I call it a sin and a shame, Mr. Gardner, that a man may go about armed to the teeth, provoking peaceable men to affairs of this kind, and compelling them either to lose their lives outright or risk them in order to defend themselves."

"I'm entirely of your opinion, madam," said Gardner, "and it is for that reason that I came to ask Mr. Blair to swear to an information—"

"That is entirely different, Mr. Gardner. Mr. Blair, having accepted the challenge made so irregularly, it is true, could not now, as a gentleman, do otherwise than accept the consequences. It would be dishonourable to do otherwise."

"You see, Scott," said Blair; "you see what little fire-eaters our Southern ladies are!"

He looked at her in the security he felt in her passionate loyalty and devotion, and in the pride he had in the fact that she should be his wife, that he should have won her love. He thought of all this after Gardner had gone, and he sat for a while alone in the waning afternoon, before going back to the bed of which he was growing so tired. Lucretia, after he was convalescent, had had his bed set up in the sitting-room that opened off the dining-room, because from its windows he could have a view of the street, and of the life that passed in it, though in a quiet street like theirs, sparsely built up as yet, there was not much of life to pass. Still, it was something—if only a narrow strip of grass, a picket fence, the sidewalk and the elms he had set out along the kerb, still in their protecting boxes, and not yet tall enough to shade the sidewalk along which a few neighbours passed at regular intervals, morning and afternoon, turning their heads to greet him as he looked out of the window. Now, with the autumn, the leaves of his unpromising little elms were shrivelling up in an anaemic yellow, and he wondered if they would survive the winter that so soon would beat upon them. He must have them bundled up in straw; he would speak to Lucretia, and she would get Moss, their negro man-of-all-work, to attend to it. He was beginning to grow restless, to long to get out of doors again, to go up town to his law-office, or, better still on these crisp autumn days, to go shooting in the woods where the quails would be so abundant. He was eager to be on the back of a horse once more, to mount Kitty and canter out to Congreve's farm and look at the stock, and see Dolly D., growing old and misshapen from breeding, passing her declining years in a pasture, switching the rather pitiable remnant of her once flowing tail . . .

Lucretia never went riding any more; she was always having a baby, or about to have one. But she never grumbled about the deprivation, as he was always doing. Well, women were different, that was all. But God, what a woman she was, Lucretia! He wished that she would come and talk to him; these autumn afternoons were gloomy and depressing, with their swiftly enfolding twilight, the glittering sun fading suddenly into a steely grey light, and a chill coming over the world. He wished that she would come and cheer him up. But Lucretia, just then, had a caller in the parlour, Sallie Congreve, he reckoned, by the sound of her voice, though he could not hear what she said, and Lucretia's voice was so low that he could scarcely hear it at all. Sallie was staying a long time. Blair was growing a little jealous of her, and beginning to feel slightly abused.

Still, when at last Sallie did go, when the interminable adieux were over—they still talked when together as they used to when they were girls—and Lucretia had gone with Sallie to the door and come back again and entered his room, he did not complain. The fact was that he always stood more or less in awe of Lucretia; there was something in her manner, a certain reticence, a slight shade of pride, her air of a great lady, that imposed a kind of formality on their relations. He had always looked up to her in awe and adoration ever since that morning when she had dashed up to Grow's store to buy the stockings, and, whenever he thought of it, it still seemed incredible to him that she should ever have stooped from her inaccessible height to him. He had always felt inferior to her and unworthy of her, and ever since this wretched business of the quarrel with Tom Nash and its outcome that had so closely grazed fatal tragedy, he had felt more unworthy than ever, and at times, when he dwelt upon the tenderness and devotion she had shown throughout his illness, and all the while in a pathetic ignorance or innocence of its cause, he had felt an unworthiness that was like a shame.

Just now, as she entered the room softly, he felt this shame more acutely than ever, when she said:

"Was I long away? I trust that you have not needed me? Sallie Congreve has been here—full of gossip."

"Anything new or startling?" he asked wondering, a little fearfully, how much Sallie knew, and how much she had told Lucretia.

"Well," Lucretia was saying, "Mr. Tom Nash has gone away."

"Gone away?"

"Yes; left town for parts unknown. Gone out West, they say."

"I'm not surprised."

"Colonel Nash, it seems, supplied him with money to go, and was considerably relieved when he went."

"No doubt." He wondered how much else Sallie had told her, and did not dare to inquire.

"I told Sallie," said Lucretia, speaking with that hardness which he was always so surprised to find in her gentle nature, "I told Sallie that I should think the West was precisely the place for the exercise of his peculiar talents as a shot, and his propensity for duelling."

But this hardness, this lack of sympathy, or even pity, in her, he reflected, was apparent only in matters concerning himself. She was as logical and as just as the Supreme Court in everything—until his interests or his actions were involved, and

236

then she was invariably as biassed, as prejudiced and as unjust as the most unblushing partisan of the worst cause in the world could possibly be.

He laughed fondly, and said:

"My dear, he can't shoot half so well as I can. You, I know, thought my shooting was all chance—as in the case of the set of dishes I won. You remember that, don't you?"

"Now, Mr. Blair!" she reproached him. He frequently teased her about that incident, and often told it when she was present, and he had an audience, as a good joke on himself.

"Now, Mr. Blair!" she said, blushing in a pretty embarrassment. "In this instance chance was on the side of justice."

"No, there was no chance, Lucretia."

She looked up in a sudden access of alarm.

"What do you mean?" she asked.

"Lucretia, I'm a wicked man, a murderer at heart. I aimed at that button on Tom Nash's coat. It was shining in the sun—I can see it now—and I dropped my arm—"

"Don't!" she suddenly cried, closing her eyes and shaking her head. "Don't, I pray you! I don't want to talk about it or hear about it, or think about it."

They sat in silence for a moment in the twilight that was stealing into the sitting-room.

"I only meant to show you," he said, "that I am not worthy of you."

Should he go on, he asked himself, and tell her now? It would be easier in the mood they were in, there in the twilight. It would distress her, of course, but it would relieve him. Now that it was all over and he was getting well, and Tom Nash had gone West, it was the moment to unburden his heart and clear his conscience. He had grown accustomed to the luxury of having someone to whom he could unburden his heart of all its woes, someone on whom he lay all his doubts and fears and troubles, and have them borne for him. He would tell her now, and never have to think of it or be troubled by it any more; life could then have no surprises for him, never catch him napping or take him unawares again. Was this selfishness masquerading as truth and loyalty? Well, of course, he couldn't bring himself to tell her all— those nights in that little upper room at Grows' and Gertie—no, not that! Men and women were different; there was one way, one life, one rule, for men, and another way, another life, another rule for women. 'Man's love is of man's life a thing apart.' Of course. And yet—

"There are other ways in which I am unworthy of you, too, Lucretia. I've thought perhaps that I owed it to you to—"

But instantly, with an impulsive and charming gesture, she put up her hands and stopped her ears.

"I won't listen!" she said. "I won't listen!"

"Do listen, Lucretia!"

But she shook her head, determinedly.

"No, I won't, I won't!" she kept repeating.

He went on, however.

"I am not worthy of you, I know," he said. "But ever since the day you rode up to the store—"

He saw, dim as the light was, that she had taken her fingers from her ears in order to hear.

"Ever since that day I've tried to be. But suppose—suppose I were to tell you that before that time, before I had ever seen you—"

"Sh!" She hushed him imperatively, got up and crossed the room to where he sat and, standing behind his chair, put her arms about his neck and placed her hands upon his lips. And bending over she said, in a voice which, though hardly above a whisper, moved him by a passion he had never been conscious of in her before: "It is useless for anyone—even you—to try to tell me anything, no matter what, that would reflect in the least on you! I just wouldn't listen! I would never, never, never believe them! I know you better than you know yourself!"

She held him a moment in a tense embrace, and then she spoke, or began to speak again. "These last days—these weeks of anxiety, of fear—" she said, and then her voice broke, and in silence she held his head against her breast a moment, and when she laid her cheek against his, it was wet with her tears.

BOOK III

I

Blair served two terms in the Legislature, and saw a great deal of Tom Corwin. He was admitted to the charmed circle that used to gather round the roaring fire in the Executive Chambers and listen to the genial Governor talk whilst he smoked his morning cigar. The Constitution of Ohio, framed on the jealous democratic principles laid down by Mr. Jefferson (as it was still customary to call him) did not allow the Governor many powers, so that he had plenty of time to talk, but it did invest him with that attribute which "is enthronèd in the hearts of kings,"[43] and—having nothing else to do, as he explained—Governor Corwin pardoned many a poor wretch who had been sent to the State's prison. It brought down a great deal of criticism and abuse upon his head, but he didn't mind, or else pretended not to mind. And one morning after a particularly vicious outburst of this criticism, as the Governor, sitting before his fire, was pretending not to mind and smoking his cigar as serenely as ever, Blair, detecting the pain that now and then showed in the dark and sensitive face, suddenly recalled the lines that Tom Corwin had recited to him on a memorable occasion years before.

"Thy godlike crime was to be kind,
To render with thy precepts less
The sum of human wretchedness—"

And the Governor, from those deep black eyes had flashed a sudden glance of gratitude for a comprehension that he did not always find, even in that enthralled circle of devotees.

The Governor, of course, could usually turn aside the shafts of criticism with his own instant wit, and Blair often recalled with a satisfaction that was due in part to his own inherited dislike of Yankees, a retort of Tom Corwin's at a time when the penal code of the state was under discussion. It was proposed to establish the whipping-post on the ground that it was less expensive than to build gaols and maintain prisoners in them. Corwin, who knew that the degree of culture achieved by a state is reflected in its penal code, had indignantly opposed this measure. A member of the Legislature who had come to the Western Reserve from Connecticut, had cited the experience of that state, saying that when men were publicly flogged they generally left the state afterwards. To which Tom Corwin had replied that he had observed that a great many men were coming to Ohio from Connecticut, but that he had never known before why they came.[44]

Now it was 1844; the Whigs had at last nominated Henry Clay for the Presidency. The Whigs were jubilant and certain of success, so certain that Lemuel Sanders, one of Blair's friends, made a public vow that he would never shave or cut his hair until Clay was elected President. Blair was not so reckless, but he flung himself into the campaign with an ardour that Lucretia—who distrusted enthusiasm—said was an invitation to disaster.

"I mean, Mr. Blair, that I don't much like to see you set your heart so on anything. Remember how disappointed you were when Governor Corwin was defeated for re-election."

Yes; he suddenly remembered the bitterness of that disappointment. Tom Corwin—defeated by a man like Shannon—a demagogue! However, he could always reassure himself, take things by the easiest handle, and he said:

"There is no danger of that, my dear. Do you think it possible that an unknown man like Polk, whom nobody ever heard of before, could defeat Henry Clay?"

The emphasis with which he pronounced the name of his idol showed how great was his infatuation.

"Did you ever hear of Polk before?" he went on. "Did you ever hear of anyone named Polk?"

"Well," she replied, in her calm and somewhat literal way, "there were Polks in Goochland county—quite a large connection."

"But this Polk is from Tennessee."

"No doubt the family came from Virginia."

Blair laughed.

"You seem to think, my dear, that the only qualification necessary to render a man eligible for the Presidency is that he belong to one of the First Families of Virginia."

"There might be standards less exacting, Mr. Blair." She set her lips rather firmly after this speech, and Blair said no more about Virginia. There were moments when he felt a little afraid of his wife. It was best, after all, not to risk offending her State pride; when it came to their native states people were apt to be rather touchy. He had felt that way about Kentucky, though in the new country of Ohio, where the democratic feeling was more assertive and Southern men had to associate with Yankees, even though they disliked them, and men from the East, no one set so great store by a man's birthplace or cared so much where he came from. But Lucretia's residence in Ohio and her contact with a civilization which, in its purely social aspects at least, was, as compared with Virginia, crude and unrefined, had only served to intensify her aristocratic feelings. Secretly Blair was glad of the fact and vastly proud of her on account of it, though four years of Ohio politics, with two terms in the Legislature and his candidature in the present campaign for the State Senate, had developed in him, or encrusted upon his manner, that democratic familiarity which is essential to political success.

"I don't pretend to the slightest knowledge of politics, Mr. Blair, as you know," Lucretia went on, speaking as though the thing were beneath her, "but I remember how deeply you were disappointed when Governor Corwin was defeated. There are those dreadful abolitionists—Free Soilers with their Liberal Party, as I believe they call it, and their Mr. Birney."

Lucretia spoke with a contempt unusual in her.

"Yes, I remember." And he thought of Grow and the others like him who had defeated Tom Corwin. "But they have more to expect from Henry Clay than from Polk, and there isn't the slightest chance in the world of electing Birney. Why!" he suddenly burst forth, as the mere possibility of such a prodigious catastrophe presented itself to him, "it is preposterous to think of Henry Clay's not being elected! He is sure to be elected, my dear!"

"Pray send he may," she said calmly, going on with her sewing.

Blair, having been reared in Kentucky, had grown up in the devout belief that Henry Clay was the greatest statesman in America, and so, of course, in the world. He had never seen Henry Clay since that day in boyhood when he had heard him speak at Paris; his feeling for him was, therefore, an impersonal feeling, a cult, as it were. But his feeling for Tom Corwin was intensely personal, an ardent human affection. And as Lucretia had reminded him, they had beaten Tom Corwin, an incredible thing, come to think of it—as incredible as if they were to defeat Henry Clay now. And yet Lucretia seemed to think that possible. Lucretia of course, as she said, knew nothing of politics; women never did. And yet, a good deal went on in that delicately poised little head, and somehow or other she was always right.

He glanced at her as she sat there in her low chair on the verandah of their new house in the late August afternoon. She sat erect, stiff in her stays, and straight as though strapped to a backboard, the flowing skirts of her white muslin gown billowing

241

about her. Slight and dainty as her figure was, the dignity and reserve and a certain positiveness in her manner gave her, as Blair had so often observed, an almost formidable air. Especially if she thought he was chaffing her, or poking fun at Virginia. Her eyes were downcast, fastened upon her sewing, for her hands were never for an instant idle; she was always sewing or knitting or darning or mending something; just now it seemed to be a frock for one of the children; they had three now, Jamie, the eldest, and Corrie (Thomas Corwin Blair) now three years old, and Penelope, a year old.

Blair could now realize himself as a family man, a solid citizen, a consequential personage in Macochee and Gordon county. Four years, flown by with the incredible swiftness of happy times, had wrought a change in his position. He had been successful at the bar, and they had been able to build the addition to the house, or, to state it more accurately, to build the new house to which the old was an addition. And they had bought a farm in the Marmon Valley, 160 acres of rich loam, Pretty Prairie, he called it. The new house had been built largely with his fee in the Purcell case, his successful defence of old man Purcell in the Court of Common Pleas having won him as well a considerable reputation as a criminal lawyer. The farm had been bought, or the first payment on it had been made, with his fee in the Crewe case (Crewe v. Weaver, 23 0., 407.)

The consciousness of this success and the dream of the larger success it seemed to promise for the future, was generally present with Blair, and perhaps it showed now and then in his manner, though he had sense enough to try not to let it. But undoubtedly it did give him a little more assurance, a little more impressive bearing as he went in and out among the people of Macochee. He wore broadcloth; he had a velvet waistcoat; his hair he wore as long as in his youth; he was beginning to grow a trifle perhaps too fat; he did not ride so much as he should have liked, (Lucretia never got to ride at all, poor thing, a baby had always just come, or was just coming) though he had three horses in the stable. Still, he did not mind growing fat; Henry Clay, to be sure, was lean, but Tom Corwin was fat. A leading lawyer, a member of the Legislature, and a prominent citizen who was always referred to in the newspapers as "the Hon." and who, in a few weeks more after the elections were over would be addressed as "Senator," would find it no disadvantage at all to have a corporation; it was the symbol of prosperity and added vastly to one's dignity.

242

As they sat there on the verandah at the close of the hot August day, Blair could glance around and dwell with considerable satisfaction on the evidences of prosperity that were all about him. Everything was going on well; everything was growing, developing, like the elms he had planted along the street before his house; they were high enough now to cast a bit of shade, and the rose-vine that Lucretia had brought from Virginia was climbing one of the pillars of the verandah. Along the side of the house her beds of pinks were blooming, their spicy odour scenting the air. Behind the house there was a great vegetable garden, and when they went into supper presently its produce would be hot upon the table—the new potatoes and golden ears of sweet corn, and spoon bread or beaten biscuits. Yes, he could hear already the sharp staccato of Elvira's blows as she pounded the dough with a potato-masher. And then for dessert there would be sillabub, or perhaps as he hoped, a strawberry shortcake with rich yellow cream. Lucretia had brought Elvira from Virginia too, like the rose vine, and transplanted her. She was a slave, or had been until Lucretia had manumitted her and fetched her to Ohio, recording her certificate of freedom and obtaining two freeholders to give security for her good behaviour, in accordance with the Black Laws.[45] Not that it made any difference to Elvira whether she was free or not; she would never consent to be far from Lucretia's side. And then there was the long grape-arbour that covered the path from the kitchen down through the garden to the paddock, and in time the large blue Concord grapes and the tiny sweet lavender Delaware grapes would begin to ripen.

The new house which overtopped and reduced the old to a subordinate position as a west wing, was build of brick, and in the Southern or Colonial tradition, with a wide hall, dim and cool on these hot days, and a parlour on one side; behind the parlour was Blair's library. The library was not as yet filled with books, any more than the grape arbour was covered with vines and filled with grapes, or the verandah embowered by Lucretia's rose-vine from Virginia, or the street overarched by the elms. But all these slow, silent processes were in motion, and all these things were to be, and Blair sat there under his own vine and fig-tree, with a proud consciousness of his prosperity and an assurance of security. No matter what happened they had this, he and Lucretia, this home in the town, and those acres out at Pretty Prairie. And all these things that contributed to his purse, his comfort, his satisfaction, came from the ground, from the Earth whence all came and to which all in the end must return. "Go and buy 160 acres of land," Tom Corwin had advised him, "or if you can't buy it, squat on it—and live like a freeman." Well, he had done that, and better than that. He had married Lucretia, and however strong this consciousness of prosperity and success, and however he might fail from time to time in his attempt to hide it, there was, deep down in his heart, another consciousness, stronger than all the rest, and that was that he owed all this, or at least the organization of it, to the little woman sitting there so quietly at his side . . .

The feel of evening was in the air, the air that was dusty and stifling after the long day's heat. People going by on their way home called out their greeting in a pleasant homely, neighbourly way.

"Good evening, Mr. Blair. Been a hot day. Good evening, Mrs. Blair, ma'am."

Lucretia returned these salutations with a grave inclination of her head. She never called out to anyone, no matter who.

"Hadn't you better be getting ready for supper, Mr. Blair?" she suggested.

Yes, he had; there was Moss fetching home the cow from the pasture. She shuffled slowly through the dust, switching her tail and tossing her head to drive off the flies, flinging long streams of saliva from her mouth by the movement. The air was perfumed by the sweet odour of her breath as by a field of clover blossom.

And then, there was Elvira in the doorway behind them.

"Supper's on de table, Mis' Lucretia," she said, in her indifferent way, as though announcing a fact that might possibly interest her mistress.

"Very well, Elvira," said Lucretia, folding up her sewing, and getting up.

"I'm 'fraid you won't be able to eat the sho't-cake Mis' Lucretia," Elvira continued as she stood aside to let them enter the hall and then followed Lucretia towards the dining-room. " 'Pears lak it hain't fitten to eat, it sho' dew. Umph-humph!"

Lucretia smiled. When Elvira said, as she often did, that some dish she had just prepared wasn't "fitten to eat," they knew that she had produced a masterpiece of Southern cooking.

II

Blair began to suspect, however, as the campaign wore on that perhaps his wife knew more about politics than ladies were supposed to know, and to fear that the prospects of the Whigs were not so bright as he liked to think them. His hopes indeed were pretty badly chilled when one morning he encountered Grow in the town. He did not often see Grow; they had no interests in common and their paths of late years seldom crossed. Grow still published his newspaper, *The Torchlight,* though it was not so much a newspaper as an organ for the spread of anti-slavery sentiment and radical Abolitionist principles. Blair was a regular subscriber to the journal and occasionally read it, but material success had made him conservative, and so far as slavery was concerned he stood with Henry Clay and Tom Corwin and other conservative Whigs, was in favour of compromise and, deep down in his easy-going nature, rather resented the intrusion of the subject in politics at all. Grow, on the contrary, instead of becoming more conservative with age, reversed the order of nature and became more radical all the while. He, too, had prospered in the only sense in which he cared to prosper, that is, he had seen his cause grow and his newspaper become the recognized organ of the Free Soilers and Anti-Slavery Whigs in that part of Ohio. To material prosperity he had an indifference that was almost contemptuous. He had his small house and those few acres on the Blue Jacket turnpike west of town, and that, with the small gains *The Torchlight* brought him, was enough to satisfy his material wants, however short it fell of the desires of his family, which consisted now of his wife and Gertie and her boy. The Nashs had disowned their daughter-in-law and grandson, and Tom Nash, lost somewhere in the illimitable and mysterious West, had never given sign of his existence since he had disappeared. Gertie and her mother did all of the work in the small house, and most of the work that was necessary to cultivate the land about it. Gertie, so Blair had heard, had been converted at a Methodist revival, and apparently found consolation for her frustrated life in religion, which he thought just as well, religion being a good thing for women. This division of labour in the Grow family left the old man—as most people called him though he could not have been very much over fifty—free to devote himself to the cause of freedom, as he called it. It was pretty hard on his family who did not enjoy much freedom, for the small house was a station on Levi Coffin's Underground Railroad and was frequently called upon to harbour runaway slaves from Kentucky, and even to withstand sieges on the part of their owners and the minions of the law who came with them to recover the fugitives. However, Grow enjoyed it all immensely in his dour and gloomy way, and led a full and satisfying, if somewhat tumultuous life, organizing and addressing abolition meetings, corresponding with Levi Coffin, James G. Birney, and Joshua R. Giddings and Ben Wade and Salmon P. Chase,[46] writing flaming leading articles for *The Torchlight,* urging resistance to the law, engaging in violent arguments with Democrats and Conservative Whigs, denouncing everyone who disagreed with him, and driving long and lonely miles by night in his buggy to convey some runaway negro a stage further along the road to Canada and freedom.

The present campaign with its interest and excitement, its stimulating effect on the curiosities and the passions of men, offered an occasion which Grow could not miss, and he was, as Giles Paten once remarked to Blair when over their morning dram at Tappan's, "as busy as a boar killing snakes."

And then it happened that Blair encountered Grow at the Post Office. Grow had his arms full of that week's issue of *The Torchlight,* wrapped and addressed and ready to post to subscribers in the county. By his side, conscious of the importance of his functions, marched his grandson, Thomas Nash, his arms likewise full of wrapped and addressed copies of the inflammatory journal.

"Enlightening the world as usual, eh, Mr. Grow?" remarked Blair, with the facetious humour of the candidate.

But Grow, never at any time in jocular mood, was evidently more than ever serious that morning, and turned on Blair a dark look of rebuke for his lightness in such an hour of crisis.

Even the little grandson, Blair thought, looked up at him as he passed with an expression of aged and disapproving gravity.

"Yes, Blair," said Grow, "enlightening it a little more than usual—as you will learn when you read my leading article."

Then he strode on, followed by his young aide-de-camp, and thrust his armful of papers through the window to Crane the Postmaster who, as a Democrat, was glad to receive and speed them on their errand of disruption. Blair waited until Grow came back, and then said:

"I haven't seen my copy of your paper, Mr. Grow, this week; anything new and startling in it?"

"Well, sir," said Grow with a certain emphatic satisfaction and

246

a note of challenge in his voice, drawing from his pocket a folded copy of *The Torchlight*, "just take a look at that and see."

And striking the paper with his fingers he almost rudely thrust it under Blair's nose. Blair took the sheet that still smelt of its fresh ink, and glancing at the column that Grow had struck with the back of his hand, he glanced down the double-leaded editorial in which Grow advised all lovers of liberty and human rights to vote the ticket of the Liberty Party and elect James G. Birney President.

He felt for an instant as though Grow had struck him in the face. The shock of the announcement which meant, of course, that the free-soil Whigs were going to bolt their party and vote against Henry Clay, was sufficient of itself to unnerve him for an instant, but Grow's belligerent and offensive manner was like a personal insult. For a moment he felt the hot blood of his anger and resentment surge upwards to his head, and spin dizzily round and round, but of late years he had been trying to curb his violent temper and not fly off the handle in his old impetuous way. Besides, this was a public place and he mustn't forget that he was a candidate for office. And so, with a noble effort he swallowed his resentment and, giving Grow back his paper, he remarked:

"Well, that's very interesting, I'm sure!" And he smiled, knowing that a smile always irritates an antagonist. "But," he went on, "since you know perfectly well that Birney hasn't a ghost of a chance to be elected, and that every vote he gets will be a vote drawn from those who support Senator Clay, would you mind telling me just how you expect to advance the cause of freedom by defeating a great statesman who believes in emancipation, and by electing an unknown politician who believes in slavery?"

"Believes in emancipation!" exclaimed Grow, contemptuously. "Believes in emancipation! But when?"

"When? Whenever it can be brought about by peaceable and orderly methods, conserving the rights of everybody without disrupting the government, disorganizing the life of the nation."

"Blair, look 'e here," said Grow, settling himself as it were for an argument, "I'm sorry to have to come out against you; you know that personally I always liked you, and do still—"

"Oh, never mind me!" exclaimed Blair, in sudden anger, "I don't give a damn about that side of it—"

"Well, just hold your hosses," said Grow; "don't get mad. This is no personal matter; this is far above such considerations; this is a matter of principle."

It was the hour when everybody gathered at the post office for the distribution of the mail brought up from Dayton that morning by the stage, and as Blair and Grow became more and more deeply involved in their political argument, the crowd that gathered round them craning forward curious and eager faces to hear, became more and more dense until finally the two antagonists were uncomfortably face to face. Blair could scent the musty odour of Grow's breath as he talked, his eyes blazing, his long beard wagging with the motions of his argumentative jaw; near by he could see the faces of friends, Giles Paten, Fowler Brunton, Lem Sanders. Crane abandoned his duties behind his lettered pigeon-holes and came out to enjoy the fun, and there, almost between him and Grow, stood the young Thomas Nash, a boy of seven and tall for his age—a year older than Jamie—very grave in his peak-cap and his long hair, his short jacket and grey trousers, and looking up out of great blue eyes and solemnly weighing the arguments as they were advanced.

Blair did his best to defend Henry Clay and Tom Corwin from Grow's criticisms and attacks; both of them, he showed, were in favour of gradual emancipation, as he himself was. But at this, Grow, who was constitutionally opposed to making any reform gradually, almost leapt at him in his excitement.

"You!" he exclaimed. "You! Why, Blair, you are the worst of the lot! For four years you've had a chance to do something. You've had a chance to introduce in the Legislature a Bill repealing the Black Laws which constitute a foul blob on our state, and you never did a thing, you never said a word, you never so much as lifted your little finger!"

"I am not the Ohio Legislature, Mr. Grow," said Blair. "I'm only one member of it. You know that at no time has there been the slightest chance of a majority in favour of the repeal of those laws."

"That doesn't exonerate you of your personal responsibility, or of the blame we lay upon you. You should have stood up for it, and stood out for it, whether anyone else was for it or not!"

The light of his uncompromising fanaticism was blazing in Grow's eye as he denounced the Black Laws, the abhorrence of the Free Soilers.

"I'm just as much opposed to the Black Laws as you are," said Blair—an admission for him!—"and I'm ready to vote for their repeal whenever there is any reasonable likelihood of its being brought about, but in the meantime, having at heart other measures in which the people are interested, I'm not going to compromise their chances by a Quixotic fanaticism. I'm in favour of liberty, but I'm not a damn fool."

The discussion raged for an hour, and Blair was put to it to hold his own with Grow, who had greatly improved in the art of dialectics since that evening long before when he had held a joint debate with Colonel Nash at the Mechanics' Institute. Blair felt that he should have come off better, indeed, had not Grow, when the arguments had all been exhausted and the disputation was coming to an end, adopted the patronizing tone of an elder man and begun to give Blair personal advice.

"These are times that try men's souls," he said, raising his hand and waving a monitory finger under Blair's nose, "these are times that try men's souls—"

"You're quoting Tom Paine now, Grow," chipped in Giles Paten, itching from the first to take part in the discussion. "I'm surprised that you should quote that wicked man."

"No matter who said it," Grow went on, "it's true to-day and you, Blair, will find it out. It's time that you quit straddling this question, quit this miserable time-serving. You cannot serve God and Mammon, and I want to see you come out flat-footed and on the right side. Don't wait until it is too late or you'll regret it. For the people are tired of compromise and temporizing and timid vacillation; they are not going to be satisfied any longer with the oratorical platitudes of Henry Clay and the jokes of Tom Corwin; they're sick and tired of you paltering Whigs, and they are ready to spew you out of their mouths!"

Grow spit out this last phrase in Blair's face, turned, thrust the crowd aside and stalked out of the Post-Office, followed by his grandson.

III

Whether his brush with Grow had injured his chances for election or not, Blair did not know. Grow was still considered by the community as wild and impractical and a little ridiculous, and may have been no more influential than he ever had been; but it was evident, nevertheless, that the extremists were gaining ground, and that the Free Soilers everywhere were going to cut the Whig ticket. The outlook, therefore, was not so encouraging as it had been. However, an event occurred that consoled Blair for all this; he was asked to make a few speeches in the Southern part of the State, and for two or three days travelled about with Tom Corwin and spoke from the same platform, and after this experience his fears were all allayed, and all his hopes revived. For one glance at those enormous audiences roaring and rocking with laughter at Tom Corwin's jokes, or rapt in sudden silence at his eloquence, or weeping when he touched their emotions — one glance was enough to dispel any doubt of the result in the Buckeye State.

Blair was not certain to what, precisely, he owed the distinction of accompanying Tom Corwin on a stumping tour. Was it Corwin's old interest in him, dating from the call at Lebanon? The Byronic song written in the Log Cabin and Hard Cider campaign? Those pleasant hours of companionship in the Governor's chambers at Columbus? Or did little Corrie Blair, the mere fact of him, have something to do with it? Or could it be that he himself was becoming such an important figure in the political life of the State that—but no, he wasn't so conceited as all that. But at any rate, whatever the reason, here he was, appearing on the same platform with Tom Corwin.

Blair, of course, always spoke first, the big gun being reserved for the final bombardment. He had his old cherished ambition, shared with every young lawyer in Ohio, to speak like Tom Corwin. He longed to become a silver-tongued orator; longed for the ability to speak for hours at a time, lost in an ecstasy of eloquence, and when he was done to seem as limp as a rag and drenched in perspiration, with a large wet spot in the middle of his back between his shoulder-blades. But he could never rise to such heights; he had never been able even to sweat down his collar. And then, there were the witticisms, the flashes of humour, which were as natural to Tom Corwin as breathing. The thought of them filled him with envy and despair.

He could, of course, indulge in rude banter with the crowd, as he did in the meeting at McConnelsville where they stopped on their way up the river from Marietta. It was an open-air meeting, held in the afternoon in the public square. Blair had been speaking for half an hour when a man in the crowd interrupted him; there was a little clash of wits in which Blair easily had the best of it. The crowd laughed, and the man interrupted him no more, and for some time afterwards Blair kept up a fire of facetiousness which kept the crowd laughing. He felt rather well satisfied with himself. But as they sat at an early supper in an inn the fact of Blair's having joked with the crowd came up in their conversation, and Tom Corwin grew suddenly very serious.

250

"Don't do it, my boy," he said, "don't do it. Remember that the crowd always looks up to the ringmaster and down upon the clown, though in nine cases out of ten the clown is the better man of the two. The crowd will laugh at his jokes, but it won't respect his judgment. If you would succeed in life, and especially in public life, you must be solemn, solemn as an ass. All of the great monuments of earth have been erected over the graves of solemn asses."[47]

He was very serious, and Blair perceived that he was sinking into one of those moods of melancholy that were temperamental with him. They were to take the steamboat and go up the Muskingum to Zanesville, where they were to address a large meeting on the morrow. They went aboard at eight o'clock, and for a long while that evening they sat on deck in the shelter of the boat's cabin in the melancholy dusk of the autumn evening, smoked their cigars and talked in low tones. The little Ohio hills, their silhouettes just distinguishable against the sky, moved darkly by on either hand, the waters of the Muskingum flowed darkly past, and to Blair there was something mysterious in the moment—the willows along the river bank, the silence, save for the sniffing of the steam and the splash of the stern-paddles, and the soft voice of Tom Corwin sitting there muffled in a cloak. He talked to Blair that evening with an intimacy he had never shown before, and of subjects on which he had never opened his heart. He talked of life, not as at the supper-table of how to get on in it, but of its tragedy, its insoluble mystery, its brevity and futility, and the cruel irony of its inevitable frustration to one who thought deeply, fearlessly and honestly about it. He recited long passages from the Book of Job; he seemed to know it all by heart. And then he was silent for a while, sitting and gazing out over the dark waters of the river. A chill came across them, and the Governor shivered slightly, flung his cigar into the river, shook his head hopelessly, and said:

"All thought is sad—sad, sad!" Then they turned in.

But the next afternoon at Zanesville there the Governor was, joking with the crowd again.[48] Blair, having made his speech— and no jokes this time!—sat on the platform and watched him with amazement and delight. The meeting had been made the occasion for a general holiday; the crowd was enormous, gathered from all that part of the state. Excursion steamers from all the towns along the river came loaded to the guards; there must have been five thousand people there, and when Blair faced the vast concourse and felt the intoxication of all that enthusiasm, he was certain that it was all up for Polk; he had no doubts now that Henry Clay, at last, was about to achieve the ambition of his life.

Tom Corwin had never been in better form. How on earth did he do it! Blair sat there with little thrills running up and down his spine; he felt gooseflesh all over his body; something would suddenly catch in his throat, and tears would flood his eyes; then he would burst out laughing. Tom Corwin had devoted a long, eloquent period to a description of Henry Clay, his career, his achievements, his long services to his country. Such, he said, was the candidate presented by the Whigs. The crowd hung spellbound on his words.

"And now," he said, "whom have our Democratic brethren placed in nomination for the high office of President?" He paused an instant, and said: "One James K. Polk."

Then slowly, with vast and solemn deliberation, and with a look of serious inquiry on his face, he turned his head slowly from side to side, looking all over the enormous crowd as though seeking someone, and at last, in the attentive, anxious, painful silence, he said:

"After that, who is safe?"[49]

The crowd laughed and laughed, and started laughing again and again even after Tom Corwin had resumed his speech and grown serious. It was a long speech, and it was towards evening when the whistle of a steamboat warned the excursionists that it was about to start down the river. And as men and women reluctantly turned away, they would pause and turn round and try to catch just one more phrase from the lips of Tom Corwin.

IV

The defeat of Henry Clay was a blow to Blair from which he felt he could never recover. When the news came he refused to believe it. It was incredible, impossible! He almost wept, as did Colonel Nash and many another staunch old Whig, at the downfall of their old idol. The fact that he himself had been elected to the State Senate was not much consolation. There was a kind of bitter irony in it, a gratuitous and almost flippant insult of the fates. It gave him a feeling of guilt, as though he had committed a treachery. When political friends came to his office to congratulate him he hastened to explain, almost to apologize; he said that he would much rather have gone down to defeat with Henry Clay; it would have been a greater honour. And the sad countenances of these friends showed something like agreement. He was disgusted with politics and all the nasty mess of their deceits and betrayals; he would have nothing more to do with them; he was out of politics. But when in the cynicism and bitterness of his disillusion he made this grave announcement to Lucretia, she merely said:

"You'll feel differently about it later on."

And so, indeed, he did. His wife's prediction, of course, was based on general principles rather than on specific facts, but shortly afterwards when it was apparent that the Whigs were to have a majority on joint session of the General Assembly it turned out to be true. For now they could elect Tom Corwin United States Senator from Ohio. There was, after all, some hope for the future of the Republic.

But there was another cause for congratulation. Tom Corwin's election would make old man Grow angry as the devil; old man Grow would rather have seen Salmon P. Chase get it, even if Chase was a Democrat. Ever since the election Blair had been filled with rancour against old man Grow. For him Grow embodied the forces that had defeated Henry Clay; he was the archetype, the original model of the radical abolitionist with his insane insistence upon immediate and absolute solutions of political problems that had perplexed statesmen from Washington and Jefferson downwards, and his constant interference with the calm and logical evolution of political events, upsetting the calculations and orderly programmes of peerless leaders like Henry Clay, and turning the country over to uninspiring mediocrities like "one James K. Polk."

Grow, indeed, was one of those political zealots who find more satisfaction in defeating a candidate who, while approving their cause, rejects their programme, than in electing one who accepts both their cause and their programme. As often as not, indeed, elections turn on the question who shall be defeated rather than who shall be chosen, democracies in general deriving more joy in the defeat of the loser than in the victory of the winner. And Grow was obviously in this humour when Blair encountered him for the first time since the election. They met by chance in the Court House. Blair was on his way to the County Clerk's office and Grow was just leaving the Treasurer's office; he was accompanied, as he seemed always to be of late, by his grandson. When he saw Blair, Grow actually began to smile, if the expression that relaxed his grim, saturnine features might be described as a smile.

"Well, Blair," he called out as he came down the long corridor, "and how d'ye like the elections?"

His manner and the little cackle of triumph that followed this needless and derisive question were of course irritating to Blair. But he controlled himself, and said:

"Well, no need to ask how *you* like it! But I should like to ask you one question, Mr. Grow; just what do you fellows expect to gain by your action in defeating Senator Clay? You have elected Polk, but what will he do to help your cause?"

"Help our cause!" cried Grow. "Help our cause! How long have we waited on Henry Clay and Tom Corwin and Carter Blair to help it?"

"You do me too much honour," said Blair, making a mocking little bow, "in coupling my name with those distinguished—"

But before he could achieve his speech Grow had snatched it from him.

"No one is so small or so insignificant, Blair, but what he has some influence."

And having thus hastily divested his allusion of all complimentary intention, he went on in his old familiar strain, the old burning argument, and they were soon launched on the old debate.

"With us lovers of liberty, Blair, no half-way measures will do. It's the whole hog or none!"

"Yes," replied Blair, "and since the country won't go the whole hog all at once, you throw away your votes."

Having said this Blair was startled by a strange, piping young voice at his side.

"No vote cast for principle is ever thrown away," it said.

It was Grow's grandson, the young Tom Nash, who had spoken. He had been standing there listening solemnly to the argument, without saying a word, and now, having spoken at last, and having gravely uttered this solemn aphorism, he stood looking up at Blair out of his large blue eyes, an expression of gravity and wisdom on his long, sober face, far beyond his years. Blair felt somehow embarrassed. Ordinarily he would have felt like slapping a boy who talked like that. The wise aphorism, of course, could not have been original; the lad had picked it up parrot-like from Grow, who was full of such wise saws, and yet, damn it all, the lad had known when to cut in with it, and precisely where it fitted into the argument. There was something disconcerting in that, as there was in the lad's steady gaze.

254

"And so you take an interest in these questions, too, do you Master Tom?" asked Blair.

"Yes, sir."

Blair noticed then that Grow was gazing down at his grandson with an expression of human affection that he had never seen in that dour old face before. Grow, so far as he could recall, had never looked at Gertie in that way, or at his wife. He remembered how he used to wonder whether Grow ever showed any tenderness to his wife, ever caressed her, ever kissed her when, for instance, they were alone in that bedroom off the dining-room in the small house in Locust Street.... He didn't like to think of the small house in Locust Street, and of what went on in its bedrooms ... Especially in the presence of this boy, this strange, mature, and almost aged boy whose own father wouldn't own him—this boy whom everybody in Macochee, except Grow, and perhaps Lucretia, suspected was his, Carter Blair's. He wondered; but he would not search for resemblances or admit the possibility of such a thing, even to himself. Certainly there had been no such premature wisdom and gravity in him when he was a boy, shooting squirrels in the woods of Kentucky, or breaking his father's colts to ride, or sassing schoolmasters who were unjust ... Grow had laid his hand on the lad's head, as in benediction, and was looking down fondly on him.

"He is being raised to love liberty, Blair."

"Anyone reared in your house, Mr. Grow, would hear that word often."

"Yes, I expect they would," said Grow absently. He gazed at the boy who, made thus suddenly the centre of interest and subject of discussion, was suddenly overcome with confusion, blushed, and hung his head.

"I want he should go to Granville and get an education as soon as he's old enough," Grow went on. "They are sound on liberty at Granville, you know." And then he gave the lad a gentle little push and said: "Run along, Sonnie, and wait for me at the door; I've got something to say to Mr. Blair."

The boy went on to the door—thin, tall, too tall for his age, and as Grow's eye followed him, the old man said:

"Think of a man not wanting a boy like that for a son, Blair! He's a good boy, a fine boy. I'm trying to raise him right—teach him to love liberty and temperance. I'm raising him in the country, out in God's own country. Man made the city, but the devil, Blair, the devil himself made these small towns! They are no place to raise boys in; they are too wicked, too full of temptations at your own doorstep—these hell-holes of grog-shops, for instance. We shall have to 'tend to them as soon as we settle slavery. Lord, I'd rather see that boy in his coffin than to see him enter one of them!"

Grow paused, and stroking his wisp of a beard gazed down the long, dark corridor at the boy for whom he had found this mysterious and touching affection. The boy stood in the doorway, his thin, adolescent form silhouetted against the greyish silvery light of November outside.

"You've got a boy of about the same age, haven't you, Blair?"

"Yes, two of them."

"What are you going to make of them?"

Blair hadn't thought of that. He admitted as much and then, excusing himself with a little laugh, he said:

"I leave that to their mother; she's better qualified to rear them than I am."

But Grow shook his head a little doubtfully.

"Women spoil boys; especially their mothers."

Blair found Grow's theory on this, as on other subjects, at variance with his own, but there was no use in getting into another argument with the old man, and he went no farther in maintaining the integrity of his own opinion than to say:

"Oh well, mother love has an instinct for—"

"Yes, an instinct!" said Grow, interrupting him; "that's all it is! It isn't necessarily intelligence, it's too apt to be mere sentimentalism."

Perhaps, Blair reflected, Grow founded his theory on observation of his own wife and daughter, and with two such flibberty-gibbets as examples, there was something to be said for it.

"My boy's got no father," Grow went on. "Never a word from that Tom Nash. He's—God knows where, somewhere out West, I guess. And Colonel Nash won't give a picayune towards the boy's board and keep. So it all falls on me—raising and all. I want to do my duty by him; I want that he should have an education; I want that he should go to Granville. I'm trying to prepare him. I've grounded him pretty well in Latin. He's read Caesar. But the Greek's harder. I'm not up in Greek as I'd ought to be. It's a nuisance, Blair, an infernal nuisance, that we've got to spend so much of our lives worrying about this wretched business of money-getting, when there are so many really important things to do! Here I am, with a great cause to serve, and yet compelled to take so much thought for the morrow that I have hardly time to do the things that really count! It's strange!"

256

And Grow shook his head at the injustice of it.

"Still, Garrison managed it, and so does Birney, and so does Levi Coffin. Think of the thousands of miles he has tramped over this land, North and South! And so I guess I can. And that brings me to what I wanted to speak to you about. If I could get the job this winter as, say, Assistant Secretary of the Senate, that would help out. It wouldn't interfere with my getting out my paper, and it would fetch me in a little extra money."

"Yes, but your paper, since you've bolted the Whig ticket, might interfere with your getting the job. Had you thought of that?"

"Oh yes, I'd thought of that," replied Grow, with an air of indifference, "but you'll all be coming over to our side before long; another election and we'll win! Anyhow, if you could say a word for me with other Senators—I won't ask you to vote for me. I won't ask anyone to vote for me. I never asked a man to vote for me in my life, and I never will. And I won't make any political bargains; I'm no place hunter, but if I could get one of those clerical positions I could fill it and it would help me just now. You might just think it over."

Grow, without waiting for a reply, started to rejoin his grandson in the portico of the Court House and as they went down the corridor together, Blair said:

"I shall be glad to vote for you, Mr. Grow, and to do what I can. I haven't forgotten that you gave me my first position."

"Thank ye, Blair," was all that Grow said. Blair realized how much Grow's pride must have suffered in making this request of him. But the strangest thing was that in spite of their political disagreement, in spite of Grow's opposition at the polls, and in spite of the rancour he had felt ever since election, he should have felt a sudden sympathy for Grow and a desire to help him.

V

Blair stood in the portico and watched old man Grow and his grandson go down the broad walk and out into the street. He watched their backs move in and out among the shifting groups of aimless, shambling men that were always forming near the Court House. Their backs looked very much alike, only one was a large back and the other small. But they were both bent, bowed as by a burden, and both

old. It was funny, come to think of it, how characteristic and significant people's backs could be. He suddenly recalled a saying
of old Wesley, on the farm in Bourbon County: "Ah knows him
by de back!" Well, he should know old man Grow anywhere just
by his back. But the boy! Good God! "A vote cast for principle is
never lost!" to talk like that at seven years of age! The boy ought
to be smacked! If one of his boys, Jamie or Corry, should ever
talk like that, he'd give him a trouncing he wouldn't forget. But
of course such a thing could never happen with Lucretia there to
look after their boys.

He could not get the boy, this queer, unwanted child, out of
his mind. They had stopped, the old man and the boy, to talk to
someone at the corner, under the barren maple tree that grew
there; Blair could still see their expressive, symbolical backs, old
Grow's thin beard twitching over his shoulder with acerbity as he
talked and laid down the law, the boy looking up gravely at his
grandfather as Elisha might have looked up at the prophet Elijah.
He had a vivid recollection of the lad's face as it had been turned
up to him, the large blue eyes, the expression of aged gravity and
ripe wisdom, and the look of rebuke as he parrotted his
apothegm. It was silly, and it was impertinent for a child to speak
like that to any man, much less to a leading Whig, a member of
the bar and State Senator elect. In his day children were seen
and not heard. But after all, that wasn't the point. The point was
that there was something almost uncannily knowing in the boy's
eyes, deep down in their blue depths, a look that was embarrassing and made him feel ill at ease. In short, it was as if the lad
knew more than he let on. But of course that was nonsense; the
boy might be as wise as Solomon, but he couldn't know what no
one else on earth knew. It was a wise child indeed that knew his
own father! But did the lad know, for instance, that he and Nash
had fought a duel, and that at this very minute as he stood there,
the chill autumnal air was causing the old wound to ache a little
with rheumatism? No telling.

He felt sorry for the little wretch, of course; no childhood, no
companions of his own age, no play, no fun—nothing but a silly
mother and a whining, complaining grandmother, and old Grow
and abolition politics and Latin conjugations and declensions.
What a life for a boy! And what would old Grow make of the lad
when he grew up? How would he turn out? Well, probably as an
abolition fanatic, or a temperance lecturer, or a ranting Methodist
preacher, calling sinners to repentance and threatening them
with hell fire and brimstone. But he couldn't help it; obviously

there was nothing that he could do. His own theory that the rearing of the child should be left to the mother was sound, based originally, no doubt, on the fact that nature, cruel as she was in most ways, never held the male responsible for his offspring.

Just then, as Blair was following these random reflections and trying to put Tom Nash's son out of his mind, Fowler Brunton came up, a little drunk, as usual.

"How does your corporosity seem to sagatiate?" asked Brunton by way of greeting.

They stood there, gossiping idly, after the leisurely manner of lawyers when they meet at the Court House, and as they gossiped Blair noticed that Brunton's gaze wandered now and then to the group on the corner.

"That's old Grow and his grandson, ain't it?" observed Brunton.

"Yes." There could be no doubt of that relation, at any rate.

"Getting to be quite a young shaver, heigh?"

And Brunton glanced at Blair with a peculiar, knowing look. He wouldn't have done so, Blair knew, if he hadn't been slightly tipsy. It was of no consequence, of course, but it only went to show what popped into people's minds whenever they saw young Tom Nash and him in the same company. The legend had begun; and it would spread and flourish and become a part of local history.

VI

There wasn't much to do at the session of the Legislature that winter, after they had elected Tom Corwin to the Senate of the United States, a simple ceremony, unrolled on the stark and barren stage of the mean brick building that served as a State House, but abundantly significant and moving to Carter Blair as he watched the new Senator, just turned 51, standing there in his black broadcloth and ruffles, his black hair combed like a schoolboy's ready for Sunday school, his solemn, swarthy face slightly pale as he made his speech of acceptance.

Afterwards when Blair saw him in the crowd that thronged the plush and gilded elegance of the Neil House[50] parlours, Tom Corwin singled him out with especial marks of friendship and favour, the light of old affection in his dark eyes, and his irresistible smile, laid his hand on Blair's shoulder, and called him "my boy." And that, Blair said, when he wrote to Lucretia that night to give her an account of the doings of the memorable day, was the greatest moment for him.

But after that they could look forward to nothing more exciting than the accidental clashes of conflicting interests to break the monotony of the daily routine of a legislative session. The Senate sat every morning; in the afternoons there were committee meetings to attend; in the evening Blair and a few friends would drink and talk politics in the barroom of the Neil House and then in a room upstairs play poker until dawn.

There was one man at Columbus who, Blair was sure, looked upon these latter dissipations with a bilious disapproving eye, and that was Ethan Grow. For Grow was there in his new quality as Assistant Secretary of the Senate, and what was even more interesting, Grow's grandson, Tom Nash, was there too. Grow, doubtless because of the fear his tireless and radical activities could inspire, had mustered enough influence not only to secure his own position as clerk, but the appointment of his grandson as a page as well. He did this, he explained to Blair, because he thought it was part of his education as a citizen to learn how laws were made, and as Grow was there to keep an eye on him, the boy learnt this without being contaminated by those corrupting influences which sometimes affected the process.

As Blair sat at his desk on the right of the chamber, made cheerful on frosty winter mornings by the great wood fires that blazed in its two wide fireplaces, he could find considerable interest and amusement in watching Grow, sitting with the other secretaries at the long green table below the President's dais, his glasses far down on his long nose, as in the old days in the dry-goods store, engaged in his interminable writing. It was not the official record of the Senate's proceedings that he was compiling, but that more illuminating, if less unbiassed, account of its doings which appeared in *The Torchlight* each week, and in other papers in the State for which Grow wrote a weekly letter. That this journalistic enterprise interfered with Grow's official duties made no difference; there were, as always in any government office, clerks enough and to spare, and besides, no one dared object because of fear of Grow's sharp, unsparing pen. Grow would sit there scribbling away during the hours of the daily session and even after the Senate had adjourned, and his grandson, shy, timid and embarrassed on that public scene, would lean against the table beside him until some Senator clapped his hands for a page, and then, if no other page responded, Tom would sidle out from behind the table and slip up the aisle to where the Senator sat.

One day when Blair had clapped his hands it was young Tom who responded, and as Blair gave the lad a document to deliver to the secretary, he glanced into the boy's face and said:

"You are one of my constituents, aren't you?"

"Yes, sir," said the lad, and then he blushed and smiled. It was the first time that Blair had ever seen any expression as natural and boyish as a smile come to that aged little face. And Blair smiled, and gave the boy an affectionate little pat on the shoulder, and the boy grew red with embarrassment and his large blue eyes danced with pleasure, and Blair looked at him long, searching his features until he saw that the boy was becoming confused, and then he desisted.

But after that, whenever he called a page, it was always young Tom who leapt into the aisle, and flew to serve Blair, and was disappointed and jealous if any other page preceded him and got there first. And so a kind of friendship grew up between them. The boy ventured oftener from his grandfather's side, grew more and more at home in the Senate chamber, and often leaned against Blair's desk, as he had leant against his grandfather's table, and with the same sense of patronage and protection.

Blair, when he had overcome the initial difficulty of talking to a child, who is a citizen of a world in which a grown-up person is a stranger and an alien — Blair found to his relief that it was only in the presence of his grandfather that the boy talked in that preposterously solemn and elderly manner. When alone with him the boy spoke like any other boy, though perhaps with more precision and a somewhat larger vocabulary. And Blair felt that it was unjust that this boy's life and intelligence should be deformed by the dark and tyrannical mind of the fanatical old man sitting there before them, ready and willing to plunge the world into chaos if he could not have his own way about everything in it. Blair pitied the boy, and longed to do something for him, and as he could think of nothing else to do, he one day gave him a Spanish dollar. The boy took it and as it lay in his open palm he gazed at it with eyes that widened with wonder and shone like stars. Doubtless he had never owned a dollar before in all his life. For a moment he could not speak, and then he looked up and asked, as if still doubting:

"Is this for me, sir?"

"Yes."

The boy tried to thank him, stammered something, blushed, and ran away.

But the following morning, after the Lieutenant-Governor had called the Senate to order and the Chaplain had offered prayer, Blair saw the boy coming towards him down the table. The boy came slowly, and not with the quick skipping step that usually was his when he came on any errand to Blair, but slowly now and reluctantly. He came and stood beside Blair's desk and timidly held out his hand with the old Spanish silver dollar lying in it. Blair glanced up at him in inquiry.

"What's this?" he asked.

"My Grandfather says I mayn't keep this, sir," the boy said in a low, breathless voice, his face blushing deeply, "I'm to give it back to you. But I thank you, just the same—"

Then he paused and bit his lip, and his blue eyes suddenly filled with tears.

"You mean—?" Blair for the moment hardly understanding what it all was about.

"I'm not allowed to keep it, Sir. My Grandfather won't let me."

Blair, in a sudden flash of irritation and injured pride at this spurning of his gift, was, for an instant half angry with the boy, though an instant later he realized how unreasonable this was. Then he glanced at old Grow, sitting there at the Secretary's desk, writing his interminable screeds, but nevertheless, with a dour and sullen look of disapproval and menace on his gaunt face, glancing over his spectacles at the little scene. The glance had been familiar to Blair in his youth when he was working in Grow's store. However he took the dollar, perhaps a little petulantly, and put it in his pocket, with an indifferent:

"Oh very well, as you like."

But the boy still stood there, with a woebegone expression in his face that wrung Blair's heart.

"You don't blame me, Sir, do you?" the lad said.

"Why of course not," Blair assured him, and gave him a little pat of affection. And as he looked at the child he saw in his face, in the look of his eyes and the poise of his head, a swift, fleeting resemblance to someone, but for the life of him he could not tell whom. He glanced at the lad curiously, but the resemblance had fled as suddenly as it had come.

"It's all right, my boy," he said. "We'll have to find some other way. I shall speak to your Grandfather."

"That will do no good, Sir," said the boy, with an air so convinced and solemn that it made Blair laugh.

All that morning he was haunted by that resemblance, and he cudgelled his memory, trying to recall who it was that the boy looked like. But he could not bring it before his eyes again.

When the Senate rose at midday, Blair intended to speak to Grow, but Grow had gone. He had no opportunity to speak to him that afternoon, for he loitered so long at the Neil House after dinner, drinking with some convivial members of the Legislature, that he missed the afternoon session. He was a little tight therefore when, towards evening, coming out of the bar, he encountered Grow by accident in the lobby, and said to him, somewhat arrogantly:

"Look 'e here, what do you mean by making that boy give back a little present I had made him? Did you think I didn't know what I was doing? Or that I haven't got the right to do what I like with my own money?"

"Blair," said Grow, with a black look on his face, "I don't want that boy spoiled; I don't want that he should get silly ideas and big notions into his head. I don't approve of giving boys money. If it had been a bit, now, but a dollar, no, that's too much."

The old anger and resentment flared up in Blair.

"Don't want the boy spoiled, don't you?" he burst out with a sneer. "Well, there's more than one way of spoiling a boy, and your way is the worst of any, for with your system you'll crush all the life out of him, turn him into a contemptible little prig, and in the end make him grow up a cold, snivelling damned Presbyterian hypocrite."

Grow looked at him narrowly an instant, then said, in his harsh, rasping voice:

"Blair, you're drunk."

"And you're insane," Blair retorted, "and for all I care you can go to hell."

Late that night, as he sat in an upper room of the Neil House playing poker, suddenly, for no reason, the face of young Tom Nash came before him, and that strange, wistful expression he had noted in the morning, and the mysterious resemblance, and as suddenly he was able to identify it; the boy looked like his brother, Joe Blair.

Notes to *The Buckeyes*

1. Used here with reference to a breed of horses from east of the Blue Ridge, Virginia. Diomed was the winner of the first English Derby in 1780.

2. A nick-name for a Kentuckian.

3. In the short MS version of *The Buckeyes* (p. 27), Whitlock refers to the *Moselle* as a steamship whose boilers soon burst, killing two or three hundred people. In *Cincinnati A Guide to the Queen City and its Neighbors* (Cincinnati: The Wiesen-Hart Press, 1943), p. 58, compiled by workers of the Writers' Program of the Work Projects Administration in the State of Ohio, we learn that the *Moselle* blew up in a race near Cincinnati on April 25, 1838, killing 136 passengers. Subsequently the Federal Government appointed inspectors to enforce safety regulations on such vessels, whose boilers frequently exploded at great cost to human life. "Brag" here is used in the sense of "fine" or "first rate," as in the following quotation from Mitford Mathews' *A Dictionary of Americanisms* Chicago: University of Chicago Press, 1951): "The Moselle was a new *brag* boat and had recently made several exceedingly quick trips." (1838)

4. A type of broad-brimmed hat named after the Venezuelan patriot Simon Bolivar (1783-1830).

5. The first edifice of the First Presbyterian Church, located near the corner of Fourth and Main Streets, was replaced by the second in 1815. It was called the "two-horned church" because of its two cupolas.

6. Lebanon House was one of several names by which the famous Golden Lamb Inn, built 1815, was known. The oldest inn in Ohio, the brick building in which the Lamb still flourishes was built by Ichabod Corwin, the first settler in Lebanon and the uncle of Thomas Corwin, soon to be introduced in this novel.

7. Senator Emory is evidently one of Whitlock's inventions.

8. Martin Van Buren (1782-1862), eighth president of the United States (1837-1841) was born in Kinderhook, N. Y. He was called "the red fox" of Kinderhook because of his political ambition and cunning. The novel opens in July, 1836; in point of fact, Van Buren was not elected President till December of this year.

9. These facts of Corwin's education are set forth by Josiah Morrow, ed., *Life and Speeches of Thomas Corwin* (Cincinnati: W. H. Anderson & Co., 1896), pp. 12-16.

10. The concluding stanza of Demogorgon's final speech in Act IV of *Prometheus Unbound* (1820).

11. A widely distributed, fragant bush appearing with small yellow flowers in early spring, followed by red berries. It grows in moist woods, thickets and along streams.

12. An abolitionist newspaper published by William Lloyd Garrison (1805-1879) from 1831 to 1865.

13. An anti-slavery weekly published in Ohio—first in New Richmond, then in Cincinnati—from 1836 to 1847. Destruction of this newspaper's press and printing office by a mob in July, 1836, gained numerous adherents to the cause of abolition. The *Philanthropist* was first published by James G. Birney, then edited by Gamaliel Bailey.

14. Paten's kinship with Falstaff, evident in the former's obesity, libertinism and wit, is here reinforced by Prince Hal's description of Falstaff freely quoted by Winship to describe Paten (Henry IV, I, Act II, Sc. 4).

15. While returning to England from Bermuda via United States in 1804, Moore was presented to President Jefferson, who "gazed down on him in silence." Offended, the diminutive Moore returned the President's imagined affront by "per-

petuating in his verse epistle to Thomas Hume the Federalist libel that Jefferson had a black mistress."

This epistle, published with Moore's *Epistles, Odes, and Other Poems* in 1806, is referred to by Howard Mumford Jones in *The Harp That Once*—(1937; rpt. New York: Russell & Russell, 1970), p. 79. (Later, in 1816, Moore "recanted his views" [p. 85].) In a subsequent footnote Moore accused Jefferson of not living up to the nobility of the President's house (then incomplete), but of living meanly in a corner of it, abandoning "the rest to a state of uncleanly desolation."

16. Whitlock evidently chose this particular folk song about the outrageous antics of a virile bull because it was a favorite song of the legal profession, as Carl Sandburg observes in *The American Songbag* (New York: Harcourt, Brace & Company, 1927), p. 164. He quotes from *The Illini* by Col. Clark E. Carr, an early settler of Galesburg, Illinois, in 1852: "The song became a favorite with lawyers traveling the circuit in those days, and was often sung on convivial occasions. It is said that at one time, at Knoxville in our county, when some good news that caused universal rejoicing had been received, the court was adjourned, and judge, lawyers, jury, spectators, paraded around the public square singing, 'De ol' black bull kem down de medder.' "

17. That is, making fun of him, mocking him. "Quiz" is also used, as in "he's a great quiz," for one who mocks or ridicules others.

18. I have not been able to find any reference to a periodical called the *Humanitarian* at this period.

19. Apart from Sir William Blackstone (1723-1780) whose *Commentaries on the Laws of England* are of course still highly regarded, these eighteenth and nineteenth century lawyers and judges, together with their texts, have been swallowed up in the "dark backward and abysm of time." A remarkable fact, from a twentieth century viewpoint, is that none of these legal authorities was American; despite the American Revolution, the Ohio frontier remained securely colonial in its legal orientation. Joseph Chitty (1776-1841) wrote *A Practical Treatise on Pleading* (1809), Thomas Starkie (1782-1849) wrote *A Practical Treatise on the Law of Evidence* (1824), William Tidd (1760-1847) wrote *The Practice of the Court of King's Bench* (1790), and Issac 'Espinasse wrote *A Digest of the Law of Actions at Nisi Prius* (1790). Judging from the numerous editions of each of these works in the first half of the nineteenth century, these must have been standard law texts of the period, as Whitlock implies.

20. "Sweat" here evidently means "control" or "manage"; I have been unable to find a dictionary definition of "sweat" that exactly fits Whitlock's use of the word.

21. Mechanics' Institutes, modeled on their English counterparts of the same name, were organizations designed to provide education in the form of lectures and debates for industrial workers. Following their growth in England in the early nineteenth century, they became popular in the U.S. in the 1830's. I have found no evidence that one actually existed in Urbana, however.

22. Sir Thomas Lyttleton or Littleton was an eminent fifteenth century English jurist on property law. His book *Tenures,* much expanded by Sir Edward Coke (1552-1634), was a standard law text up to the nineteenth century.

23. Literally "bubble," referring collectively to the foam which collects on beer and some kinds of wine; its application to freshly poured coffee seems a bit idiosyncratic, one of Mrs. Grow's numerous provincialisms or solecisms, perhaps.

24. Byron's *Don Juan*, I, stanza 214.

25. Lavinia Talbott, the real-life counterpart of Lucretia Harris, was born April 7, 1813 at Newton, Frederick County, Virginia, married Joseph Carter Brand in Champaign County, Ohio on July 4, 1832, and died Nov. 2, 1905 in Urbana. She

was the daughter of John Talbott (1790-1861), also born in Frederick County, and Margaret Hickman Talbott (d. 1823). Margaret was the daughter of William Hickman and Rebecca (Harris) Hickman of Calvert County, Maryland. Rebecca's maiden name of Harris provides a clue as to where Whitlock may have got the fictional Lucretia's maiden surname. (The above information was summarized for me by Mr. Edwin L. English, Sr. from a family record in his possession entitled "Talbott Family of West River, Maryland.")

26. The use of "whilst" here and elsewhere in *The Buckeyes* constitutes a peculiar archaism evidently designed to give an old-fashioned flavor to the events described.

27. The O.E.D. gives no instance of the verb "crape" being used, as here, intransitively. "Craping" here evidently refers to the draping or covering of a hat or gown with crape; the common funereal associations of "crape" are lacking.

28. Catharine Maria Sedgwick (1789-1867) was a Massachusetts author who wrote romantic novels realistically depicting early nineteenth century customs and domestic virtues. *Hope Leslie, or Early Times in the Massachusetts* (1827) tells of colonists' adventures with the Indians, and *Clarence; or, A Tale of Our Own Times* (1830) contrasts the fortunes of a sensible and an adventurous girl in New York City and its environs.

29. "Syllabub" or "Sillabub" is a dessert made from milk or cream mixed with cider or wine to form soft curds.

30. A cake made silently and with appropriate rites by young ladies on St. Agnes' or St. Mark's Eve in order to foretell, as by a dream, what men they will marry.

31. Like dumb cake, "salt and egg" refers to a folk ritual of divination described by Edwin and M.A. Radford in *Encyclopedia of Superstitions* (New York: The Philosophical Library, 1949), p. 112: "...if you take an egg and roast it hard, take out the yolk and put salt in its place and eat it fasting for your supper when you go to bed, you will dream of your future husband." The custom of tying a girdle round the bedpost, alluded to by Brunton, is obscure in meaning, apart from its obvious sexual symbolism.

32. Whitlock presumably derived this name from a white man named Marmaduke Swearingen who became a Shawnee chief named Blue Jacket. When captured by the Indians at age 17, Marmaduke was wearing a blue hunting shirt, hence the name "Blue Jacket" given him by the Shawnee. (*The Ohio Guide*, pp. 587-588.) Before Bellefontaine, Ohio, 18 miles north of Urbana, was settled by white men, it was a Shawnee village called Blue Jacket's Town in honor of the chief.

33. The famous tornado of March 22, 1830, passed through the northern part of Urbana, according to Howe's *Historical Collections of Ohio*, I, 374. "It demolished the Presbyterian church ... and materially injured the Methodist church. Two or three children were carried high in air and killed...." As well as reporting the lifting and the killing of three children and the damage done to the Methodist church, Mrs. Grow adds to the tornado legend her characteristically homely detail about the chickens, and momentarily clarifies the somewhat confused chronology of Book I. If "seven years ago" was 1830, then the setting of Grow's abolition convention and of Blair's summer courtship and fall marriage to Lucretia would appear to be 1837. But later, at the opening of Book II, the courtship and marriage are referred to as having taken place in 1838 (p. 170). This discrepancy seems not to have been satisfactorily resolved in the novel.

34. Whitlock may have taken the name *Torchlight* from the title of a newspaper called the *Torch-Light* published by the poet and songwriter Otway Curry (1804-1855) from 1843 to 1845 in Xenia, Ohio. Later in the text Whitlock quotes from Curry's "Buckeye Cabin Song" (p. 185), perhaps the most popular of many songs written for the Harrison campaign of 1840.

35. Whitlock's use of the word "round" here is puzzling; none of the standard definitions seem exactly to fit the context.

36. Thomas Metcalfe (1780-1855) was Governor of Kentucky from 1828 to 1832, state senator from 1834 to 1838, and a member of the national Whig convention of 1839.

37. In 1826 John Cleves Symmes (1780?-1829), nephew of the great Ohio land speculator of the same name, propounded the fascinating but fantastic theory that the earth is made up of habitable concentric spheres with vast openings ("holes") at each pole. After the theory gained fairly wide acceptance, President Jackson rejected the proposal that Congress finance a polar expedition to test Symmes' proposition. After the theory was disproved, a popular joke went the rounds at Symmes' expense. If things or people, like Tom and Gertie in this case, had disappeared, some wit would explain the disappearance by saying, as here: "They've gone down into Symmes' hole." (*Cincinnati,* pp. 508-509.)

38. In firearms the "anvil" is the resisting cone, or bar against which the powder in a cartridge is exploded. Here the term is extended to refer to a cannon, apparently.

39. Harrison campaign songs quoted here and on previous pages (*pp. 183-187*) are discussed by Josiah Morrow in *Life and Speeches of Thomas Corwin,* pp. 35-36. The "ball" referred to in the song here quoted by Whitlock was typically a huge sphere perhaps ten feet in diameter on which campaign slogans, etc., were inscribed. Sometimes the ball was rolled along by two men at either end of a long pole inserted into the ball's "axle." Whitlock attributes to Blair a campaign song written in honor of Thomas Corwin; such a song, "Success to You, Tom Corwin," was actually written by John W. VanCleve of Dayton.

40. I can find no record of a tornado having hit Urbana (Macochee) in this year.

41. *Don Juan,* 1, stanza 194.

42. Morrow, p. 38.

43. *Merchant of Venice,* Act IV, Sc. 1, l. 194.

44. Morrow, pp. 139-148 gives a speech of Corwin's against corporal punishment delivered in the House at Columbus on Dec. 18, 1822 upon the bill to punish petty larceny with whipping, but the speech contains no reference to this anecdote in *The Buckeyes.*

45. Laws, hateful to the abolitionists, assigning Negroes an inferior status to Whites. Many such laws were passed in the North from 1839 to 1850 in an effort to secure an acceptable compromise with the Southern view of slavery.

46. More or less well known anti-slavery leaders. Levi Coffin (1789-1877) became a station master on the Underground Railroad at his home in Newport (now Fountain City), Indiana. Birney (1792-1857) came from an aristocratic, slave-holding family in Kentucky. After selling his slaves, he moved north to Ohio to join the anti-slavery forces there. He is best known for his newspaper the *Philanthropist* and for his Presidential candidacy for the Liberty Party in 1840 and 1844. Joshua R. Giddings (1795-1864) became a successful abolitionist lawyer from Jefferson, Ohio, representing the Western Reserve in Congress from 1838-59. A Free Soiler in 1848, opposing the extension of slavery into territories acquired from Mexico, he became a Republican in 1854. Wade (1800-1878) was a protegé of Giddings. Salmon Chase (1808-73) defended so many runaway slaves that he became known as "attorney general for fugitive slaves." He was prominent in the Liberty Party, the Free-Soil Party and eventually in the Republican Party. He held the political offices of Senator, Governor of Ohio, Secretary of the Treasury, and finally Chief Justice of the U.S. Supreme Court.

47. Quoted by Morrow, p. 90.

48. The *Western Citizen & Gazette* of Aug. 20, 1844 reported that 20,000 Whigs gathered at Zanesville on Aug. 14 when Corwin and others spoke. I have found no evidence, however, that Brand, Blair's prototype, accompanied Corwin on the

campaign trail in support of Clay. Probably we have here one of Whitlock's departures from strict historicity in the interest of continuity.

49. Morrow attributes this witticism to Corwin in a speech made at Carthage, near Cincinnati, during the campaign of 1844 (p. 44). But Morrow, while emphasizing the humorous side of Corwin, at one point hints at a sombre side to his nature: "Those who knew him best knew that he was a profoundly serious man. He was, like Lincoln, a story-teller and a humorist, but at heart a sad man" (p. 89). The serious side of Corwin is the side that Whitlock stresses a great deal, perhaps in response to Joseph Carter Brand's interpretation of Corwin's character as well as by way of reflecting Whitlock's own increasingly pessimistic nature.

50. An imposing hostelry near the old State Capitol, the Neil House seems to have been highly favored by assemblymen as a gathering place. Howe in his *Historical Collections*, I, facing p. 617 pictures the old Neil House in 1846 before it burnt and was replaced by the new.

Additional Bibliography

Jones, Howard Mumford. *The Harp That Once*—1937; rpt. New York: Russell & Russell, 1970.

Mathews, Mitford. *A Dictionary of Americanisms*. 2 vols. Chicago: University of Chicago Press, 1951.

Radford, Edwin and M. A. Radford. *Encyclopaedia of Superstitions*. New York: The Philosophical Library, 1949.

Sandburg, Carl. *The American Songbag*. New York: Harcourt, Brace & Company, 1927.

Writer's Program of the Work Projects Administration. *Cincinnati A Guide to the Queen City and Its Neighbors*. Cincinnati: The Wiesen-Hart Press, 1943.

Index to Principal Historical
Characters, Events, Places and Topics

271